TALES TO ASTONISH

BY THE SAME AUTHOR

Gangsta
Have Gun Will Travel
Street Sweeper
Bad Boy

TALES TO ASTONISH

JACK KIRBY, STAN LEE, AND THE AMERICAN COMIC BOOK REVOLUTION

RONIN RO

BLOOMSBURY

Published by Bloomsbury, New York and London
Distributed to the trade by Holtzbrinck Publishers

All papers used by Bloomsbury are natural, recyclable products made
from wood grown in well-managed forests. The manufacturing processes
conform to the environmental regulations of the country of origin.

Library of Congress Cataloging-in-Publication Data

Ro, Ronin.
Tales to astonish : Jack Kirby, Stan Lee, and the American comic book
revolution / Ronin Ro – 1st U.S. ed.
p. cm.
ISBN 1-58234-345-4
1. Kirby, Jack. 2. Cartoonists – United States – Biography. 3. Lee,
Stan. I. Title.

PN6727.K57Z88 2004
741.5'092–dc22
2003020906

First U.S. Edition 2004

1 3 5 7 9 10 8 6 4 2

Typeset by Palimpsest Book Production Limited,
Polmont, Stirlingshire, Scotland
Printed in the United States of America by
Quebecor World Fairfield

For Stan and Jack

Chapter 1

Jacob Kurtzberg was tired of being poor.

Born on Essex Street in Manhattan, on August 25, 1917, he lived in a tiny tenement apartment on Suffolk Street on the Lower East Side. His father, Benjamin, worked as a tailor to make the $12 rent, while his mother, Rosemary, worked as a seamstress or in a bakery. Money was always tight.

Most afternoons, he'd walk to Forty-second Street, where the *Daily News*, the *Journal*, and various Hearst newspapers had their offices, and run errands for reporters. On Saturdays he'd head to the cinema, pay a dime, and thrill to gangster movies, serials, comedies, and science fiction. By now, a few of his neighbors, including John Garfield, were making it big in Hollywood, and James Cagney was in the middle of a winning streak. Jacob privately dreamed of moving out west to become an actor.

When the movies were over, he returned to the neighborhood and to feeling ashamed of his hand-me-down turtleneck sweaters and knickers.

It was a difficult time to be a twelve-year-old boy. Everywhere, kids were forming gangs. Kids on Suffolk Street became the Suffolk Street Gang and fought the Norfolk Street Gang. Then they fought Irish and black gangs. Some of his peers started running with the well-dressed mobsters hanging around the neighborhood. If he couldn't become an actor, Jacob figured, he'd do this, too, or become a crooked politician, like the ones he saw holding conferences and spending money in neighborhood restaurants.

But thoughts of the future had to wait. For now, he had to maintain his reputation and look out for his brother, David. Their mother wanted David to wear nice clothes, but velvet pants, a lace collar, and shoulder-length curly blond hair (at the height of the Depression) had made the kid a perpetual target. Five years his junior and over six feet tall, David was stocky and tough, but no match for the street-hardened gangsters stepping up to confront him. David did what he could when the gangs attacked, but sometimes Jacob would leave school, see his brother under a pile of opponents, and leap at them with both fists swinging. "I really had to whale into 'em, and I did," he said later. "And it was a common everyday occurrence. Fighting became second nature. I began to like it."

When he wasn't fighting – a rare moment; at Hebrew school he knocked out a kid while jostling to get a better window view of an airplane passing overhead – he continued spending hard-earned dimes on *The Time Machine* or comedies that starred Charlie Chaplin, Buster Keaton, or the Marx Brothers (whom he'd enjoyed from before they hit it big, when they took the stage at the Academy of Music on Fourteenth Street to perform vaudeville routines). He told his mother he wanted to pursue a career in the movies, but she said, "No, you can't go to California."

He kept seeing gangs fight and gangsters get shot in the corner candy store. He tried to find a place to play ball, dodged ice wagons and pushcarts and nomadic peddlers, and battled it out with Irish gangs that wandered over from the East Side waterfront wielding rocks, glass bottles, and clubs.

But one rainy afternoon, everything changed. Jacob noticed a pulp magazine floating toward a sewer in the gutter. "So I pick up this pulp magazine and it's *Wonder Stories* and it's got a rocket ship on the cover and I'd never seen a rocket ship." At home, he tucked it under his pillow so no one would know he was reading it. *Wonder Stories* led him to newspaper strips like *Barney Google* and *Prince Valiant*. He liked that the pages were large and colorful.

"And *Prince Valiant* – it was astonishing to see this beautiful illustration in the newspaper, and it was so different from the ordinary comics."

Soon he was writing his own stories. And though his dream of studying art at Pratt ended when his father lost his job, he kept teaching himself how to draw, studying Milton Caniff's and Hal Foster's comic strips while trying to make his own heroes even more powerful. When he watched movies now, it was to learn how directors told stories and to apply these techniques to his work.

By 1936, he wanted to create his own newspaper strip. Publishers were only beginning to slap strips together into monthly magazine titles, but creating an enduring strip, he felt, would ensure a stable income. The nineteen-year-old aspiring artist landed a job at Lincoln Newspaper Features and drew editorials ("Your Health Comes First") and forgettable daily strips under pseudonyms. "I wanted to be an all-around American," he explained. His pen names confused his parents, but he kept using them. "I felt if you wanted to have a great name, it would be Farnsworth, right? Or Stillweather. I felt Jack Kirby was close to my real name."

He left Lincoln for an assistant's job at Max Fleischer's animation studio. Here, he sat at a long table and drew what were known as the in-between steps in a cartoon. For the character Popeye to be seen taking a step, he had to create six drawings – his foot rising, moving through the air, and landing on the ground again. He drew these pictures, then passed them over to the next artist seated at the long table. This artist would then draw the character's next step.

Although the Fleischer studio paid decently, Jacob came increasingly to view this job with disdain – it struck him as being too much like his father's job in a factory. Just as he decided he wanted to create on his own properties, he began to see the earliest comic books hanging from newsstands.

Jerry Siegel (with artist Joe Schuster) had sent comic strip proposals to various publishers. "He was looking for work," says Will Eisner, who owned one of the biggest comic packaging shops in town. "He had two features called *Spy* something and another thing called

Superman. And I wrote back a letter to him when he was in Cleveland. I thought they weren't ready for prime time, that they should stay in Cleveland another year." They didn't, and Superman's immediate success birthed an industry. When DC published June 1938's *Action Comics* No. 1, fans loved the tough-talking hero in blue tights and a red cape and bought an astounding nine hundred thousand copies (other comics sold between two hundred thousand and four hundred thousand copies). A multitude of publishers quickly appeared to offer their own invulnerable flying knockoffs.

After seeing an ad in a newspaper, Jacob carried his portfolio over to Art Syndication Company on Madison and Fortieth Street. Will Eisner and Jerry Iger (born Samuel Maxwell Iger), who owned the company, liked his work and gave him a job. In the office, he was part of a staff that included a number of future legends: Bronx kid Bob Kahn (who would soon create *Batman* under the name "Bob Kane"), Lou Fine (who would go on to fame with *The Spirit*), and Stanislav Pavlowsky (also known as "Bob Powell"). "He was a quiet young man, short, small fellow," Eisner recalls. "He always resembled John Garfield and he acted like him, but he was a very hardworking person, very sincere. I enjoyed having him working for me. He was a good man."

If Jacob wasn't toiling on unremarkable strips like "Diary of Dr. Hayward," "Wilton of the West," and "Count of Monte Cristo" for Fiction House's 1939 entry into comics, *Jumbo Comics* No. 1, he was impressing Eisner in other ways.

One afternoon, Eisner was in his office when Iger let him know someone was here to see him. Flush with success, they had recently moved to a larger building across from the Daily News Building on Forty-second Street, into an office with two rooms: one wide space for the artists and a smaller room in front. Since the move, however, Eisner had been complaining about the new building's towel service and had tried to contact other companies. His visitor entered the office, a guy who, according to Eisner, "looked like he came out of Central Casting, a real Mafioso with a black hat and a black shirt and a white tie and broken nose."

"I'm in charge of the towel service," the man said.

"Well, we want to change the towel service. We're not happy with your company because the towels are not coming out white."

"Well, you know we got the franchise here."

After Eisner complained that no other company would take on their account in this building since it wasn't their territory, the guy said, "Well, you know, nobody else can service this building."

"Why not?"

"Because we got the rights to do this building." Then: "Look, we don't want to have no trouble with you. We want everything to go nice, see? You tell me what your problem is, and we'll try to fix it."

"Well, I want more towels."

"I can't get you more towels. Only four towels."

The conversation had risen in volume; Jacob emerged from the artist's room. "Hey, boss," he said. "Both of you, just a minute. I'll take care of this."

Jacob walked up to the tall, burly bruiser. "What do you want, you big ox?"

The guy realized Jacob was from the streets and explained about the towel service.

"Look, we don't want any crap from you," Jacob told him. "We don't like your goddamned towel service. Now get the hell out of here."

Eisner was nervous. He figured the guy would take the place apart. Jacob wasn't worried at all.

After sizing up Jacob for a minute, the big guy said, "Well, all right," then walked out.

Eisner never forgot the incident. "He comes back again, call me," Jacob told him. "I'll take care of him." With that, he returned to his desk, to a "Count of Monte Cristo" story he'd sign as "Jack Curtis."

In 1939, he left Eisner's studio, drew a few drawings for pulps published by Martin Goodman's Red Circle Company, then landed a salaried position at Fox Features Syndicate, where his life changed yet again.

While Victor Fox conducted his business at a glass-covered desk in a palatial office, under a high, light blue, domed ceiling, Jacob sat among rows of artists churning out newspaper strips like *The Blue Beetle* and *Socko the Seadog*. Fox was an overweight, former ballroom dancer in his late forties. He stood five feet two inches tall and spoke with a raspy British accent. He had seen the impressive sales figures of *Superman*, *Action Comics*, and *Detective Comics* (spurred on by new sensation "Batman") while working as an accountant for DC Comics and soon rented an office in the same building, a few floors below. While his salaried artists worked on newspaper strips, Fox hired Eisner and Iger's shop to create art and stories for his first few comic book titles.

To Jacob, Joe Simon resembled a politician. The former reporter from Syracuse, New York, was tall, broad shouldered, and educated and wore an impeccably well-tailored suit. Joe – whose father was also a tailor – had progressive views regarding the use of lawyers in negotiations and maintaining ownership and a percentage of profits derived from their work. "My purpose was what my father's purpose was," Jack recalled, "to make a living and to have a family. I was going to do the right thing. My dream was to have money to support it and live in the kind of house I liked." With Joe Simon, he'd achieve this.

Simon had many contacts in the burgeoning industry. He had worked at First Funnies Inc., an office in a run-down office building on West Forty-fifth Street, near Times Square. There, he'd seen artists at tables churn out piles of cardboard drawings for Lloyd Jacquet, an employee of the McClure Newspaper Syndicate who ran Funnies on the side. Simon brought the former army officer his samples and heard Jacquet describe how the company created comics for publishers who didn't want to hire editorial staffs. Funnies worked for several companies, and each page of story and art could bring Simon $7 a page. Simon's first assignment – a seven-page western created in four days – was accepted. He dropped in to see Jacquet again and learned that one of Funnies' largest clients, Martin Goodman, liked his work.

* * *

Martin Goodman was born in Brooklyn on January 8, 1908, and had dreamed of publishing since his childhood – using newspapers, magazines, scissors, and glue to create homespun magazines. Goodman's friend and attorney, Jerry Perles, recalled that while America reeled from the stock market crash, Goodman "traveled around the country, bumming in hobo camps, cooking over campfires." Upon his return to New York, Goodman worked for Independent News alongside future comic publishers and rivals John Goldwater and Louis Silberkleit and Frank Armer, who helped distribute Harry Donenfeld's *Detective Comics*. In 1932, Goodman and Silberkleit left Independent News, borrowed money, and formed Western Fiction Publishing, where they published the pulp magazine *Complete Western Book*. Decent sales inspired more of the same: *Best Western* and *Quick Trigger Western Novel*. Two years after forming Western Fiction, however, Silberkleit left. Goodman continued publishing more magazines and tried his hand at a continuing character. He premiered *Ka-Zar*, based on a Tarzan-like savage in the jungle, but canceled the title after three issues. By August 1938, Goodman was publishing twenty-seven pulps, including the sci-fi title *Marvel Science Stories* (which somehow convinced him that the buzzword *Marvel* would draw readers). A year later, Frank Torpey (whom Goodman later called his "lucky charm") persuaded him that comic books were the future – especially those created by First Funnies Inc., where Torpey worked as sales manager. By now, Funnies was delivering entire books to other companies. Goodman saw that Funnies could help Timely Publications compete with All-American Comics and National Periodicals (two publishers that would later unite to form DC Comics), Fox Features Syndicate, and Centaur Publishers. But before publishing a comic, Goodman carefully considered the lessons of the past. His sci-fi pulp *Marvel Science Stories* had flopped; he needed a new approach to his first comic magazine.

Sub-Mariner was an offshoot of an idea originally conceived for a Columbia Pictures serial. In 1936, Columbia had seen major competitor Republic Pictures score a hit with its twelve-chapter thriller *Undersea Kingdom.* Columbia planned to respond with a full-length Technicolor serial, *The Lost Atlantis*, which would present two warring amphibian factions battling for control of an undersea kingdom. The serial, Columbia hoped, would feature explosions, sinking ships, helmets that allowed fish-men to breathe on the surface, and a love story between an air-breathing human and an undersea queen. The latter two would fall in love; the queen would renounce her throne and try to join the man on the surface, only to discover she couldn't breathe and had to return to her kingdom. Columbia also planned a sequel, *Prince of Atlantis*, which would detail the adventures of the human and the sea queen's son. When the film studio eventually discovered it couldn't create the effects needed for undersea warfare, however, plans for the film were shelved.

But by now, Columbia had already asked artist Bill Everett's shop, First Funnies Inc., to create a black-and-white comic book for free distribution in movie theaters. The magazine's covers would have advertised both Atlantis films. When Columbia canceled the films, the comic, titled *Motion Picture Funnies Weekly*, was also canceled. Just as Martin Goodman began to search for stories to include in Timely's first comic, Bill Everett wondered what, if anything, to do with the character Namor the Sub-Mariner, the Prince of Atlantis. Once Goodman acquired the rights from Columbia, he scheduled Everett's work in *Motion Picture Funnies Weekly* for inclusion in what was shaping up to be *Marvel Comics* No. 1.

The comic also featured "The Human Torch" by Carl Burgos, a tale of an android who burst into flames, soared through the air, and turned his nonspecific anger into behavior as destructive as any seen in Depression-era film hits *Frankenstein* and *King Kong*. Burgos, a gifted amateur who enjoyed drawing android characters, created the Human Torch, wrote the story, and handled artwork and the lettering.

To round out his first comic, Goodman insisted on the inclusion of his failed pulp hero, Ka-Zar, the western character the Masked

Raider, and the Angel, a powerless blue-clad detective who sported a trendy thin mustache. *Marvel Comics* became a hit, and Goodman began publishing a comic magazine line under the name Timely Publications.

Goodman soon wanted to try to repeat the continuing success of "The Human Torch" with a similar character. Jacquet handed Simon a copy of *Marvel Comics* and told him all the new hero had to do was be able to set himself on fire and wear a mask. The new tale would be a fifteen-page lead feature. Jacquet added, "Pad it with lots of action and fire. Fire is easy to draw. You're getting a break."

Simon sat in a room at Haddon Hall with his drawing board and art supplies and invented the Fiery Mask, a hero who could shoot flames through his eyes. Goodman accepted it without any changes and later called Haddon Hall's front desk to invite Simon over to his office.

Timely Publications operated out of the McGraw-Hill Building on West Forty-second Street. When Simon went up to meet with Goodman, he saw the place was filled with Goodman's relatives. After waiting in the small anteroom and meeting Uncle Robbie, who dealt with printers and engravers and relayed messages to and from Martin, Joe walked past a business and bookkeeping office, where Martin's brother Abe Goodman worked. Then he passed two editorial rooms, where Dave Goodman photographed models for magazines and Artie Goodman colored the comics. Finally, he entered Goodman's headquarters.

In his thirties, with white hair and wire rim glasses, Goodman sat in a swivel chair, facing a meal of crackers and milk. Simon was as aware of rumors that claimed Goodman hadn't attended school past the fourth grade as he was of Goodman's hard-charging approach to anticipate and capitalize on trends. Goodman asked Simon what Funnies was paying for stories. Simon told him $7 a page but claimed that some companies paid $10.

"I'll pay you twelve," Goodman replied. For this, Simon would help Timely move past derivative low-selling knockoffs. Simon was freelancing for Timely when he saw Victor Fox's ad in *The New York Times* for an artist/editor.

Shortly after forming his own company, Fox had told Jerry Iger, "I want some comics." He asked for a muscular character with a cape, a red suit, and an insignia of some sort on his chest. Back at the shop, Iger told Eisner, "This is what our new customer wants."

Eisner said, "Hey, that looks a little like Superman, doesn't it?"

The shop gave Fox what he wanted, and DC promptly sued for copyright infringement.

In court, Eisner told the truth and testified against Fox. "Fox's defense was that we created it; he had nothing to do with this," Eisner recalled. "'So I'll just ask you people to give me a hero, and they gave me a hero that looked like Superman. I didn't know a thing.'" Fox lost the case and placed an ad seeking an artist/editor.

Twenty-one-year-old Jacob was working at Fox when Joe Simon arrived. At the time, DC was suing Fox, Fox was suing DC, and Fox was trying to expand his publishing line despite a flare-up with the Eisner and Iger shop, his company's biggest packagers.

As an editor at Fox, Simon received $85 a week, a sizable amount at the time. Jacob – pale, with thick eyebrows and a razor-sharp crew cut – was earning $15 a week on staff and seeking other ways of pulling in money. "He'd never seen a comic book artist with a suit before," Simon recalled. "The reason I had a suit was that my father was a tailor. Jack's father was a tailor, too, but he made pants!"

Simon was freelancing for Fox and working on projects for other publishers, including First Funnies Inc. Jacob asked if he could work with him. Simon welcomed the help. Curtis Publications, which published *The Saturday Evening Post*, teamed with Funnies for a new line of comics. The first title was *Blue Bolt*, a futuristic sci-fi adventure created by Simon that detailed how a hero used his electric blasts against the villainous Green Sorceress and her subterranean henchmen.

They rented an office within walking distance for $25 a week, and Jacob helped Simon work on the second issue of *Blue Bolt*.

After the *Blue Bolt* issue, Jacob and Simon continued to work together, with Jacob using various aliases to conceal the fact that he was moonlighting. Jacob wanted to hide this from Victor Fox, who continued to pay a regular, steady salary. Jacob's evasions got so elaborate that he wouldn't even answer a phone. ("Maybe it's Victor Fox!" he shouted.) This, he told Simon, was the real reason he signed so many fake names (Jack Curtis, Jack Cortez, Jack Kirby) to his work.

Simon kept urging him to use his real name.

"Don't you like Jack Kirby?" Jacob asked.

Simon said he did: It had as good an "Irish ring to it" as the names used by film and radio stars like James Cagney. And suddenly he understood that there was more to the fake name than a simple fear of Fox finding out he was working for rival publishers.

In the autumn of 1939, Simon left Fox's company. Three months later, Jacob did, too. Simon asked what took so long, and Jacob said he would have left sooner if he'd been born taller.

"What the hell has that got to do with it?"

"Short people have a big handicap," Jacob explained. "It's hard to make people notice you. Did you ever see a short drill sergeant?"

Within a week, Jacob Kurtzberg went down to City Hall and received an official document confirming that he'd legally changed his name to Jack Kirby.

As 1940 began, Goodman moved to end his relationship with Lloyd Jacquet and First Funnies Inc. by paying Joe Simon directly to edit Timely's comics. "Soon, we were buying only the Human Torch and Sub-Mariner from Jacquet and irritating the hell out of him with demands for script and art changes, in the hopes he would resign the features he had helped to build," Simon once recalled.

After *Marvel Comics* No. 1, January 1940's *Daring Mystery* and *Mystic* presented new heroes, only to replace them after a few stories. Publishing schedules were unreliable: *Daring Mystery* and

Mystic would vanish, then reappear months later with an all-new batch of heroes. While DC profited with Superman, Batman, and other best-selling heroes, Simon and Kirby spent their first year together contributing pictures to pulp stories or creating Timely heroes who failed to catch on: the Phantom Bullet and his ice gun, the Shadow-like Phantom Reporter, androids Rudy the Robot and Marvex the Super Robot, the cape-wearing Dynaman, Stuporman, and the Purple Mask (not to be confused with the pre-existing Green Mask, Grey Mask, Red Mask, White Mask, or Timely's own Fiery Mask). Simon helped create Marvel Boy – who fought a Hitler stand-in whom Goodman, for fear of a lawsuit, named "Hiller" – but this was another turkey. About the only character in *Daring Mystery* to make a dent was the Fin, a foolish-looking aquatic hero who wore a two-foot-high fin strapped to the top of his head. "He was really just a frogman," explained creator Bill Everett.

Mystic fared just as poorly. Readers were unimpressed with generic heroes like Master Mind Excello, Merzak the Mystic, Flexo the Rubber Man, the 3 Xs, female star the Black Widow, and the Blue Blaze (which lasted only four issues).

March 1940's the Vision managed to make up for some of these flops. The uncanny, green-skinned mystic who appeared in clouds of smoke was inspired by the fact that Jack and Joe smoked cigars in their cramped office. When the Vision's debut helped *Marvel Mystery Comics* No. 13 become Timely's first true sales hit, the duo were vindicated. (After the first issue, Goodman added the word *Mystery* to the title to spur sales.) Only months later, however, in August 1940, their winged hero Red Raven proved to be Timely's lowest-selling character to date. "I did it for the money and I got the money, but the strip only lasted one issue," Jack later said. "The Red Raven, boy, it was a real dud!"

Despite a few heroes, Timely still couldn't compete with *Superman*'s sales figures (or those of DC's Batman, Green Lantern, The Flash, Wonder Woman, or the consortium they formed in *All-Star Comics*). In fact, except for a new quarterly *Human Torch* magazine, Timely was really publishing nothing more than *Marvel*

Mystery Comics. Simon and Kirby, who already had a few flops to their credit, needed to come up with a winner.

On September 1, 1939, Nazi Germany invaded Poland. The United States was shipping arms and matériel overseas to Allied nations while trying to adhere to an isolationist policy. As Adolf Hitler's forces continued to march across Europe, American newspaper headlines screamed about concentration camps and brutal Gestapo tactics. By spring of 1940, Hitler's forces had sacked Poland, Denmark, Norway, the Netherlands, Belgium, and France. Congress realized America might soon be at war and encouraged various publishers to promote literary themes that inspired national patriotism.

Joe Simon, however, was already thinking about using Hitler and his Gestapo in a comic book. *Marvel Mystery* No. 4 had presented the Sub-Mariner battling a Nazi submarine, and *Human Torch* No. 1 had shown the Torch combating Axis powers. But Simon had more ambitious plans. "There never had been a truly believable villain in comics," he noted. "But Adolf was alive, hated by more than half of the world." With a villain in mind, Simon started thinking about a hero.

At the time, he and Jack were working on *Blue Bolt*. But the thought of a hero defeating Hitler burned in his mind.

The new hero, Simon finally decided, would have superpowers, but he would also be a member of the armed forces. In addition to allowing Simon to humiliate the Nazis, this idea could bring in good money. One night Simon sat at a sketch board to design a star-spangled hero whose alter ego was a timid army private in khaki uniform.

He outlined a human figure and added bulging muscles, an armored jersey, tights, gloves, and boots. "I drew a star on his chest and colored the costume red, white, and blue," he explained. Then he gave him a shield and red-and-white stripes on his torso (under a blue chest). The final drawing worked, but the hero needed a sidekick. Simon sketched a boy with matching colors and a simpler costume design. He wrote the name "Super American" on the bottom of the first sketch but immediately changed his mind. "Captain

America," he wrote over it. And the boy would be "Bucky," named after the star of his high school basketball team.

By the summer of 1940, Jack's family had moved to the first floor of an attached brick home in Brooklyn. One day, he was playing stickball with his brother and some friends when his new upstairs neighbors arrived. Jack, wearing bathing trunks, noticed that seventeen-year-old Rosalind Goldstein and her older cousin Pearl were watching them play.

Pearl told her, "I'll take the older one and you take the younger one."

Roz answered, "I don't want him. You take him." While they bickered over who would get him, and moving men hauled their furniture upstairs, Jack's parents sat on the stoop and got acquainted with the new neighbors. Jack walked over and politely introduced the girls to the group. The other guys all wanted Pearl, Roz remembered, but Jack engaged her in conversation. He told her he was an artist. "Would you like to see my etchings?"

Rosalind was confused.

"My drawings," he added.

She said, "Oh, sure."

She accompanied him to his bedroom – secure in the fact that her parents were right outside – and saw the drawings on his walls and table. Then he showed her his pages from *Captain America*.

He and Roz started dating, and he got to know her parents better. Her father worked in a factory as a seamstress on women's dresses, and her mother did contract sewing at home and cared for the children. "I never slept well at night, so I would sit there sewing things for hours with her," Roz recalled. "We did a lot of that. I still can sew very well – hand sewing."

Some nights she'd come downstairs to the Kurtzbergs' railroad-style apartment, which had the living room leading right into the dining room, kitchen, and bedroom, all in a straight line. She and Jack would sit on the couch in the parlor with his parents right behind the glass door leading into the bedroom and fool around quietly until her father lugged a huge trash can downstairs at three A.M., peeked in, and asked, "Oh, Roz is still up?" Taking the hint, she'd hurry upstairs.

As months passed, Jack couldn't bear the thought of Roz being with another man. When Joe and his girl wanted to see a show or concert in Times Square, Jack brought Roz along. And when he learned a piano player was trying to put the moves on Roz, he stood behind the guy while he played for a crowd and said, "It would be terrible if the piano lid closed on your fingers. That would be painful, wouldn't it?" Before the guy could answer, Jack added, "You belong in Hollywood, out west. You play too well." The guy took the hint, and Jack and Roz continued their courtship: riding horses (she tried unsuccessfully to teach him), enjoying swing music, attending Sinatra's big show at the Paramount Theater (amid hysterical bobby-soxers screaming their hearts out for the young crooner), and seeing each other practically every night.

"I discouraged all of them. I knew when I saw Roz that I wanted her and nobody else." He'd dated all kinds of women, but none were as dignified as Roz. She was intelligent, considerate, and quiet. She came from a wonderful family. Everything about her was right. During their courtship, his protectiveness grew to include her sister, Anita. Sometimes he'd come home and see three or four of "the wrong kind of guys" waiting for her to come outside. If he saw them sitting with her inside the house, he'd upend their chairs, knocking them to the floor, and kick them out.

Rosalind's parents, meanwhile, were happy about the fact that Jack had a stable occupation. "If Michelangelo weren't making enough, they would have thrown him out," he joked. They were also happy that Roz had finally found someone to love her. During her childhood, she had suffered from asthma, "always very bad lungs." The Goldsteins frequently had to call ambulances to bring her oxygen. Following an attack, she would recuperate in bed with two aunts standing over her, crying and telling each other, "Oh, she won't live to get married."

After a while, she had internalized this message, come to believe it. But doctors learned how to treat her allergies, her health improved, her confidence returned, and her parents saw her looking and feeling good. On her eighteenth birthday, sitting beside her on a park bench, Jack pulled out an engagement ring. "He didn't say 'I love you' and all that kind of schmaltz," Roz quipped. "He says, 'I don't want you seeing anyone else,' and he put the ring on my finger." She thought his proposal was cute and accepted immediately.

Martin Goodman was aware of the flag-colored hero trend. At Timely, he'd send Uncle Robbie down to the newsstand with bundles of Timely books and trade them for books by the competition (giving newsstands three Timely books for every one received). MLJ Comics had enjoyed considerable success with their patriotic hero the Shield. And in the news, more headlines in two-cent newspapers were screaming about Hitler's aggression in Europe. Said Joe Simon, "The United States hadn't yet entered the war when Jack and I created Captain America, so maybe he was our way of lashing out against the Nazi menace."

Simon submitted the character design to Goodman with a short note at the bottom: "Martin – Here's the character. I think he should have a kid buddy or he'll be talking to himself all the time. I'm working up script – send schedule. Regards, Joe."

Goodman told Simon, "Let's do it. We'll give Captain America his own book."

Simon mentioned that he'd like "a piece of the action." Goodman agreed to pay 25 percent of the profits (15 percent for Simon and 10 percent for the artists), and they shook hands on the deal, Simon recalled. But Goodman worried about using Hitler as a villain. The Nazi leader might be dead by the time the book hit stands.

Simon had to put a rush on putting it together. When Jack heard Simon had asked artists Al Avison and Al Gabriel – whose work resembled Jack's – to work on the first issue, he asked why. "You're still number one, Jack," Simon told him. "It's just a matter of a quick deadline for the first issue."

Jack said he'd make the deadline.

Jack and Joe were working on the first issue of *Captain America* when Uncle Robbie entered the office with an awkward seventeen-year-old boy. "This is Stanley Lieber, Martin's wife's cousin," Robbie told Simon. "Martin wants you to keep him busy."

Joe immediately felt that hiring Stan was an act of nepotism. Stan, however, said that he had never been close to Martin Goodman. Goodman, said Stan, was nice, but "a little bit cold." He was "very pleasant, very intelligent, and he was the boss." Though Goodman was married to his cousin, he "had never been that close" to her. He'd met Goodman only once or twice when he was a kid. "He owned the company. So I didn't have much to do with him, really."

Like Jack, Stan didn't exactly have an easy go of it during his childhood. He was born on December 28, 1922, to Jack and Celia Lieber, who came to America from Romania for a better life. They gained citizenship and made ends meet with what Jack Lieber earned as a dress cutter in the garment district. When the Great Depression began, Jack Lieber lost his job and couldn't find another. He tried to open his own business, a diner, but the plan failed and he lost his savings. As a child, encouraged to pursue dreams by his mother, Stan couldn't help but note how sad his father looked while sitting at a table and looking for a job that, unfortunately, just wasn't going to come. The sight of his father wrestling with secret sorrows instilled in Stan an indefatigable drive to succeed, a superhuman work ethic, and the unshakable belief that a man must always have work to do: He's got to stay busy. He's got to become indispensable at his job.

As the Depression stretched on, and his parents gave birth to a second child – Larry Lieber – Stan noticed how his mom and dad lavished attention on their children but barely interacted. "They must have loved each other when they were married," Stan revealed in a passage from his autobiography, *Excelsior*, "but my earliest recollections were of the two of them arguing, quarreling incessantly. Almost always," he added, "it was about money, or the lack of it."

At this young age, he watched poverty continue to take its toll on a marriage: his parents worrying about having enough to buy food or pay rent; his mom cleaning their tiny apartment on West End Avenue in Manhattan while his dad sat day in and day out in the living room, going through the paper and looking for work. Once the phone service had been cut off, Jack Lieber would head out on foot with an optimistic smile on his face, only to return hours later looking hopeless and dejected.

Like many children raised in poverty, Stan found an escape through reading: During meals, he always kept a magazine or book nearby; if none were around, he'd read labels on kitchen products. His mother soon installed a little plank on the kitchen table so that he'd be comfortable while reading and, occasionally, finishing his meals.

By the time Jack Lieber moved the family to cheaper quarters in Manhattan's Washington Heights, Stan's passion for reading inspired his first attempts at writing and drawing comics (stick figures and straight lines serving as horizons; cheap, homemade stages for escapist dramas).

In school, he was a loner. His mother wanted him to hurry up and finish learning, to get out there and find work. He skipped grades, studied with older kids, and entertained himself for hours after school with his beloved two-wheel bike. By now, his face showed that he was going to be something, whether the world wanted it or not. His smile was vibrant, as if he knew a secret no one else was privy to; his posture and demeanor were confident and brash; nothing was going to get him down, not even the fact that the windows in the new apartment, located in the rear of the building in Washington Heights, faced a depressing, immovable brick wall.

During the summer other kids went to camp, had the time of their lives; he was alone. He turned to comic strips for solace, and fantastic novels by H. G. Wells, Arthur Conan Doyle, Mark Twain, and Edgar Rice Burroughs. He read more Hardy Boys and fifty-cent hardcover mystery novels. Then he turned to the classics – Poe, Dickens, Omar Khayyám, Émile Zola, and the occasionally indecipherable but wholly satisfying flowery wording of Shakespeare. Like Jack, he found diversion and inspiration from movies featuring the swashbuckling, devil-may-care Errol Flynn, the quiet but heroic Roy Rogers, the slow-moving but quick-witted Charlie Chan and his loyal number one son, the perceptive Sherlock Holmes, the raging Frankenstein monster, the monstrous Moby Dick and his pursuers, the pathetic comic Everyman Charlie Chaplin, the sympathetic giant King Kong, and the unrelenting Gunga Din.

Soon, Stan was writing letters to a reporter for the *Chicago Tribune*, and by age fifteen he was entering and repeatedly winning writing contests held by one of New York's best-selling papers, the *Herald-Tribune*. After three of his five-hundred-word essays about the "Biggest News of the Week" won first prize in three consecutive weeks, an editor suggested he consider writing as a profession. Instead, he worked as an usher in a movie theater, attended DeWitt Clinton High School in the Bronx (once his family moved there from Washington Heights), used his developing oratorical skills to sell classmates subscriptions to the *Herald-Tribune*, and studied acting in the WPA Federal Theatre Project (one of many programs created by President Franklin D. Roosevelt to provide the unemployed with hope, direction, and new skills). Though he briefly considered a career in law or advertising, he worked as an office boy in a shop that made and sold men's trousers. Upon graduating from Clinton in 1939, the energetic, self-made seventeen-year-old took the advice of his uncle Robbie and stopped by Timely for a job. After seeing the first issue of *Captain America* – the first comic he ever enjoyed – he hoped to interact more with the book's creators.

For the first three weeks, Stanley saw nothing of Kirby but the top of his head. "He was a very hard worker," Stan recalled. "I can't remember him doing anything but sitting at his board and working. There must have been times when he got up and walked around and went for a sandwich or a smoke or something, but my only memory of him was sitting at the drawing board, drawing and occasionally talking to Joe Simon, because Joe was the editor at the time." Stan added: "They were a very close-knit team, although I think Jack did more of the artwork, because Jack was always at the drawing board and Joe did a lot of walking around."

Both of them, however, kept Stan busy. "I was just a guy who did whatever had to be done," Stan explained. They had him running down to the store to fetch sandwiches or coffee, erasing pencil lines from inked drawings, and proofreading pages. "And then, if I found a sentence that didn't make sense, they'd say, 'Well, see if you can rewrite it.'"

Simon and Kirby's *Captain America* was a departure from National's formula, but just as profitable. The first story set a stunning pace: They introduced the hero, killed his creator (an Einstein stand-in named Dr. Erskine), featured a rousing fight scene, and included a cameo by President Franklin Delano Roosevelt. The new hero battled German saboteurs posing as mind-reading performers (Von Krantz, alias "Sando" and Omar); Nazis Rathcone, Herr Kameleon, and Strangler; and one of comics' greatest villains, the Red Skull. (Simon claims he created this villain, while Jack later described freelance writer Ed Herron as this character's father.)

Captain America Comics No. 1, dated March 1941 but on sale in December 1940, immediately sold a million copies. Its cover presented the Captain – the first Timely character to debut in his own title – socking Hitler on the jaw.

That many young readers would soon be in the army ensured the book's success, as did the presence of kid sidekick Bucky, an eager young hero assistant readers could identify with. "*Captain America* was exceptional, a sellout," Simon noted. "We were up to, after the first issue, close to the million mark, and that was monthly." *Captain America* was the first Timely book to be in the same league as *Superman* and *Batman*. "We were entertaining the world."

Not everyone, however, was thrilled about *Captain America*. MLJ

Comics publisher John Goldwater was furious. Before *Captain America*, the company had enjoyed success with their red-clad superpatriot the Shield. Now, Goldwater felt Captain America's shield plagiarized the chest insignia of his character. Goldwater let Goodman know he was planning to file a lawsuit. Goodman smoothed things over by asking Kirby and Simon to change Cap's identical shield motif. Jack was happy to oblige. He'd never liked Simon's concept of a shield. In the second issue, April 1941, Cap was seen carrying and throwing a round one.

Other people were also upset with *Captain America*, but for different reasons. Among them was homegrown Nazi group the German American Bund, a New York–based group that supported and dressed like Hitler. The German American Bund objected to Simon and Kirby depicting their Führer and their own group as punching bags (in *Captain America* No. 5's story, "Killers of the Bund"). They inundated Timely's mostly Jewish staff with hate mail and telephoned death threats. Initially, the staff didn't take the anti-Semitic threats seriously. This changed when some employees returned to the office with tales of seeing strange men outside of the building on Forty-second Street. Soon, some workers were afraid to leave the office for lunch, and the police were called. Just as police guards arrived to patrol the hallways and office, the receptionist summoned Joe Simon over to the telephone switchboard. She said Mayor La Guardia was on the line, asking to speak with the editor of *Captain America*. Joe took the call, and the mayor said, "You boys over there are doing a good job. The city of New York will see that no harm will come to you."

After the first issue, Simon asked Jack to join him in Timely's art department as the company's art director. Jack accepted, and they moved out of their modest office on West Forty-fifth Street and saved $25 a month. Simon then hired inker Syd Shores to be Timely's third employee.

During the next two months, Joe and Jack crammed their stories with new creations, including love interest Betty Ross; Oriental giants ("That Wouldn't Die," the title screamed); Adolf Hitler, Hermann Göring, and their Nazi stronghold; a mayor who was really the villainous Wax Man, the hunchback who terrorized Hollywood; and the evil Butterfly and his Ancient Mummies.

By the third issue, Stan Lieber made a habit of sitting in a corner and playing notes on his ocarina for appreciative Uncle Robbie. "Jack and the guys would throw things at him," Simon explained.

Stanley also kept asking for a chance to write. To give him something to do, Simon let him handle two pages of text that every publisher needed to include in comics to qualify for second-class mailing privileges. "Nobody wanted to do that stuff because nobody read it," Simon remarked, "so Stan did it, and he treated it like it was the Great American Novel." Within two days, Stanley showed Joe a few one-page prose adventures for his debut in *Captain America* (May 1941's "Captain America Foils the Traitor's Revenge").

Noting the signature, Joe asked, "Who's Stan Lee?"

Lieber said he was. He was changing his name, for "journalistic reasons."

After *Captain America*, Jack and Joe were invited to work on an issue of Fawcett Publications' *Whiz Comics*, which starred Captain Marvel, a crippled newsboy given supernatural powers by an ancient wizard he met in an abandoned subway tunnel. When Billy yelled, "Shazam," he became a caped adult hero who could fly and fight evildoers.

Ed Herron, a young writer who had worked for Fox Features Syndicate (Simon claimed to have given Herron his first writing assignments when he was new to the city – broke, desperate, and practically homeless), called Joe Simon at Timely and said executives at Fawcett wanted to meet with him and Jack. Jack and Simon walked to Fawcett's offices two blocks away and met Herron, two editors, and art director Al Allard, who showed them a drawing of Captain Marvel. The editors explained that he was a new character readers seemed to enjoy and that Fawcett was "hoping to make him into another Superman."

Simon and Kirby agreed to create the first special issue. After working all day at Timely, they wolfed down sandwiches and then headed for a rented hotel room to develop *Captain Marvel.*

They called in inkers and letterers and had it finished in a week. Jack asked, "What about the byline?" Simon thought the book would flop. They didn't sign it, and *Captain Marvel*'s first issue became a hit to rival *Superman.*

Chapter 2

Goodman sat at his desk and faced Joe Simon. "We've got a lawsuit on our hands." Goodman raised a copy of *Captain America* No. 6 (cover dated September 1941) and flipped to a page that showed the villain the Hangman. "John Goldwater has a character named the Hangman. John is very upset over this. Our Hangman is nothing like his. He hasn't got a case, but lawsuits are expensive and we'd better go over there to talk to him."

The character died by the story's end, but Jack, Goodman, and Joe still had to catch a cab down to MLJ's office on Lafayette Street. After six issues, *Captain America* was routinely outselling many of chief rival National's books and yielding almost as many imitators as *Superman*. MLJ's the Shield couldn't compete anymore, and MLJ was a little disappointed.

After comparing the similarities of the two Hangmen, Goodman assured his old co-worker Goldwater that Timely wouldn't use the character again. As the meeting ended, Jack saw Goldwater tap Joe on the shoulder. "You guys have the touch," he said amiably. "If you want to make a change, we can make the deal." Outside, Goodman was furious.

By the time Jack was working on the ninth issue of *Captain America*, tensions with Timely came to a head.

During the previous eight months, he and Joe had filled *Captain America* with more eye-opening concepts. Cap defeated Herr Snupp and his flunkies the Unholy Legion, a contemporary Ivan the Terrible, Counterfeiters ("The Case of the Fake Money Fiends"), Dr. Grimm and Gorro (who died in their "Horror Hospital"), the Ringmaster and his circus of crime, and "Fang, the Arch-Fiend of the Orient." If Cap needed help in these battles, Joe and Jack threw in their new creation, the Sentinels of Liberty, a multiracial group of patriotic kids led by Cap's sidekick, Bucky. The series continued to be Timely's biggest hit and one of the most imitated.

One afternoon, Timely's accountant, Morris Coyne (the silent third partner in MLJ Publications), approached Simon when no one was in the office and said that Timely was paying Simon less than the agreed-upon 25 percent. Coyne claimed Goodman was piling salaries and overhead on the title and that Simon and Kirby wouldn't be able to do anything about it.

Joe felt Goodman had reneged on the handshake agreement for 25 percent of *Captain America*'s profits. Instead of confronting Goodman, however, he reached out to Jack Liebowitz, the recently installed head of Harry Donenfeld's DC Comics. Liebowitz was thrilled to hear from a creative duo whose fame and sales figures matched that of Siegel and Schuster. By now, Joe and Jack had helped *Captain America* and affiliate titles *USA*, *All-Winners*, and *Young Allies* sell close to a million copies each month. "When can we get together?" Liebowitz asked.

In less than a year, Jack had gone from obscurity to industry star to meeting with the uncontested market leader. In DC's office at 480 Lexington, he faced an enormous six-foot painting of Superman in the waiting area. Liebowitz – late thirties, slim – ushered them into his office with a warm greeting. "This is Harry Donenfeld, my partner," he said, indicating a short, older man pacing around the room with a huge chauffeur in tow. Within seconds, Liebowitz told them that Simon & Kirby – their brand name – should work for DC. At Timely, their *Captain America* sold over a million copies a month, and Goodman paid Jack $75 while Joe received $85. Now, Simon faced Liebowitz and said they wanted $500 a week ($250 each) and a one-year contract.

Liebowitz said he'd have it drawn up. "Have your lawyer get in touch with us."

Standing near a bottle of scotch on a tiny swivel table in the corner, Donenfeld said, "Have a drink, fellas." After the chauffeur poured the scotch and they toasted, Jack and Joe raced out of there. "Donenfeld was still toasting when we left," Simon recalled.

The next morning, Jack sat at his drawing table in Timely, trying not to let on that they were thinking of moving. He noticed how many of Goodman's relatives actually surrounded him each day. He didn't want them all angry with him. After a full day of work, he and Joe once again rented a nearby hotel room and spent the evening churning out cover sketches for heroes like the one Joe Simon called Super Sherlock Holmes.

Soon, he and Joe were leaving Timely's office for lunch but heading over to their makeshift studio to work on ideas. After wolfing down sandwiches and coffee, they talked about comics or the new deal while drawing. Back at Timely, young Stan Lee wondered what was up. They weren't sending him out for lunch anymore, and he wanted to know if he'd offended them. The duo assured him nothing was wrong. But one day, while heading for their room, they noticed Lee right behind them. Joe said he shouldn't come with them, but Stan kept pace. "You guys must be working on something of your own," he said.

"Go back to Uncle Martin, kid," Joe said. "You may be an editor soon."

"Come on, I'm your man," Stan said. "You guys need me."

They let him tail after them and also let him in on the fact that they were moving to National. Now, when they left the Timely office after work, they usually found Stan waiting at the hotel. Joe seemingly resented his presence, but Stan was eager to help: If they needed him to run errands, he did for no pay. When they finished sketches and ideas, he held them up with wide-eyed awe.

If they weren't developing concepts for DC, they were in Timely's offices, finishing the tenth issue of *Captain America*. They didn't tell Goodman they were leaving and kept working for Timely in an effort to avoid burning any bridges. They wanted Goodman to continue to pay their share of *Captain America*'s enormous profits. If Goodman found out they were practically out the door, they felt, he'd immediately stop issuing checks. They were also waiting for their lawyer to change a clause in the DC contract that said their work had to meet the company's standards. They wanted it to read that they'd meet their usual standards. After signing the deal – which called for them to deliver twenty-five pages a month and receive additional pay for anything over that – they brought Liebowitz the proposals they'd worked up. Liebowitz faced the Super Sherlock pages and said DC's lawyers would investigate whether they could use this sort of character. Ultimately, he said they couldn't and that they should focus on original ideas.

While they kept working up ideas in their hotel room, Jack wondered how wise it was to have Stan around. He kept telling the kid, "We expect you to keep this all in strict confidence, Stan."

Stan would answer, "What kind of guy do you think I am?"

Within days, Jack thought he learned the answer. He was at his desk at Timely when he noticed the mood change. Goodman's relatives slowly formed a group and approached. Soon, Goodman's brothers and uncles surrounded Jack and Joe.

Uncle Robbie yelled, "You guys are sneaking behind our backs, working for someone else. Martin is furious!"

"We're not going to deny it," Joe said. "I guess it's time for us to leave."

Abe Goodman asked, "Aren't you ashamed of yourself? You're fired!"

Another Goodman added, "But first you have to finish this issue of *Captain America*."

They completed the latest batch of stories, emptied their desks, and carried their supplies out of Timely. No one said good-bye.

Kirby wondered how Goodman learned of their deal. A lot of people knew about their plans, but Joe Simon remembers that Jack suspected Stan. When Simon told him Stan claimed he had nothing to do with it, Jack replied, "The next time I see that little son of a bitch, I'm gonna kill him."

After a cordial greeting, the maître d' quickly led Jack Liebowitz and his all-star entourage to the best table in the house. It was a popular Hawaiian restaurant on Lexington Avenue. Kirby glanced at the hula girls and then at Simon; Liebowitz; DC's tall, blond, thirty-something senior editor, Whit Ellsworth; two younger editors, Mort Weisinger and Jack Schiff (recruited from pulp magazines); and Jerry Siegel and Joe Schuster, co-creators of Superman. Siegel had recently been described as wealthy and sophisticated in *The Saturday Evening Post*, but the duo, who created Superman while attending Cleveland's Glenville High School in 1934, were beginning to regret selling National the first Superman adventure – and rights to the character – for $130. "They brought them along because they were trying to impress us," Simon explained. "They didn't have a lot to say."

Eventually, Liebowitz wanted to talk about whether Simon and Kirby would create new titles or work on established characters. By now, they'd been on staff for a few weeks. They'd worked up new characters, drawn salaries, and rented a larger studio in Tudor City that overlooked a dock on the East River.

They sat at the drawing tables positioned around a Murphy bed that could fold into the wall and waited to hear what DC wanted. "They didn't know what to do with us," Simon explained. "We were on the payroll, and we had been trying to come up with characters." After DC rejected Super Sherlock Holmes and other ideas, the company began to send Simon and Kirby scripts for lesser-known features. Various editors also suggested that they mimic the style of current DC creators. They tried, but everything inevitably resembled Captain America. "Artists in the DC bullpen had to retouch or redraw the figures and faces," Simon recalled. "We were a dismal flop."

Simon and Kirby were soon dragged into another controversy, this time involving Fawcett's *Captain Marvel.* After *Captain Marvel* began actively to compete with *Superman* (enjoying sales of almost one million each issue), Fawcett unleashed a line of clever spin-offs: *Mary Marvel,* featuring a teenage girl in the thunderbolt-emblazoned costume; teenage boy *Captain Marvel, Jr.*; and a book starring the entire brood, *The Marvel Family.* That sales continued to climb enraged National Comics, especially since the *Captain Marvel* franchise was affecting their film deals. When National couldn't reach a deal with Republic Pictures for a *Superman* serial, and signed with Paramount for a cartoon series, Republic quickly filmed *The Adventures of Captain Marvel.*

On September 5, 1941, National filed a lawsuit against Fawcett and Republic, claiming infringement and unfair competition. Jack and Joe ran into Jack Schiff, one of the young editors who sat with them at the Hawaiian restaurant, one morning in the lobby of the DC office building. Schiff said he was on his way to see the lawyer right now. Joe asked why they were filing a lawsuit.

"Captain Marvel," Schiff replied. "He's a copy of Superman."

Joe noted that everyone was copying the hero. Schiff nodded and explained that Fawcett's variant was "getting too big. Fawcett is too big. Donenfeld wants to make a test case of Captain Marvel." Jack wanted to stay out of it, but then Schiff remembered that Jack and Joe had actually produced the first *Captain Marvel* special. Schiff told them that National's lawyer, Louis Nizer, should talk with them. When Simon asked why, Schiff said, "Didn't they ask you to copy Superman?"

Simon was evasive, noting again that everyone was copying Superman. But Schiff wouldn't let it go. "We can always subpoena you," he mentioned.

Once again, Jack and Joe were heading to a lawyer's office.

Nizer, then one of the country's best-known attorneys, was a sharply dressed, extremely organized, excellent speaker. Joe and Jack had to help Nizer's capable staff prepare his case. Already, his staff had compiled stacks of research on comic book heroes and the medium.

For days, Jack had Nizer coach him on his testimony. Some nights, he sat with Nizer and most of National's staff, preparing for a cross-examination. "It was my understanding that he was basing his case on one major basis: that Captain Marvel, in flying without wings or artifacts, plagiarized Superman," Joe Simon said.

Ultimately, Jack didn't testify. At the trial, he watched Simon approach the witness stand. Simon was the only artist called; he spoke against the Fawcett executives in the crowd who had hired him and Jack to create the special. After a pithy cross-examination, Fawcett's lawyers got down to business, pointing out dozens of fictional characters who came from other planets; that DC failed to include proper copyright notices in some cases; and that Superman and Captain Marvel had different types of powers. Fawcett won the case but would soon see another court reverse the decision and rule against the company and Captain Marvel. In the end, Fawcett would settle out of court, paying National $400,000 in damages and killing off the Captain Marvel line.

After they failed at editor-assigned ghosting jobs, Simon and Kirby were instructed by Liebowitz to "just do what you want. You guys are getting paid." They started by revamping a hero called the Sandman, who wore tights and emerged from dreams to fight crime. Their new Sandman, however, resembled a lean Captain America clone. Next, they worked on Manhunter, which borrowed the title of a recent film. In Simon & Kirby's version, however, Manhunter was pursuing Adolf Hitler. While this was yet another Captain America look-alike, readers didn't care. They snatched up copies of both *Manhunter* and *The Sandman*.

Chapter 3

America's entrance into World War II meant higher defense spending, millions of Americans finding work, and more children having nickels and dimes to spend on comic books. *Publishers Weekly* and *Business Week* both reported that Americans were buying fifteen million comics a month; publishers, ever watchful of trends, offered even more military-oriented features.

Jack and Joe were still working out of their studio in Tudor City, in a luxury apartment building with a late 1920s art deco design, located on the present site of the United Nations. At the time, kid gangs seemed to be the way to go. Before leaving Timely, they had created the Sentinels of Liberty, a wartime gang led by Captain America's mascot, Bucky. Now they created the Newsboy Legion, a Dead End Kids–style group led by a police officer in a Captain America–like blue-and-yellow costume, toting a shield. Meanwhile, Stan Lee continued to write stories that pitted the Young Allies against supervillains and the Axis.

Inspired by headlines of daring raids by courageous British commandos, Jack and Joe then created The Boy Commandos, a kid gang comprising members from each of the Allied countries: France's André Chavard, England's Alfie Twidgett, Dutch member Jan Haasan, and the star, "Brooklyn," a violent Kirby stand-in American kid who carried his tommy gun in a gangster-style violin case. The kids, the story went, were mascots on U.S. Army bases in Britain, until Captain Rip Carter gathered them together, put them in uniform (except for Brooklyn, who wore a green turtleneck and red derby), and led them into battle against the Nazis. When young readers saw Brooklyn, they went crazy. After *The Boy Commandos* premiered in July 1942, the title continued to sell over one million copies each month. It was one of DC's three biggest hits, along with *Superman* and *Batman*. As with some of their earlier work, however, *The Boy Commandos* also inspired death threats. When Jack answered the telephone, he would hear someone growl, "We'll wait for you downstairs, we'll beat the bejabbers outta ya!" Jack responded by drawing five pages a day, adventures in which the Commandos cheered, "Let's give Hitler the bum's rush!"

Jack Liebowitz, however, knew that any day now Jack and Joe would both be drafted. Already many industry talents were in the military (including Stan, who patriotically volunteered and was stationed in New Jersey, writing scripts for army training films). If Simon and Kirby were gone, other creators might not be able to handle their characters the same way. With this in mind, Liebowitz asked them to work faster and start building an inventory of stories. To accomplish this, Jack and Joe filled their studio with inkers, letters, colorists, and writers, striving to create a year's worth of tales. "I was hired to do as many Boy Commandos, Newsboy Legion, and Sandman stories as I could," said artist Gil Kane (born Eli Katz). "They gave me scripts and they would do the splashes and they would have it inked." Much of the work was rushed in places, but they sent it in anyway, Kane explained, "because they knew they were both going into the service and they just wanted to get as much money together as possible."

By late spring of 1943, Simon entered the Coast Guard. Jack gave up the studio and worked in DC's office until midsummer. "It was a very, very lonely time," he explained, "because Roz and I would walk down Broadway, we'd go . . . anywhere we'd go, we'd walk around Brighton Beach, and there were no young people there. It was a ghost town." The sight of young people in uniform made them feel strange about wearing civilian clothing, and soon nighttime curfews curtailed their late-night walks.

On June 7, 1943, Jack was drafted. He learned this the usual way – by telegram – and reported to the draft office, located in the same building as DC, with a card stamped "Navy." "And then some guy came in and he said, 'We need six guys for the army.'" Jack was one of them. The next stop was basic training at Camp Stewart, Georgia. It was a hot and humid summer. Jack was unprepared for drill sergeants, stern orders, and army discipline. Everywhere he turned, it seemed someone was yelling, "Stand straight! Get up! Lie down!" At two A.M., they'd wake him up. He'd get dressed, get his full pack on, reach for his rifle, and hike twenty-five miles in one direction, then twenty-five back. The experience was nothing like what he'd seen in the movies. The same applied for the people he met.

He heard people speak with southern accents and learned that some were Jewish. He met people raised on farms who had never traveled to the city. He met Texans who never rode horses and who believed all New Yorkers had money to burn. Some people didn't like Jews, but they learned to work and live together in close quarters. In this way, he felt, the war did a lot to unite the country. Encountering people from Florida, Michigan, Utah, and Texas also opened his eyes to how diverse America really was.

In August, they boarded a huge, crowded ship heading for the port of embarkation, which was surrounded by an escort of baby battleships and destroyers. He joined the other soldiers on the deck, stretching out, exhausted. During every minute of the trip, ocean waves made them seasick, whether they were asleep or awake. The ship reached Liverpool, England, at night, and Jack saw the widespread destruction caused by German Stukas and bombers during the Blitz. People were reduced to sleeping in subways. Before he could fully absorb the destruction, they were on the move, heading for Gloucester on foot. While walking or waiting for orders to continue, he faced the English countryside close to the embarkation area near Dartmouth. It looked like an enormous garden. "It was the most beautiful thing I have ever seen," Jack recalled. Two days later, he left for France and landed on Omaha Beach ten days after the D-Day invasion.

He stepped off the boat and marched toward the beach, "and the bodies were still there. They didn't clean it up." Everywhere he turned, he saw thousands of bodies lying in the sand. "We were rushed off those boats, and they tried not to give us time to think about this, but we did."

He was moved quickly into hedgerow country and onto a waiting truck, then taken from this vehicle after a few miles and placed on another. After bypassing Paris, he joined the other forces being assembled for General Patton's devastating march across France.

Jack was in northern France, close to the border of Germany and Belgium. His outfit was lined up and watching Patton yell at their cowering colonel. Apparently, someone had told Patton that Jack's outfit had been killed. Patton arrived with replacement troops and saw Jack and his men alive and well. No one could explain what happened; the general was livid.

Jack and the men were shivering in their boots. By now, they knew heavy coats wouldn't keep them warm during a French winter. Walking might warm them up, but until Patton stopped yelling, they had to stand at attention.

Freezing, Jack stood and watched Patton spread a huge map over the hood of a jeep. Patton faced Jack's outfit and yelled, "What the fuck are these guys doing here?" He jabbed a finger at the map again. "What is this? What is this? You're fouling up the whole fucking thing!"

The tongue-lashing continued. "I heard that Patton ordered replacements," Jack said later. "He thought my outfit had been wiped out. So some foul-up, I guess, signals crossed, messages mixed up; it happened quite a lot during the war." The mix-up, however, could affect Patton's schedule and ability to predict events on the battlefield.

Ultimately, Jack's outfit joined the general on his march against the enemy, and Jack came to regard Patton as a great general who knew you couldn't win a war by digging in. "He kept his troops moving constantly so the Germans never got any rest. Never, at least not in my sector." In addition, Patton made sure his men received the best meals and medical care. And if his colonels needed more troops, he'd bring them himself.

One day, in a command center, a lieutenant called him over. "Private Kirby?"

"Yes, sir."

"Jack Kirby? The artist?"

"Yes, sir. I drew *Captain America . . .*"

"And *The Boy Commandos*. So you can draw?"

Jack figured the officer wanted a portrait. "Yes, sir. Of course I can draw."

"Good," said the lieutenant. "I'm making you a scout. You go into these towns that we don't have and see if there is anybody there. Draw maps and pictures of what you see, and come back and tell us if you find anything."

Back then, advance scouting was one of the most dangerous duties soldiers could have. Their radios barely worked. Germans kept cutting their telephone lines. Though they were covered under the Geneva Conventions, scouts were treated like spies upon capture: beaten or killed. Advance scouts knew they wouldn't live very long.

Like many Americans, Jack thought the war would be a carefully planned event with groups of professional soldiers facing one another in columns, aiming rifles, and waiting for their commanding officers to give the order to shoot. In the field, however, he saw that in his sector, the Germans were acting like guys from his neighborhood, only with bombs and guns.

During this war, the danger was always real. The Germans weren't an unknown enemy sneaking up on them. The battles were very personal. He'd see their faces and fight them in close quarters.

Many German soldiers, he learned, knew English and enjoyed taunting the Americans. They'd been fed Hitler Youth propaganda since childhood and believed they were superior to other fighting forces.

"We called each other names all the time," Jack explained. "We were cursing each other in English, German, French, Hebrew. I had quite a large vocabulary by the time I got back – I could cuss somebody out in four different languages." Sometimes opposing armies would meet and do nothing but yell "Go to hell" or "Go shit on yourself!" But everyone understood that insulting someone's mother could lead to gunfire.

War was a sequence of events. There were long periods where Jack did nothing but wait. He walked a lot. Then he faced situations where he knew that any second now, it'd be curtains. During a ferocious shelling from the enemy, Jack sat in a foxhole and steadied his nerves by sketching in a notepad. But a shell landed near his foxhole and hit one of his friends, blowing his head clean off. Jack returned to his sketch later on and saw that some of his friend's head was on his drawing. He was on patrol often, and on patrol you see the strangest things.

One day, Jack and three other soldiers arrived at a field with high grass on each side of a narrow path and a nine-man German patrol one hundred yards away on the other side. Jack and the three men ducked and hid behind grass. On patrol, men on both sides didn't shoot unless they had to or unless an officer ordered it. Jack and Mitch, a furniture dealer from Michigan, swapped insults with the patrol until Mitch pointed at a tall German. "I'm going to get me that first one. I'm going to get him right in the eye."

"You're crazy," Jack said. There were nine of them.

"No, I'm going to get me one of them."

You couldn't use the standard issue M-1 to hit a bucket at ten yards. It wasn't a sniper's rifle. It also bucked in your hand. Jack figured Mitch would either miss or nick the tall guy, and then the Germans would put fifty holes in them. Jack hunkered down in the grass and noticed Mitch's eyes hardening. He yelled louder this time: "Get in the goddamn fucking jeep!"

Michigan crept into the open. "No!" The Germans saw him raise his rifle. "Watch me do it." He fired from one hundred yards with an M-1 and smacked his target square between the eyes.

All hell broke loose: The Germans returned fire, and Jack's patrol took off like "big-assed birds." For all they knew, there might have been fifty Germans swarming after them.

During another sweep, an old guy with a little gray beard ran over to him. The guy had tears running down his cheeks and was visibly amazed. He met Jack's stare, blinked a few times, and then said in a thin little voice, "You're Jewish."

"Yeah, I'm Jewish."

"Come with me."

Jack ran after the little old man. The rest of his squad followed. They rushed down a long road, past farm buildings and a factory. Though he wondered if they were being led into an ambush, he kept going. I mean, what would the Germans be doing with this little graybeard? he asked himself.

They came to a walled-in stockade. The old man pointed. "There, there."

Jack stopped. He saw dozens of German guards fleeing the structure, jumping over the wall, using any escape route they could find. The Germans knew that an advance scout usually had a huge division right behind him. While running away, the Germans looked over their shoulders to shout, "Fuck you!" in English. "They all said that by that time. They thought it was a big insult, but I don't think they really knew what the word meant."

When the Germans were gone, Jack and his buddies got to work opening up the stockades. He figured they'd find a few prisoners of war, some of their guys caught in the early fighting. What he saw pinned him to the spot. Most of the inmates were Polish Jews who had worked in nearby factories. The place didn't have a name like Auschwitz, but it was a smaller, equally horrific concentration camp.

There were mostly women, a few men. They looked as if they hadn't eaten for God knew how long. They were scrawny and in tattered, filthy rags. The Germans had left them behind to starve like dogs. Jack watched them leaving their cells and kept thinking, What do I do? Until his squad caught up with him, he just stood there, shaking his head and saying, "Oh, God."

The enemy comprised Hitler Jungen, the Hitler Youth. Since childhood they had been exposed to propaganda and Nazi training. Now they were battle-ready, dyed-in-the-wool eighteen-year-old Nazis. "They were little duplicates of Hitler," Jack noted. But the SS was far worse. The SS would torture and kill prisoners. During another patrol, Jack was sweeping an empty, bombed-out building. He sat on the steps for a moment and saw six SS emerge from hiding. They started coming over, shouting insults at him, then they saw his tags. One SS man asked, "You're Jewish?"

"They gave me the works, every dirty name they could think of," Jack explained, "and they got me sore 'cause they said something about my mother – and I blew up." Jack raised his M-1. The men raised their weapons. Bullets flew all over the place, and everyone rushed to get the hell out of there.

Most of the time the Germans shot at them with their antiarmor guns. These 88s were effective antipersonnel weapons that could fire hundreds of rounds in sixty seconds. A battery of big 88 shells churned the ground underfoot and pulverized brick walls. One day, Jack and his men were in a town occupied on one side by Germans and on the other by Americans. No one was making any moves. Suddenly a German man rode by on a bicycle. The Texan soldier near Jack raised his rifle and shot him. Jack turned on the Texan. "What the hell did you do that for?" The guy was on a bike. It wasn't a real attack. The Texan didn't care. But the German soldiers did. "They opened up on us with a machine gun. We opened on them with a machine gun. A half hour later, five machine guns are in action and two rifle platoons are involved."

Jack hid behind a rock wall as machine guns pounded everything in sight. Chunks of wall and big clots of dirt were flying. Caught on the ground, Jack was still trying to figure out why this guy had shot the bicyclist. A while later, his sergeant crawled over and grabbed his feet. Jack almost shot his head off. The sergeant said, "Pick out five men and go see Marlene Dietrich."

Jack was confused. "What for? What's going on? Are you kidding?"

"If you don't want the detail, then I'll get another guy."

"All right, all right," he replied. "I'll take the detail." He couldn't believe it was true, and the five men he picked out couldn't, either; nevertheless they all crawled a hundred yards and walked another four hundred to a waiting truck.

Jack joined other GIs who were climbing on board; they rode seven miles from the action to a tiny church. "And sure enough, there she was, Marlene Dietrich, along with Bing Crosby, Martha Raye, and some other actors." Jack sat in the audience and watched as celebrities told jokes, performed vaudeville routines, and sang and danced in the middle of this hell on earth. It was hard to believe, but after a while, he wasn't even thinking about the war. Even though the Germans deepened their defense and were sending fire close to the church, Marlene Dietrich came out in GI underwear, and the men went crazy. Jack felt the concussion of the nearby blast. Bombs got closer. The sound of gunfire was much clearer. Even so, the actors kept performing as if nothing else mattered. "It was a real morale booster for us," he said.

At some point, he dozed off. Someone woke him up and told him it was time to go. Jack rushed out of the church and onto the truck and rode back to the battlefield. The Germans were now using even more 88s. The Americans were using 105s. Because of one guy on a bike, the whole place was being blown apart. His division, he saw, was pinned down. With 88s buzzing past his ears like high-speed mosquitoes, he crawled toward a jeep and snuck underneath it. In between blasts, a few German soldiers were trying to get closer, firing and killing some of the men. "I was lying there just shooting away with my rifle – that's all I had." Jack stayed there until American artillery cleared them out. But by then a bunch of Americans had been killed. "It was a holy mess."

Between battles, Jack would write to Roz, who worked in a lingerie shop and tried to escape loneliness by moving in with her mother. She'd received his "V-letters" (or "V-mail") and send him a letter a day. After going behind German lines into towns nobody had entered yet, running into German patrols and mixing it up with them, he'd get back to American lines in time for mail call. He'd still be heated, dazed from battle, reading mushy poems Roz copied when she ran out of things to say. "They were so beautiful that I couldn't believe it," Jack explained. That he was still decompressing, still wanting to get back at the Germans he ran into, and reading these beautiful poems sometimes made him burst into hysterical laughter. Other times he'd pass the notes around to the entire squad.

Soon it was the middle of winter. The ground was covered with snow, and high winds made it even colder. In the field, there was no place to sleep but the frozen ground. His outfit was about to move into Bastogne, then head into Belgium and Metz, but much of the unit was withdrawn. The men were beat up. Jack himself had severe frostbite on both feet and legs. Replacements would take over.

He was taken to a hospital in London, where he spent several months worrying about his legs. They were completely frozen. During his stay, he couldn't write to Roz. He also couldn't read her older letters. He'd faithfully tucked them into his pack, but hospital employees had rifled through his belongings when he'd arrived. He would never see most of his stuff again – although one merciful thief did allow him to keep a German pistol he wanted to bring home.

Each day at the lingerie shop, Roz looked forward to getting home and reading his latest note. She began to wonder why he didn't write. One day, someone from the hospital called her long distance and told her that his feet had frozen. "The first thing that came through my mind was, Thank God he's okay," she recalled.

"The next thing I thought was, Thank God it's his feet, not his hands."

Jack's legs were just as black as his toes, and the doctors considered amputation. Luckily, his legs returned to their normal color. The hospital sent Roz a telegram saying he was all right, and he started writing to her again. He was supposed to ride back to the United States on the *Queen Mary*, but he caught a cold in England and they wouldn't let him aboard the boat. Instead, he was placed on a hospital tug that rocked side to side during the entire trip. Passengers were offered excellent meals, but he was too seasick to eat. He almost starved to death.

During the nine-day trip (the *Queen Mary* would've reached America in three), he wheeled himself out to the deck, where he saw other passengers lying around like dead men. He didn't see any nurses. One lieutenant had gotten one of his testicles shot off. Other men didn't have arms or legs. Some men had deep, gruesome scars. Some had lost their noses, eyes, or ears. Others had "half a face," and he could see right into part of their heads. More than a few suffered from psychological damage. He was doing all right comparatively.

As the slow-moving ship continued across the ocean, Jack wheeled his chair over to a table and entered a poker game with paratroopers. Although off the battlefield, these guys still had the killer instinct. Everyone was in wheelchairs, but Jack knew they were a bunch of killers. They played with fierce intensity, ready to murder anyone who won a jackpot they could have sent home to their families. In this game, however, the pot wasn't that large, maybe a couple of hundred dollars, or a few French coupons, or occupation marks they'd picked up along the way. As the pot got bigger, however, the guys grew quieter, more intense. Even worse, Jack was winning. When he raked in his prize money, the other men got angry. Jack made a run for it. Wheeling himself down the deck, he looked over his shoulder to see the other men's chairs close behind. Suddenly the money went flying through the air. Jack kept going without looking back.

* * *

In January 1945, Private First Class Jack Kirby returned to the United States and was shipped to South Carolina to spend his remaining six months in the motor pool. When he wasn't working on trucks, he looked forward to Roz's visit. It felt as if he hadn't seen her in decades. The day she arrived, however, he learned that because of a recent late return to the base, he now couldn't get a visitors' pass. Undeterred, he took an insurance card, the same color as the pass, and joined a crowd of guys walking toward the guards and their own wives and girlfriends. Jack held up the card, flashed it quickly, and then passed the sentries. He walked out with the crowd and headed for some quality time with his wife ("We didn't even close the door," he joked). Back at the base, he learned that a negative comment about his unauthorized leave would be included in his official record. He didn't care. He had only a few months left, guys were going over the fence all the time, and he'd been able to see his wife.

After being honorably discharged on July 20 and receiving a combat infantry badge and a European/African/Middle Eastern Theater ribbon with a bronze battle star, he took a train home. As he stepped onto the platform, Roz was waiting. When he'd entered the service, he had weighed about 175 pounds. Now he weighed about 129 pounds. He was thin as a rod and still hobbling a little. He'd need disability for about a year; and on cold days, his toes would still tingle. But in late 1943, he was happy to be alive and even happier to finally be home. He moved in with Roz's parents. She became pregnant with their first child, Susan. Though the war soon ended, it was never far from his thoughts. There was nothing anyone could call "romantic" about war, he felt: Movies and media painted a big picture of fellowship, but the cost in lives and to the human spirit was simply too high. Still, he reasoned, the world had had no other choice but to destroy Hitler.

Chapter 4

Stan became editor of his cousin's husband's publishing company when Simon & Kirby left for DC back in 1941. Though he had only a few stories to his credit, the seventeen-year-old temporary editor tried to lure readers with creations like Headline Hunter (a reporter behind enemy lines) and the Destroyer (a blue-faced hero with a skull insignia on his torso, who killed his enemies). But with the exception of changing Simon & Kirby's Sentinels of Liberty group into the Young Allies, none of his ideas matched the success of *Captain America*. He was writing stories for this title as well now, with former inker Syd Shores penciling it, but his characters Mephisto (a human spy), the Looter, the Vulture, the Yellow Claw, and the Vampire were a bit dull. Not even including Hitler could spice things up.

Even so, Goodman kept him on as editor, and Stan continued to present generic heroes like Father Time (a guy in shorts, cape, and mask) and the Witness (a blue, red, and yellow vigilante) under the pseudonyms Neel Nats, S. T. Anley, and Stan Martin. He also kept playing his ocarina in the office. "He'd make us wait while he finished whatever tune he was playing," said Vince Fago, who was then a twenty-eight-year-old animator. "He'd even go into Martin Goodman's office and blow it at him."

While Stan's stories were nothing special, the war meant higher sales all around, so Goodman was able to move Timely out of the McGraw-Hill Building and into the fourteenth floor of the Empire

State Building. In 1941, however, Stan volunteered for the army and spent the next few years writing training films. "He was stateside the whole time," Fago remembered. "Stan told me that he had to pick up cigarette butts on the ball field."

When Stan returned to Timely four years later, everything had changed. During his absence, Goodman had had replacement editor Fago churn out dozens of imitations of Disney's funny animals. Goodman spent most of his days sleeping on the chaise longue in the corner, near the windows and the spectacular view of Manhattan. When Fago came in with artwork, he'd open his eyes, sit up, glance quickly at the covers, and tell Fago to run with it. "He was counting his money," Fago felt. "He had been a hustler who'd had a rough life, and he was trying to live it up."

After derivative titles *Comic Capers*, *Krazy Kow*, *Komic Kartoons*, *Silly Tunes*, *Ziggy Pig*, and *Silly Seal Comics* tapped a new audience of children, Goodman wanted to reach female readers. By now, a female version of Captain America – the stars-and-stripes-clad Miss America – had debuted in *Marvel Mystery Comics* to high sales; he'd chucked the title characters and offered readers twelve-issue subscriptions of her new title for a dollar. And within two weeks, he'd seen twenty thousand one-dollar bills arrive at the office and a beleaguered Fago trying to find somewhere to put all this money (eventually pulling artwork from bins and shoving it in there). And with overall comic sales reaching a staggering twenty-five million by December 1943, he saw DC now consider Timely a threat. "The DC people looked down at us," Fago remembered. "They were snobs. They thought they were higher class than we were."

Regardless, Goodman continued to expand his audience. By 1944, Republic Pictures handed him a buck and agreed to stick Captain America into a preexisting script for a thirteen-episode serial written for another company's character. The serial didn't have much to do with the comic – producers armed Cap with a holstered pistol and threw him in low-budget tights (and had his alter ego be a generic district attorney named Grant Gardner) – but for a while sales improved.

By the time Stan returned in the fall of 1945, funny animal comics were going the way of male superhero characters. Goodman axed *USA Comics* (which featured Captain America as lead character) and asked for *Millie the Model*, *Nellie the Nurse*, and *Tessie the Typist*. Where Timely covers once featured the Human Torch, Captain America, or Sub-Mariner tearing Nazi tanks apart with their hands, they now showed women in roller skates, women bowling with their boyfriends, and women in bikinis posing on the beach with male admirers punching beach balls around. "He was always telling me to create characters in the vein of whatever was selling," Stan explained.

Stan had always liked superheroes, however, and threw Marvel's Big Three (the Torch, Captain America, and Sub-Mariner), along with the Whizzer (a costumed Flash-like speedster granted his powers after a transfusion in the jungle that involved mongoose blood) and Miss America, into a team called the All Winners Squad. Goodman saw low sales for two months and canceled the book.

Stan wouldn't give up. In November 1946, with most wartime patriotic superheroes gone, he tried to change Captain America for postwar audiences. Issue No. 59 showed Steve Rogers and Bucky Barnes (Cap's and Bucky's alter egos) receiving honorable discharges from the army. Then Stan revealed that Steve Rogers had actually been a schoolteacher in civilian life and showed him returning to his job at Lee High School. When Rogers wasn't lecturing his class about math, science, or history – or getting involved in their lame personal problems – he fought generic mobsters and arsonists. Goodman, however, was more excited about Blonde Phantom, another writer's new heroine, who fought crime in a long red dress and domino mask.

Jack Kirby wasn't having any trouble drawing fans. Even after the war, the Simon & Kirby byline continued to translate into higher sales. Joe had arranged for them to work at Harvey Comics, for a decent percentage of whatever comics they delivered. But now Jack and Roz had a daughter (Susan, born December 6, 1945); Jack wanted to buy a house and get his family out of Roz's mother's place, so he started working faster, doing crime comics like *Justice Traps the Guilty* and children's books like *Punch & Judy* for Hillman Comics, Harvey, and Crestwood (also known as Prize). After everyone went to bed, he'd sit at the drawing table in the bedroom, working until three or four in the morning; at dawn, Roz would approach to wish him good morning.

While Timely was struggling to attract teenage readers with their women heroes, Jack and Joe stumbled onto the idea of romance stories. After trying one in Hillman Periodicals' July 1947 issue of *My Date*, they worked on a follow-up for women who liked "true confession" magazines. When Crestwood/Prize Publishers Teddy Epstein and Paul Blyer saw their melodramatic stories about marriage problems in pages for the first issue, they cut a deal with Jack and Joe that gave them 50 percent of the profits. And once September 1947's *Young Romance* No. 1 sold millions of copies, becoming Jack and Joe's biggest hit in years, Crestwood started printing three times as many copies and preparing a spin-off, *Young Love*. Timely, Fawcett, Quality, and even Fox Features Syndicate soon delivered knockoffs like *Love Confessions*, *Romance Tales*, *True Stories of Romance*, and *My Love Secret*. Despite the imitations, Jack and Joe continued to sell five million romance comics a month and to earn more than enough to buy their own homes. By 1948, their search had led to tree-lined Brown Street in Mineola, Long Island, where a developer building houses on sixty-by-one-hundred-foot plots had two homes diagonally across from each other. After paying a $3,000 down payment for the $11,000 house, Jack and Roz ordered beds, kitchen tables, and pots from Macy's and moved in with Susan and their second child, Neal (born in May 1948). Joe and his family moved in across the street. From then on, Joe would come over to smoke cigars and discuss new gimmicks with Jack. "They both stunk up the house!" said Roz. "My walls were yellow, my drapes were yellow, all the books were yellow."

At Timely, young Stan continued to oversee eighty-two separate titles and to work with a stable of artists that included Human

Torch creator Carl Burgos, Captain America's Syd Shores, Dan DeCarlo – who eventually became famous for *Archie Comics* – and talented newcomers John Buscema and Gene Colan. Since Goodman wanted more Blonde Phantom–like heroines, in April 1948, Stan wrote *Captain America* No. 66 and gave Cap a new partner. "I've always hated teenage sidekicks," he explained. "I always felt if I were a superhero, there's no way in the world that I'd go around with some teenager. At the very least, people would talk. Why would a grown man pal around with a teenager? I'd get another grown man to pal around with." If it were up to Stan, Cap wouldn't have anyone by his side. "I read Tarzan and loved it, and there were no teenage sidekicks," he tried to tell Goodman. "And I loved Sherlock Holmes, and he didn't have a teenage sidekick. Robin Hood didn't have a teenage sidekick." Goodman never agreed. And now he wanted more women for teenage girls to identify with. At his typewriter, Stan typed a story about Bucky getting shot and dying in a hospital and Cap meeting his new partner, Golden Girl (a brunette in a generic dress and mask).

Then he oversaw the creation of female versions of *Sub-Mariner* and *The Human Torch*. After three issues, however, Goodman canceled *Namora* and *Sun Girl*. After nineteen issues he canceled Bill Everett's *Venus* (a Wonder Woman–like Roman goddess who posed as a human reporter). And in March 1949, Stan saw the boss decide superheroes were old hat and cancel *The Human Torch*. Then in June, after ninety-two issues, Goodman got rid of *Marvel Mystery Comics* and *The Sub-Mariner*. "I felt a slap to my pride, I guess," Everett said later. "What the heck! You mean *The Sub-Mariner*; it's not selling? I don't believe you. It's impossible! My character, my baby – he's not selling? This is ridiculous! This just doesn't happen!"

Captain America was next. Stan used every trick to keep the book alive – new villains, schoolteaching, killing Bucky, Golden Girl – but Goodman was unconvinced. And though he already had mediocre knockoffs like *Justice Comics*, *Crimefighters*, *All True Crime*, *Official True Crime Cases*, *Lawbreakers Always Lose*, and *True Complete Mystery*, Goodman told Stan to pull Cap from his own book, change the title to *Captain America's Weird Tales*, and fill it with crime stories.

And then he wanted the book gone.

Stan followed orders and kept moving forward. There was no time to consider why he'd failed to keep the heroes alive. Not when he had to start working on books that emulated Jack and Joe's million-selling *Young Romance*.

Chapter 5

Goodman continued to keep Stan busy with hackwork. After deciding romance comics were out, and canceling all but three of eighteen genre entries, he asked for more crime, western comics, and war stories about Korea. Ignoring that the public might not be as supportive of this "police action" – U.S. soldiers fighting under the banner of the United Nations to help South Korea resist North Korean and Red Chinese troops – Goodman gave Stan a laundry list of titles he wanted. "*War Comics*, *Battle Comics*, *Combat Comics*, *War Battles*, *War Combat*, *Battleground*, and *Battlefield*," Stan recalled, sighing. "Anything that had 'war' or 'battle' became a title."

Flooding the stands with Korean War–themed comics was a miscalculation on Goodman's part. "It was five years after World War Two," said artist Joe Sinnott. "The mood wasn't as gung ho as it had been in World War Two, where everybody was behind the effort. I don't think we had the same effort in Korea because mainly it was never a declared war; it was a police action." In addition, "It was a different type of war, with a lot of restrictions put on the service personnel." Korea, he added, was "one of the bad wars." Many Americans somehow sensed that the nation wouldn't win. They were right. During the next three years, fifty thousand American troops would die; the army would feel that the tone of many comics about the conflict was discouraging and keep many, including titles from Goodman, out of its PXs; the United States would emerge as neither winner nor loser when an armistice was declared in July 1953.

With war comics not selling as expected, the mood in the office remained unstable. One day, after finding hundreds of unpublished pages in a closet, Goodman gave Stan an earful. Why pay writers and artists for substandard pages and then hide them all in a closet? "No more staff, only freelancers," Goodman announced, and while he was golfing down in Florida, he wanted Stan to fire everyone.

A few months later, everything changed again. Stan could call some freelancers back because Goodman was about to get rid of distributor Kable News and form his own national distributor, Atlas News Company. Soon, Goodman moved the company – now called Atlas – into smaller offices at 60 Park Avenue. But in his new windowless cubbyhole, Stan kept doing most of the work: writing most of the comics, editing, art directing, designing covers, composing copy, and dealing with the production department.

That June, just when Stan was getting used to war comics, Goodman said, "Stan, let's put out some science-fiction stories." With a sigh, Stan created *Strange Tales*, *Mystic Spellbound*, *Journey into Mystery*, and *Adventures into Weird Worlds*. "I was one of the world's biggest hack writers, and I never thought anything of it," he recalled. "Whatever had to be written. See, the way we worked at our company, my publisher had a theory: He never wanted to be first with anything. He wasn't much of an innovator." Every few months, Stan had to leave one genre for another. Still, it was a job. And he sort of enjoyed doing it.

But he never quite forgot the superheroes. Though their last new hero, December 1950s revival of Joe Simon's Marvel Boy, had lasted only two issues (readers didn't enjoy its mix of heroes, flying saucers, and alien communists who were called "Comrade" before being slugged), Stan told Goodman they should bring heroes back. With *Superman* on television and more people buying comics, Goodman agreed to let him stick a few into the December 1953 issue of *Young Men*.

At his typewriter, Stan came up with a new twist on the big three.

For years, first-term Republican senator Joseph McCarthy (from Wisconsin) had continued to make national headlines. He burst onto the scene after a 1950 speech in Wheeling, West Virginia, where he held up a sheet of paper he claimed contained the names of 205 known communists working in the State Department. He never backed up his claims but continued, with his assistants Roy Cohn and David Schine, to level wild accusations, destroy reputations, and rail against fellow politicians, commies, and homosexuals. With most Americans supporting McCarthy's hunt for communists and un-Americans, Stan positioned the revived heroes as staunch anticommunists. After nuclear fission revived him, Stan wrote, the Human Torch had to battle aliens with nuclear devices (stand-ins for Russians, who'd had nuclear weapons since 1949). The Sub-Mariner no longer hated humans: Instead, he wanted to defend them from communists disguised as aliens trying to steal America's nuclear secrets. Captain America, meanwhile, was joined by Bucky (who hadn't been killed by a gunshot, Stan revised) in a bold new title, *Captain America: Commie Smasher.*

Though Stan and artist John Romita created stories like "Striking Back at the Soviet," readers didn't warm to this new Cap. After a few issues of *Young Men*, and three issues of his revived *Captain America* series, Goodman told him to once again cancel the book. "Patriotism was a dirty word for a while," Romita recalled. Then, after a story set in a North Korean POW camp, Goodman decided to cancel *The Human Torch. The Sub-Mariner* would have also been canceled after its third issue, but producers were considering a television adaptation with Richard Egan as Namor. When a deal failed to materialize after ten issues, however, Goodman told Stan to cancel *The Sub-Mariner*. Stan just wasn't having much luck with heroes.

By 1954, Simon & Kirby had created a few series for Harvey Comics and worked on their own line of books out of Harvey's offices on the fifteenth floor of 1860 Broadway. With the arrival of his third child, Barbara, born November 1952, Jack kept working faster and appreciated the deals Simon found, which paid them 50 percent of the profits. Once they saw Atlas revive Captain America, Jack and Joe handed Crestwood/Prize a new patriotic hero called Fighting American. "We were, of course, I'll say bitter, about not owning Captain America," Simon recalled. "We thought we'd show them how to do Captain America."

They did – coming as close to Cap as possible. They gave the hero an identical costume with stripes and little wings and a teen sidekick named Speedboy, who resembled Bucky. Miraculously, Martin Goodman didn't sue. "I think they didn't because they would be embarrassed in the courts because of the shabby way they treated us," Simon said.

After a Captain America–like origin – a young man emerging from a test with superpowers – Fighting American and Speedboy spent their first star-spangled issue grimly pursuing communists in America. Jack didn't really know much about communism, but he felt that since Senator McCarthy was decrying Red Americans, it was the right thing to do. All he knew about communism, really, was that it was foreign to democracy. "And here I was, I had been fighting for democracy and always aware of two political parties and brought up in that kind of atmosphere." Anything different was dangerous, he felt. If communists prevailed, no one knew what would happen. "So communism became the doorway to chaos, and the doorway to chaos was the doorway to evil. Your family might be hurt. Your friends might be hurt. You didn't want to see a thing like that."

After the first issue failed to sell many copies, Jack and Joe faced another new enemy: New York psychiatrist Fredric Wertham, whose nonfiction book *Seduction of the Innocent* blamed comics for everything from murder to dyslexia and sexual perversion. Wertham's claims were so persuasive that the Senate formed a subcommittee to investigate comics and potential ties to juvenile delinquency. During these televised hearings, Wertham implied that superheroes promoted same-sex relationships. Echoing McCarthy's earlier claims, he said, "If Batman were in the State Department, he would be dismissed." Wertham also claimed that the "protruding breasts" on Timely's harmless characters Millie the Model and Nellie the Nurse inspired young girls to stuff their bras with tissue paper. After announcing that over a billion comics were sold in the United States each year, chairman William Langer of South Dakota repeated Wertham's claims. Committee executive director Richard Clenenden, meanwhile, held up a copy of an innocuous Stan Lee comic. "The next comic book is entitled *Strange Tales* and has five stories in which thirteen people die violently," he said. Clenenden then insinuated that Goodman's use of different companies to publish magazines and comics was an attempt to conceal his identity.

The entire industry was worried. "Remember that comic books didn't enjoy the same prestige as, say, *Collier's* magazine or *The Saturday Evening Post*," Jack explained. "In the fifties, if you went to a newsstand and bought a *Saturday Evening Post*, they'd say: 'There goes a good American.' If you bought a comic book: 'That guy, he shoots pool.'" With the industry receiving more bad press, Jack hoped the hearings wouldn't impact upon his ability to support his family. And though he found some of Wertham's tactics distasteful, he tried to stay out of it. "The only real politics I knew was that if a guy liked Hitler, I'd beat the stuffing out of him and that would be it."

When the latest Red scare continued into May 1954, Jack changed his opinion of McCarthy. This guy was nothing but a hunter. He'd cut down anything in his path. And if he kept this up, who knows? Maybe people who didn't fit his definition of an American – including Jews – would find themselves being dragged from their homes. After all, McCarthy was targeting the United States Army, and Army Secretary Robert Stevens, for abuse during nationally televised hearings, and no one dared to say anything.

Along with twenty million other television viewers, Jack watched the outspoken senator accuse respected officers of being communists. McCarthy's faithful assistant Roy Cohn helped present evidence that made these accusations seem slightly plausible. But the president of the United States, army veteran Dwight D. Eisenhower, had

had enough. He was there to help the army defend itself. Meanwhile, witnesses and the army's lawyers let the public know what was really happening: McCarthy's real problem with the army was that it wouldn't give his former assistant David Schine special privileges after he'd been drafted.

For 187 hours over 36 days, television stations broadcast unedited clips from the hearings that showed McCarthy berating his thirty-two witnesses. The public eventually grew weary of seeing him point his finger at Secretary of the Army Robert Stevens or the president of the United States and bully, harass, and level groundless accusations against witnesses.

Finally, when McCarthy attacked Fred Fisher, who worked in the same office as the army's chief attorney, Joseph N. Welch, soft-spoken gray-haired Welch rose to his feet. "Until this moment, Senator, I think I never really gauged your cruelty or your recklessness," he said. "Let us not assassinate this lad further, Senator. You have done enough. Have you no sense of decency, sir, at long last? Have you no sense of decency?"

"He sounded logical to me, more temperate," Jack said of Welch. "You didn't feel like the storm troopers were going to knock on your door the next day when you listened to this guy." Welch's attack threw cold water on McCarthy and reminded him "he was just a politician" and "was never going to be a Hitler."

Public opinion veered against McCarthy so quickly, Jack and Joe had to rush to change the direction of *Fighting American*'s next issue – from bashing commies to attacking McCarthy. "The hell with it," they decided, and made the book a satire. They also felt that the first issue was pretty stupid and naïve, Simon later revealed.

But the backlash against comics continued, and several publishing houses closed their doors. Printing companies panicked. At Crestwood/Prize, salesman George Dougherty Jr. tried to drum up business by urging Jack and Joe to start their own company. They accepted Dougherty's offer of credit, formed Mainline Comics, and set up shop in the offices of Harvey Comics at 1860 Broadway. Since readers still enjoyed westerns (*Shane* had won an Oscar the year before), they published the action-packed *Bullseye: Western Scout*. EC Comics and Atlas did well with war comics, so they created *Foxhole*, promoted as being written and drawn by actual veterans. *Young Love* continued to spawn imitators, so they devised *In Love*. *Police Trap*, meanwhile, mimicked EC's crime comics but claimed its stories were true, based on accounts from police officers. After inking a distribution deal with Leader News, which also handled Bill Gaines's best-selling EC line, Jack and Joe started working on their new line and the handful of titles they continued to create for Crestwood/Prize.

Though Mainline Comics was nothing like EC or the other horror comics under attack, Jack still saw Wertham hold up copies of *Bullseye: Western Scout* and *Foxhole* for a nation of television viewers. "Jack was always very angry about it," said Roz. "He called Wertham all kinds of names. But life went on. There wasn't anything he could do about it." Instead of individual titles, Wertham attacked the entire industry and caused the public to believe every comic was obscene and immoral.

As if this weren't bad enough, one of Joe's ideas led to more trouble. For whatever reason, Joe tried to save the cost of artwork for an issue of *Young Love* by recycling an old story already published by parent company Crestwood. After giving it a new title, he wrote a new story around the art. "I thought that was very clever," he later explained. "I was proud of myself."

But a Crestwood employee recognized the art, and the publishers soon contacted the company attorney. Nothing in the Mainline contract prohibited Simon from doing this, so Crestwood retaliated by delaying payment of what it owed Jack and Joe. They then had to hire accountant Bernard Gwirtzman to search Crestwood's financial books for the last few years.

That November, attorney Morris Eisenstein arranged for Gwirtzman and other accountants to set up shop in Crestwood's office until they finished going over the books, and Crestwood, now hostile toward them, had their own accountants present during the two-week audit. A few days after the inspection, Jack accompanied

Joe, Gwirtzman, and Eisenstein to a meeting in the office of Crestwood's attorney. Across the conference table, Crestwood publishers Teddy Epstein and Paul Bleier, and Crestwood's general manager, M. R. Reese, frowned at them. Then Eisenstein stood and read a letter on behalf of his clients, demanding whatever money Crestwood, Feature Publications, and Headline Publications, among others, owed them. Jack and Joe felt that they hadn't been paid all of their advances, royalties, and other monies for *Fighting American*, *Young Brides*, *Black Magic*, *Young Love*, and *Young Romance*, Eisenstein explained.

Rising to his feet, Teddy Epstein said that they had paid everything and had never withheld royalties. Gwirtzman said he was talking about overseas sales, used plates, and "other incidentals." Crestwood's publishers laughed until Gwirtzman added that over the past seven years, the company had failed to pay $130,000. Crestwood's people left the room in a huff, but their attorney returned thirty minutes later to say Crestwood didn't have the money, and if this went to court – with business as bad as it was – Crestwood would simply close down. That day, Jack and Joe left the office with ten grand and the payments Crestwood had recently delayed issuing. And, amazingly, they went right back to work on their line for the company. But the relationship between Jack and Joe, said inker George Roussos, was strained. "I don't know the extent of what really took place, but there was a point when they split up when they were working at Crestwood," Roussos said. "Joe took the business end of it and Jack would do the artwork."

Where Jack once viewed Joe as an older brother – though never a close friend, Roz said – they now barely spoke while working in the same room. At this point, however, it didn't even matter. Attacks on the industry had taken their toll. Publishers folded in droves, and the number of comics published dropped from 650 to 250. "They fell because of the Kefauver investigations and that . . . psychiatrist," said artist Carmine Infantino, an old friend of Jack's who then worked for DC. "The publishers in those days, my old boss Jack Liebowitz, and Martin Goodman from Timely, and the people from Archie [MLJ], got together and created the Comics Code, which promised parents they would have no more blood and stuff like that. They responded to the efforts of Kefauver and Wertham and comics kept publishing, but they were hit so badly. Sales were terrible, and we tried everything to get them back."

Even with publishers self-censoring their books through their new Comics Code Authority, EC closed down, starting a chain reaction that nearly destroyed an already shaky industry. With EC gone, distributor Leader News no longer had enough money to advance to small companies like Mainline. When Leader imploded, it took Mainline and other publishers with it. "I never dealt too much with the business end of that," said Roz. "But it was tough times. Like nowadays, the books weren't doing well. If you put money into it, you lost your money."

Mainline was gone. Now, Jack and Joe had to look for work with the industry in its worst recession ever. Joe ended their sixteen-year partnership by accepting a position in advertising. "He said the hell with it," Jack recalled. "And Joe was very good at advertising. Actually, that's his medium. He did well." Jack could have done the same, but he didn't like that field. He decided to keep trying to support his wife and three kids with comics. "So Joe went his way, and Jack went his way," said Roz. "They both had families to support, so they did the best they could. It was just economics."

Chapter 6

After Joe left comics, Jack returned to what he called "National Comics" (DC). He could have gone back right after the war, but Joe had arranged for the best-selling duo to work with his old pal Alfred Harvey at Harvey Comics instead (he even married Alfred's former secretary). Now at DC, Jack saw the company search anxiously for a way to raise sales. "We just tried one thing after another," said Julius Schwartz, a DC editor at the time and now an industry legend. "We were putting out westerns, we were putting out war books, we were putting out adaptations of radio and television shows, we were putting out cartoon books . . . we were putting out everything in desperation because the comic industry was not doing well."

"Don't forget," added artist Carmine Infantino, "the EC Comics line was the killer. When they got hurt, we all got hurt. It got so bad that we were told we had to take a three-dollar page cut or they would close the doors on the comic book business."

Schwartz, a former literary agent, knew how to turn things around. "We were putting out a magazine called *Showcase*," he said gruffly. "When a magazine came out in those days, it was distributed on the newsstands, and you had to wait about four to six months before you knew how it did." While waiting for the first issue's sales figures, he added, publishers usually spent money on a second, third, and fourth issue. "But if number one didn't sell, then the follow-up issues would sell even worse, so you took a beating. We got the idea: Why don't we put out a magazine and showcase a new character, a new theme, and a new idea, and wait four or five months until the results came in? If the results were poor, we had nothing to lose but that one issue. If they were good, we'd try it again."

It was in *Showcase* that Schwartz revived DC's 1940s fast-running hero the Flash, whose series had been canceled after 104 issues. Schwartz jettisoned everything but the name. The new Flash would have superspeed but gain the power in a logical way. "The Golden Age Flash, as I recall, had his superspeed by inhaling some hard water that fell on the floor. I thought it might be better if the chemicals had splashed on Barry Allen, the Flash-to-be, and were hit by a bolt of lightning, which travels one hundred eighty-six thousand miles a second. That would be a reasonable explanation."

Schwartz called Carmine Infantino into his office, said they were going to reestablish the Flash, and asked him to draw it and create the costume. Infantino met with writer Robert Kanigher, who gave him the first story, and then went to his drawing board. Infantino drew a simple costume with lightning bolts, but to be different, he had the new Flash leave a trail of "speed lines" in his wake, moving about the page as smoothly as an animated cartoon. After the *Showcase* issue sold well, the Flash received his own title and Schwartz asked DC's editorial director, "What are we gonna call this, issue one or a hundred and five?" Schwartz figured that with hundreds of comics competing for the same audience on newsstands, a kid would look at one hero's first issue and another's 105th and "go for one hundred and five, because he knew that was a good magazine. It lasted a hundred and four issues, at least. Number one, who knows? 'I'm not gonna spend a dime on a magazine I never heard of.'"

While Schwartz redesigned the Flash, Jack pitched editor Jack Schiff an idea called Challengers of the Unknown, the final project of the Simon & Kirby team. "After we split up," Simon recalled, "Jack took it to DC with my blessing." Schiff accepted it, and the debut of the Challengers in *Showcase* No. 6 (January–February

1957) told of how test pilot Ace Morgan, mountain climber Red Ryan, scientist Professor Haley, and boxing champ Rocky Davis survived a plane crash, felt that they were living on borrowed time, and formed a team. At the time, science-fiction movies like *Them!*, *The Day the Earth Stood Still*, *Forbidden Planet*, and *This Island Earth* were all the rage, and Jack tried to make the book as cinematic as possible: "I began to think about three words that have always puzzled me: 'What's out there?'" Jack's mix of robots, dinosaurs, aliens, and time travel hooked Schiff, who stuck the team into *Showcase* Nos. 7, 11, and 12 and asked for a full-length *Challengers of the Unknown* book. But *Challengers* alone wasn't enough to pay the bills, so Jack asked DC if he could take over a monthly title and was soon told that all of the books already had artists on board. He searched for work at other companies and encountered editors who drove him away with their nitpicking.

At Timely, meanwhile, Goodman was actually adding more titles. Inker Frank Giacoia – Carmine Infantino's buddy – tried to get work there, but Stan told him that Atlas artists inked their own drawings. "Hey, how about if I can get Kirby back here to pencil some stuff?" Frank asked.

Stan was surprised. "Great. Get him back here."

Despite whatever problems he and Goodman had over Captain America, Jack dropped by to see Stan and received assignments to draw Yellow Claw (a long-nailed Fu Manchu stand-in who battled a Chinese secret agent in a black suit) and the western title *Black Rider* (a *Lone Ranger* rip-off). He also ran into people who felt that Crestwood had underpaid them. "When some difficulties arose at Crestwood, a few artists weren't paid," explained inker George Roussos. "This caused a lot of resentment toward Joe and Jack." In an art store near Grand Central, Jack saw Roussos and asked him to walk him to Stan's office. When they reached the building, they turned around and walked right back up bustling Park Avenue and toward the enormous terminal. Jack did all the talking. "I guess it was a pent-up energy, and he was rather hurt that people took out their anger on him – unnecessarily, he felt," Roussos added.

While drawing the occasional story for Atlas, Jack kept trying to find more work at market leader DC. Schiff let Jack draw stories for the anthology titles *House of Mystery*, *House of Secrets*, *My Greatest Adventure*, and *Tales of the Unexpected* and soon asked Kirby to start drawing six-page Green Arrow stories for *Adventure Comics*. Instead of a generic masked archer who lived in an "Arrow-cave" and drove an "Arrow-mobile" (mimicking the company's successful *Batman* formula), Jack recast the character as a science-fiction hero who faced Green Arrows from other nations, alien archers shooting giant arrows into cities, mechanical octopi, and marooned Japanese soldiers who didn't know World War II had ended. His attempt to present a two-part story, however, alienated Mort Weisinger, co-creator of Green Arrow and a blustery editor who used to complain to Joe Simon about the look of *Boy Commandos*.

During editorial meetings, Weisinger and employees from the art and production departments told Schiff that Jack was ruining Green Arrow. They complained that Jack was deviating from scripts, and that the science-fiction elements he brought to the series, and his art style, were repulsive and beneath DC standards. Schiff told Jack to undo the changes he'd made to Green Arrow but let him continue to draw the series.

By summer of 1957, Stan had to tell artists they would be paid less for their work. Goodman also asked Stan to cut down on the number of freelancers he was using. With the industry shaky, capable of going under at any minute, Goodman also stopped distributing his own titles. From now on, American News Company would handle them. "Gee, why did you do that?" Stan asked. "I thought that we had a good distribution company."

"Oh, Stan, you wouldn't understand," Goodman replied. "It has to do with finance."

Stan shrugged, but within two weeks, American News Company shut its doors, leaving Atlas without a distributor. Since his decision to go with American had alienated wholesalers, Goodman couldn't distribute his own books again. He had to stop publishing immediately until he could find a way out of his predicament. For the second time, he told Stan to fire everyone. This time it was even tougher to do. Stan knew these people and their families. He had to call John Romita, who was drawing a western story. "Stop work and turn in whatever pages you have," he said. Romita went unpaid for seven pages of sketches of figures and backgrounds and told his wife, "If Stan Lee ever calls, tell him to go to hell."

Joe Maneely kept working with Stan on the syndicated strip *Mrs. Lyons' Cubs* (published by the Chicago Sun-Times Syndicate) but started drawing for DC, Charlton Comics, and Crestwood. Gene Colan and John Buscema both went into advertising. For two months, Stan wondered why Goodman was keeping him on. They weren't publishing anything. There was no Atlas anymore. Then he learned why: Goodman convinced Independent News (a distributor owned by rival DC) to distribute their titles. But Independent wouldn't let him publish forty to sixty books anymore. They'd take only eight a month, and these would contain mostly inventory work. Stan didn't like the sound of this. It was like Ford asking General Motors to sell their cars. He couldn't help but suspect that National wouldn't work very hard to sell their titles, but he watched Goodman sign the deal.

In June 1958, a year after Atlas closed its door, Stan was looking forward to calling his artists back – especially Joe Maneely, his star artist. After Atlas's shutdown, the thirty-two-year-old penciler started drawing for rival publishers and bought a new home in Jersey for his young wife and small daughters. On Friday, June 7, after joining Sub-Mariner creator Bill Everett and other laid-off Atlas artists for a few drinks, Maneely, a kind-looking blond-haired guy with glasses and a receding hairline, boarded the Jersey-bound commuter train that would take him home and somehow fell between two moving cars. He died instantly. Stan couldn't believe it. He'd known Maneely for nine years. He'd suggested he take formal art courses. He'd had him draw the newspaper strip, which could have become a hit to rival Charles Schulz's *Peanuts*. He was also about to call him back to Atlas. “It was such a shock, such a surprise,” Stan said. “He was a young guy in perfect health, and of course, he died due to an accident.” Some people believe it was suicide. Either way, if he had lived, Stan insisted, “he would have been another Jack Kirby. He would have been the best you could imagine. I’d never have let him leave.”

Jack was facing his own setbacks. While working on *Challengers of the Unknown* for DC, he had wondered privately if there was any future in comics and asked *Challengers* writer Dave Wood to help him create *Space Busters*, a science-fiction strip they could sell to a newspaper feature syndicate. The strip didn’t sell, but DC editor Jack Schiff and Wood soon asked him to draw *Sky Masters of the Space Force*, a new comic strip Jack felt was extremely similar to *Space Busters*.

Jack soon learned that Harry Elmlark, an agent from the George Matthew Adams Service, had asked Schiff if DC had any science-fiction features that could be adapted to strip forms. Since Russia’s launch of *Sputnik* a year before, American interest in the space race was high, and Elmlark could sell a good space strip. After Elmlark rejected a few DC titles and National’s executive vice president and general manager, Jack Liebowitz, told Schiff he could work on a strip himself with company freelancers, Schiff met with Dave Wood, looked over *Space Busters*, and decided Elmlark wouldn’t like it. “Dave and I then agreed to collaborate on a new story, and we kicked around several possibilities, including the idea of a strip that dealt with space rocket launchings, moon shots, and general story lines just a little ahead of current developments in the news,” Schiff explained.

Jack agreed to draw *Sky Masters of the Space Force* and incorporated his ideas into a week’s worth of episodes. Then Schiff told him and Wood to take their art samples and story outline directly to Elmlark. When Elmlark agreed to agent the project, Schiff explained, “Dave Wood said that I would naturally be getting a percentage for arranging the deal.”

Wood promised Schiff 5 percent, and Jack viewed it as a onetime gift for having arranged their meeting with Elmlark. In March 1958, however, Schiff protested and hinted that if he wasn't paid, Jack might lose work from DC. With dozens of publishers gone, and hundreds of freelancers begging DC for work, Jack didn't want to ruin the relationship with the company, which had paid him an impressive $8,000 – about seven times that, today – for fifty-six comic stories. Jack verbally agreed to pay Schiff.

In April, however, he learned that Schiff and Dave Wood expected him to pay for the strip's production costs. He wanted to deduct these costs from what the syndicate paid, then give Schiff a percentage of what remained, but Schiff wanted his 5 percent from the gross. When Elmlark sent them a deal memo from a newspaper syndicate, negotiations became even more strained.

Jack told Wood he wanted 66 percent, half of which would go to an inker. Wood refused, so Jack told him to find another artist. That same day, Wood called Schiff to complain, and Jack met with Schiff at DC to announce his departure from the project. Wood only wanted half of the money so that he could pay his brother Dick, he explained. Schiff told Jack it was silly for him to leave, implying that Jack could ink the strip himself. Jack, however, didn't feel he should do twice the work for less money. The next morning, he met with Wood in his apartment and said he'd accept 60 percent, pay the inker, and also pay for lettering and other art expenses.

Schiff thought this was fine – until he heard Jack wanted to lower Schiff's share to 3 percent. To keep things moving, Schiff agreed to accept 4 percent, and on April 15, 1958, he invited everyone to his office at DC to sign an agreement he had typed up. Though he didn't feel Schiff deserved an ongoing royalty, he worried about losing work at DC and signed the agreement.

By July, however, Schiff told Jack that he wanted 6 percent of *Sky Masters*. Then he hinted that he might actually want 10. Jack convinced him to accept 5 percent, but Schiff soon repeated that he wanted more money. *Sky Masters* debuted in over three hundred newspapers on September 8, 1958, but their lawyers still hadn't reached an agreement. In late September, the syndicate sent Jack and the Woods their first payment for the strip. The Woods quickly sent a percentage of their check to Schiff. After Jack refused to pay Schiff, other DC editors stopped assigning stories in anthology titles. As his income continued to drop, Jack tried to resolve things during a meeting held in Dave Wood's attorney's office. Facing Schiff, Jack said he'd be willing to pay $500 for a general release from the letter he had signed. He wanted a release, he added, because Schiff kept demanding an ongoing percentage instead of the onetime gift Jack and the Woods wanted to pay. Schiff refused the money and soon fired Jack from *Challengers of the Unknown*, claiming that ideas from their story conferences were appearing in *Sky Masters*. Jack continued to draw the popular *Sky Masters* strip, but on December 11, 1958, within three months, he learned that Schiff had sued him and the Woods for breach of contract. Jack asked for a dismissal, but the court denied the request. With Schiff suing him and market leader DC no longer assigning work, Jack returned to Atlas, where Goodman now had Stan shoving stories about giant monsters into *Strange Tales*, *Journey into Mystery*, and *Tales to Astonish*.

After seventeen years as editor, Stan had yet to deliver a true hit, but he kept writing scripts for artists Steve Ditko and Don Heck and then asked his younger brother, Larry Lieber, to try writing.

"I'm not a writer," Larry answered.

"You can write," Stan countered. "I read your letters in the service. I'll show you what you need."

After giving a few pointers, at times impatiently, he saw Larry reach the point where he could turn simple plots into monster stories. Since Jack was one of the industry's fastest artists, however, creating faster than Larry could write, Stan had to keep urging him on: "Jack needs another script!"

Every month, at his drawing board, Jack created a "lovable" knockoff of Godzilla or any of the other giant creatures stomping cities in Toei Film epics. "I had to make sales in order to keep myself working," he explained. The company – now operating without an official name – remained a second-rate outfit that relied on its biggest competitor for distribution. Goodman kept hinting that any minute now he'd close down the comic division, but the monster books kept selling a respectable two hundred thousand copies each. "Stan and Jack Kirby held it together in those days," said artist Gene Colan. "They worked out of a closet. Jack Kirby did all the work. Stan did all the writing. And I had to go out in the field like some of the other artists. Couldn't get any comic book work at all."

Meanwhile, DC continued to rule the marketplace with their best-selling Superman and Batman, the revived Flash, and a new version of Golden Age hero Green Lantern. "I was aware of them," Stan recalled. "I knew of their existence. Sometimes I would thumb through them just to see what the artwork was like and to see if their books looked better than ours." But he didn't read them. He didn't have time. "And there was no reason to, either. I didn't want our stories to read like anyone else's. I didn't want to be influenced by anyone else."

Before Stan knew it, Goodman asked for a new science-fiction book. Since Independent would let Goodman publish only eight books a month, one of the sixteen bimonthly products had to bite the dust. In the fall of 1958, Stan brought Goodman *Strange Worlds* and handed Jack a script called "I Discovered the Secret of the Flying Saucers." When George Roussos saw the results, he said, "You two are really going to go places."

Stan replied, "When I see the sales figures, I'll believe you, George."

While working with Stan on other stories about giant monsters like Torr, Krogarr, and Fin Fang Foom (a giant winged reptile in purple gym shorts), Jack received a call from Joe Simon. It was early 1959, and Joe was back in comics, working on *MAD* magazine knockoff *Sick* for Crestwood. Joe had just received a call from John Goldwater of MLJ comics, who had once threatened to sue Goodman over Captain America's first shield and the Hangman. "Superheroes are about to come back," Goldwater had said before asking Joe to create a few superhero titles.

Joe told Goldwater he'd invent a hero, but he really planned to resurrect an idea he'd created back in 1953. At that time, Captain Marvel artist Charles "C. C." Beck had called to announce a comeback, and Simon had worked up ideas for him to draw, including a logo for a hero called Spiderman. After asking his wife's brother-in-law, writer Jack Oleck, to come up with something a bit like Captain Marvel, Simon read Oleck's story of orphan Tommy Troy being adopted by a strange elderly couple and finding a magic ring in their attic. When a genie appeared to offer one wish, the boy wished to be a superhero. Simon changed the name to Silver Spider and took Beck's sample pages to Harvey Comics, where young editor Sid Jacobson told his boss that Silver Spider was "strictly old-hat. Almost a takeoff on Green Hornet." The story had nothing new to offer, Jacobson felt, and the Silver Spider himself should be more of a human spider: thin, wiry, long-legged, and sporting antennae on his costume; an acrobat who swung through the sky "by the use of silken ropes that would enable him to swing à la Tarzan or à la Batman." The threads "might come from a special liquid, from some part of his costume that could become silken threads in much the same way as the spider insect."

Back then, Harvey didn't do anything with the Silver Spider proposal. Now, six years later, Joe wanted it back.

A week after their first conversation, Joe met with Goldwater and pitched a hero called the Fly, who got around on a fine thread. Goldwater liked it. He also wanted a revival of his old hero the Shield, called The Double Life of Private Strong. Like Captain America, Strong would be an army private who fought crime in a star-spangled costume. "Hey, Goldwater wanted another Captain America, that's what he got," Simon once joked.

After Joe's phone call, Jack went over to discuss the characters. Joe told him that Beck had left the industry again and handed him Beck's old-fashioned sample pages. "We're doing this over," Joe explained. "Same script, only we're calling him the Fly instead of Silver Spider."

One look told Jack the idea needed work. He said the Fly shouldn't walk on buildings. A fly had wings. Joe said, "Put some on the costume." In his studio, after reading Oleck's script, Jack called Joe at two in the morning to say it had cobwebs all over it. A week later, he brought Joe a stronger costume design and other new gimmicks: the Fly climbing walls, using extraordinary strength, firing a web-gun, and taking advantage of a mysterious sixth sense that warned him of danger. They moved forward with both titles. But DC saw *The Double Life of Private Strong* No. 1 in June 1959, claimed it was a blatant *Superman* imitation, and sent Goldwater a cease-and-desist letter. Goldwater canceled the book after two issues.

Meanwhile, *Adventures of the Fly* featured the young orphan finding a magic ring in an attic. The boy would rub it while chanting, "I wish I were the Fly," and turn into an adult hero. Four issues into the run, Goldwater had in-house employees take over, replacing the orphan with an adult law school graduate who decides to use his magic ring again.

Jack and Joe went separate ways again.

Jack kept drawing stories for Goodman's company. He couldn't go back to DC, especially now that Schiff was suing him and the Wood brothers for his share of the *Sky Masters* profits. Jack countersued Schiff, offering a different version of events: Schiff, Jack insisted, was an editor who assigned him, the Wood brothers, and Eddie Herron freelance work. He said Elmlark had contacted him and Dave Wood about a "space flight comic strip" for his agency. He and the Woods had gone to the syndicate *without Schiff* to propose strips and stories, he added. He'd spent time and money drawing "cartoon strips, which the agency accepted as a basis of the *Sky Masters* strip." Schiff had had nothing to do with the agreement they'd signed with the agency or the development of *Sky Masters*. Even so, Jack continued, during negotiations, he and the Woods had offered Schiff a gift, and then Schiff had demanded more, implying that not paying him could lead to losing work from DC. Already, Jack explained, his bimonthly earnings had dropped from $1,800 to $200. This, he alleged, was why he signed the agreement – under duress.

Schiff, however, claimed that this figure was ridiculous: In 1957 Jack had earned $8,600. A year later, he received $8,146 – $454 less.

The matter went to court, and Schiff's lawyer, Myron Shapiro, questioned Jack. "Did he tell you in any words or substance that if you would not sign that note you would not get any more assignments? Yes or no?" Shapiro asked.

"I will give you his gestures."

"I want his words, not his gestures."

"His gestures were very eloquent."

"You have to give me his words. You are now under oath, and I call on you to answer that question yes or no without any volunteering or characterization."

"He said he would think ill of me," Jack answered.

"Did he say anything else besides that?"

"He said he would be unhappy," Jack explained, and that he would believe Jack was dishonorable.

"Anything else?"

"Sign it."

"Did he say anything else beside these words?"

"Sign it. That's all he said."

During the very short trial at the supreme court in White Plains, New York, Jack Liebowitz testified as a witness for Schiff. Kirby had known Liebowitz since the 1940s and during the last two years alone had drawn over six hundred pages for his company. Ultimately, Liebowitz's testimony and the signed document led the court to rule in favor of Schiff. When Jack lost, he had to leave market leader DC for Atlas, which paid some of the lowest rates in the industry.

Chapter 7

One month, Stan worked on *Battle* and *Navy Combat*, *Archie*-like teen books *Patsy & Hedy* and *Patsy Walker*, westerns *Two-Gun Kid* and *Wyatt Earp*, and sci-fi horror books *Strange Tales* and *World of Fantasy*. The next, he was given *Homer the Happy Ghost*, *Love Romances*, *My Own Romance*, *Millie the Model*, *Miss America*, *Gunsmoke Western*, *Kid Colt Outlaw*, and *Marines in Battle* to ready for the production department and printer.

With only eight slots available to him each month, and a desire to sell more copies, Goodman juggled titles like a circus performer with bowling pins. In early 1959, Stan replaced *Homer the Happy Ghost*, *Miss America*, *Navy Combat*, and *Marines in Battle* with monster-driven anthologies *Journey into Mystery*, *Strange Tales*, *Tales of Suspense*, and *Tales to Astonish*. Then Goodman decided that maybe monsters weren't as commercial as teen books and replaced *World of Fantasy* and *Strange Worlds* with *Archie* knock-offs *Kathy* and *A Date with Millie*. Soon, *Battle* and *Wyatt Earp* gave way to *My Girl Pearl* and *The Rawhide Kid*. Then *Rawhide Kid, Kid Colt Outlaw*, *Journey into Mystery*, and *Tales of Suspense* were monthly. Then *Kid Colt* and *Rawhide Kid* were bimonthly again, and *Amazing Adventures*, and *Linda Carter Student Nurse* replaced *Two Gun Kid* and *My Girl Pearl*. None of the changes, however, made any difference in sales.

Meanwhile, at National, editor Julius Schwartz continued his winning streak. After successfully reviving *The Flash* and *Green*

Lantern, Schwartz was asked by DC president Jack Liebowitz what he wanted to do next. "Well, my favorite magazine was *The Justice Society of America*," he answered. "I'd like to do that, combining so many superheroes working together."

He got the okay but said that he didn't want to call them the Justice Society. "That sounds like people gathering together for social activities," he explained. Instead, he wanted to call it the Justice League. "Everyone knows what a league is. There's a baseball league and a football league and even a league of nations, so to speak."

Liebowitz agreed to the name, and Schwartz threw Superman, Batman, Wonder Woman, the Flash, and Green Lantern – along with a new slang-talking teen sidekick named Snapper Carr (who had no powers but did snap his fingers all the time) – into a team and had them battle a giant alien starfish in *Brave and the Bold* No. 28. When Schwartz received the rating – the percentage of the print run that sold – it contained an enthusiastic exclamation point. "I immediately received the go-ahead to put it out on a regular basis."

During a golf game in May 1960, Martin Goodman heard Liebowitz brag about how *The Justice League of America* was leaping off the newsstands and asked, "Well, what's so different about the Justice League?"

"Instead of one hero," Liebowitz answered, "it's a team that works together."

Goodman returned to the office and told Stan, "Maybe there's a trend toward groups of superheroes. Why don't you come up with a group of superheroes?" Stan wasn't surprised that Goodman wanted once again to be the first to be second. "It's sort of like when *Playboy* was selling well, Guccione came out with *Penthouse*," he explained.

Nearing forty, Stan wasn't excited about the new assignment. He'd seen Goodman cancel the heroes twice. After twenty years, he wanted to quit. He figured people in the industry knew him and would offer work. When he told his wife, however, she said, "What a goof. Get it out of your system. Do a book the way you'd like to do it."

Since working on superheroes with Joe Simon, Jack had urged Goodman to bring them back. But he hadn't meant the Human Torch, Captain America, and Sub-Mariner. When he learned that Goodman wanted to include them in a new book, he said quietly, "No, we should try new characters."

After Stan and Jack discussed what a modern team should be like, Stan then sat at his typewriter and wrote a synopsis about four people who rode an experimental rocket into space. After being bombarded with "gamma rays," they survived a fiery crash and gained new powers. The plot evoked the third issue of *Challengers of the Unknown* (where Jack had that group's strongman, Rocky, gain superabilities after a space flight), but Stan's characterization made comic book history. Instead of a stock scientist, Stan typed in his outline, Reed Richards "talks too much," thinks too much, and "drives the others crazy." Though he could stretch like Quality Comics' Plastic Man and DC's 1959 creation the Elongated Man, Richards's attitude was rigid. His girlfriend, Susan Storm, was the Invisible Girl, an active and equal member of the team. Her rebellious kid brother, Johnny Storm, was the new Human Torch, more interested in fast cars and girls than saving the world. Stan figured he'd be the most popular member. The final character, the Thing, was a lumpy orange figure with a stone-covered hide. He'd be "jealous of Mr. Fantastic" and dislike the Torch because "Torch always sides with Fantastic." "I was trying to make this different from the usual type of comic books," Lee explained. "And for the first time I was trying to really be original. And it occurred to me that no team of heroes that I knew of ever had a heavy in it. All the other teams had very glamorous people. So I thought it would be fun to get somebody who is ugly, bad tempered, and tragic, but still a good guy. He was easily my favorite character in that group."

"Let's treat him so that the reader is always afraid he will sabotage the Fantastic Four's efforts at whatever they are doing," he wrote of the Thing. "He isn't interested in helping mankind the way the other three are. He is more interested in winning Susan away from Mr. Fantastic." The new team would dedicate their lives to fighting evil, but "to keep it from getting too goody-goody, there is always friction between Mr. Fantastic and the Thing, with Human Torch siding with Mr. F."

"Later I saw Stan's plot for *The Fantastic Four* No. 1, but even Stan would never claim for sure that he and Jack hadn't talked the ideas over before he wrote this," said future editor Roy Thomas.

By now, Roz was pregnant with a fourth child. If Jack wasn't dropping by the office to deliver work or pick up his latest comics from the twenty-book rack on Stan's wall, he was helping Roz care for the kids. Then, once everyone had gone to sleep, he'd enter his small office off the living room, with the World War II model airplanes hanging from the ceiling, the huge fish tank, posters on every wall, and piles of old *Yellow Claw*, *Bullseye: Western Scout*, and *Boys Ranch* comics that his nephews read during visits (when they weren't playing in his swimming pool). "I worked till four in the morning," Jack said. "I worked with the TV and radio on – it was a great setup. I was a night person and still am."

At his board, he expanded Stan's outline with new sequences that introduced each character: The Torch worked on a hot rod, then burst into flame and flew away; Susan Storm shopped for a new outfit, then became invisible; the Thing destroyed city streets and caused citizens to recoil in horror.

He also ignored some of Stan's suggestions. Instead of the others hiring Ben Grimm to fly them to Mars, Ben (Jack's father's name) became Reed's college roommate. Sue Storm wouldn't wear "a mask with a face like the one she had" ("in order to be seen"). Sue (the name of Jack's oldest daughter) would be visible until she used her power. As for the Thing, he wouldn't look "sort of shapeless," he'd resemble a stone-covered Atlas monster. Once he received the penciled pages, Stan wrote dialogue and captions and credited the writing to himself and the art to "J. Kirby." When readers saw the Fantastic Four's grim cold war origin, their horrifying encounter with atomic energy, their constant bickering, and their various handicaps, they were shocked. "There was angst, conflict, superheroes arguing, you just didn't see that in DC books," said comics historian Greg Theakston. "If Superman argued with anybody, it must have been because of 'red kryptonite.' Superman was the smiling hero. The Thing would tear you in two if he was in a bad mood."

The Fantastic Four No. 1 was the first Stan Lee story in decades to make any kind of impact. Ironically, Goodman considered replacing *The Fantastic Four* with another western or war title – until the sales figures came in. The book, he learned, was his best-selling title in years. Stan wasn't surprised. "We had never gotten fan mail, maybe one letter a year about some stupid subject," he said. "But all of a sudden we got fan mail from readers saying, 'We love this book, we can't wait till the next issue,' blah blah blah. I knew we were on to something."

By the third issue, the new team had costumes (Jack drew no-frills uniforms, and Stan penciled a memorable emblem – the number "4" in a circle – on each member's chest). By the fourth, Goodman raised the price from ten to twelve cents, Stan used the letters page to communicate with readers, and – despite the fact that DC was distributing it – the cover included the new tongue-in-cheek slogan "The Greatest Comic Magazine in the World!" ("What could I say?" said editor Julius Schwartz. "I may have used the word *copycat*.")

Every month, Jack and Stan delivered another innovation. In the fourth issue, Stan decided to revive Sub-Mariner. He had the Torch leave the group, hide in a Bowery flophouse, and defend a powerful, bearded derelict from other bums. After igniting his right forefinger and giving the derelict a shave, Torch saw that it was (Bill Everett's) Namor and somehow got dragged into trading punches on a crowded city street. In the fifth issue, they introduced Dr. Doom, a man in an intimidating iron mask who wore a cape over his suit of armor. Doom had been in college with Reed and had gotten injured while conducting dangerous experiments involving black magic and science. After chemicals exploded in his face and he was expelled, Doom traveled to the Far East and met a cult that created his costume. Jack's design for the famous costume drew on Alexandre Dumas's *The Man in the Iron Mask* and the Grim Reaper. "It was the reason for the armor and the hood," Jack recalled. While Stan implied that Doom's face was disfigured, Jack felt he was actually a good-looking guy with "a tiny scar on his cheek, but because he's such a perfectionist, he can't bear to see that imperfection." Doom didn't hide his face from the public, Jack imagined, "he's hiding it from himself."

Jack and Stan then worked on another new hero, a rampaging maniac called the Hulk, whose name was inspired by a 1940s character called the Heap. This time, they introduced readers to Bruce Banner, a scientist who was about to test his latest invention, a rocket-shaped gamma bomb. When he saw teenager Rick Jones stumble onto the test site in his convertible, Banner ran out, threw Jones in a trench, and got caught in the explosion. In a locked room that night, he changed into a mindless gray-skinned brute that was equal parts Frankenstein monster, Mr. Hyde, and a woman in a recent newspaper article that Jack had read, who had lifted a car when she saw her child trapped under it.

For this hero, Jack drew a shirtless muscleman with the same haircut the Beatles would soon popularize. He clad Hulk in torn denim shorts and drew a face that strongly resembled the makeup Boris Karloff had sported in *Frankenstein*. "I know he liked the Hulk," said Jack's friend Mike Thibodeaux. "I remember him saying he had designed the Hulk for animation. He originally did him with three fingers."

After May 1962's brutal origin story, Jack and Stan threw Hulk against a communist spy. "They were the villains to America then," recalled Larry Lieber. "So if they made the communists the villains, it was very natural." By August, Jack said he brought Stan another idea, a Norse god named Thor. Since his childhood, Jack had enjoyed reading about this pantheon, and in May 1942, he'd thrown a version of Thor into DC's *Adventure Comics* No. 76. This Thor, however, would wear a futuristic costume whose red cape, yellow belt, and ability to fly evoked Superman. It looked like a Norseman's armor, Jack said, "but he can wear that costume in 2085 if he wants to and get away with it." Unlike DC's Man of Steel, Thor would sport shoulder-length blond hair and fly by swinging a hammer, throwing it skyward, and hanging on to its handle.

At the company, now calling itself Marvel again, Stan told his younger brother, Larry, a story about alien Stone Men chasing a disabled doctor into a cave, where he finds a hammer, bangs it on the ground, and becomes the God of Thunder. "Why don't you write the story?" Stan said.

Larry did, and he named the doctor Donald Blake and his weapon "the Uru Hammer."

That summer, Jack and Stan discussed yet another new hero. According to Jack, Stan wanted an idea, so Jack gave him Joe Simon's original Spiderman, a version of which had been published by Harvey Comics in the 1959 *Adventures of the Fly*. Stan denied ever seeing the proposal, but future editor Roy Thomas claimed that artist Steve Ditko "has sort of indicated that some of that material existed, was kind of the starting point, even though Stan seems to kind of have forgotten it." The reason he might have forgotten "is that they changed it so much and went so much beyond it that there wasn't anything left really except the word *Spider*." The old proposal, Thomas explained, "was probably a starting point, so in that sense Joe Simon and Jack Kirby probably did have something to do with the creation of Spiderman. But not Spider-Man as he finally evolved."

Goodman was reluctant to publish the new hero. No one would want a geeky teenager, unpopular with girls, who dressed like a spider. But he let Stan include Spider-Man in the fifteenth issue of *Amazing Fantasy*. After Jack submitted five pages, however, Stan told him he was giving the book to Steve Ditko. "Not that he did badly, but I didn't want Peter Parker to look like a real superhero, and Jack, who was so used to drawing superheroes, made him a little too heroic."

With Ditko on board, Stan got rid of everything but the name, and he even changed that by adding a hyphen. This Spider-Man was no kid with a magic ring. If anything, he had an origin similar to the one Stan and Jack had used in *Rawhide Kid*. In that series, Johnny Bart lived with his uncle Ben, a retired Texas Ranger. After bad guys killed Ben, Bart got revenge and decided to "roam the west fighting for justice and the underdog." In "Spider-Man," Peter Parker – a teen whose haircut and glasses made him resemble artist Steve Ditko – lived with his uncle Ben. After being bitten by a radioactive spider, testing his powers, becoming a masked wrestler for money, and letting a crook escape a security guard, he learned the same crook had killed his uncle. Like Stan and Jack's *Rawhide Kid*, the first Spider-Man story ended with the new hero vowing to embark on a quest for justice.

According to Jack, he created the next hero: Iron Man. He drew a cover for a bulky, gray-armored hero, discussed it with Stan, and then waited for Goodman to add "Iron Man" to the schedule. When March 1963's "Iron Man" appeared, in *Tales of Suspense*, however, Don Heck was the artist. This time, Stan and Larry wrote an unconventional story about millionaire arms manufacturer Tony Stark being captured by the Vietcong and forced to turn a pile of junk into a transistor-powered weapon. With a piece of shrapnel lodged near his heart, Stark builds a battle suit and pacemaker and uses it to destroy his communist captors. When Stan called Heck to say, "You're going to be doing a new character called Iron Man," Heck recalled feeling nervous – until Stan said Jack had already contributed ideas (the basic plot was one he'd already used in a Green Arrow story) and a cover. Jack was terrific, he felt, always willing to help the next man out. "And as for the superheroes, the main reason they existed was Jack Kirby," Heck added.

Chapter 8

By March 1963, Goodman had replaced the tiny letters *MC* in the upper-right-hand corner of every May-dated cover (under the Comics Code seal) with the new name: "Marvel Comics Group." He wanted to move forward with superheroes – except for the Hulk. Since Jack drew the Hulk like a monster, it was hard to tell whether he was a hero or villain. Sales of the first three installments were hardly incredible, so Goodman decided not to waste a distribution slot and canceled *The Incredible Hulk* after its sixth issue. To this day, Stan claims that Hulk's replacement on the schedule was the result of a bet between him and Goodman. As Stan tells it, Goodman told him their books were selling because of buzzwords *Amazing*, *Fantastic*, *Mighty*, and *Incredible*. Stan answered that the Lee-Kirby style was responsible. Goodman insisted he was wrong, and Stan offered the following challenge: "I'll do a war book with the worst title I can come up with, but if it's done in the Marvel style, I bet it'll sell."

Artist John Severin, however, remembered Jack as the actual creator of *Sgt. Fury and the Howling Commandos*. Severin said that he had heard the idea during the late 1950s, while he smoked a cigar in a coffeehouse near Columbus Circle. "Jack wanted to know if I'd be interested in syndication. He said we could be partners on a script idea he had. The story would be set in Europe during World War Two; the hero would be a tough, cigar-chomping sergeant with a squad of oddball GIs – sort of an adult *Boy*

Commandos." After Severin turned Jack down, "we finished cigars and coffee and Jack left, heading toward Marvel and Stan Lee."

By now, Jack would tell war stories during family gatherings at his Long Island home (swapping a few with his brother-in-law and former sergeant) and had already included a few in the old Simon & Kirby titles *Foxhole*, *Warfront*, and *Battle*. Regardless of who did what, *Sgt. Fury*, "the war mag for people who hate war mags," was another departure from the norm. The Howling Commandos included derby-wearing Irishman "Dum Dum" Dugan, Jewish mechanic Izzy Cohen, southern jockey "Reb" Ralston, Italian actor Dino Manelli, Ivy Leaguer "Junior" Juniper, a gay soldier named Percival Pinkerton, and cigar-chomping Nick Fury, who resembled Jack with his cigar and haircut. Ignoring the fact that the army was segregated during World War II, Jack and Stan added black trumpet player Gabe Jones to the Howlers. Since black characters were so rare, however, the color separating company erroneously colored Jones pink in the first issue, and Stan had to write a memo clarifying that Jones was black.

Regardless of whether Stan's tale of a bet is true or not, the Lee-Kirby style was indeed responsible for breathing life into the tired war genre. Initially, *Sgt. Fury* resembled a superhero comic, with Howlers destroying Nazi planes with grenades while opening parachutes, Fury mowing down dozens of foes with a machine gun in each hand, and the unit defeating Nazi troops by throwing rocks at them. But within a few months, readers saw "Junior" Juniper die in battle (Kirby's idea) and Nazi soldiers march emaciated Jews toward gas chambers in concentration camps. The title was as controversial as it was entertaining. "We had gotten a letter from Texas or somewhere, and the writer didn't like the fact that the Howling Commandos was a mixed group of all different races and ethnicities and religions," said Flo Steinberg, then Stan's assistant. "He said we were commie pinkos – a big phrase in those days – and that he was going to come to New York and shoot us all." After the FBI had been contacted, right over on Sixty-eighth Street, an agent came by to examine the letter. He asked how many people had touched it. "Oh, about forty," Steinberg replied. The agent took the letter, a few free comics, and left. "For a while, no one wanted to go out to the front desk."

Without Jack, Stan's ideas didn't really fly. Together with Larry Lieber, Stan had introduced Ant-Man. In his debut, January 1962's Kirby-drawn "The Man in the Anthill," scientist Henry Pym drank a serum, shrank, entered an anthill, and heard ants dreaming of conquering the world. After fleeing to his home, ingesting an antidote, and returning to normal height, he destroyed the serum. Stan then decided to turn this monster story into a new hero, possibly because Marvel wanted to follow Spider-Man by covering the entire insect family with heroes and DC had revived their 1940s hero the Atom, who could also shrink. Jack came on board and gave Pym a costume (similar to that of his original Spiderman) and a futuristic antennaed helmet. He drew a few stories, but when he left, reader interest waned. To shore up interest in Ant-Man, Stan had Jack return to help introduce a curvy assistant named the Wasp. After Jack left again, readers continued to ignore Ant-Man's ten-page stories in *Tales to Astonish*.

At the same time, Steve Ditko brought Stan the character Dr. Strange, a caped mystic who looked more like a ghoul that introduced horror stories than a hero. Stan and Steve worked on a compelling origin – an arrogant surgeon emerges from an accident with shaking hands, falls into alcoholism, and becomes the disciple of a mystic in Tibet – but readers were as generally indifferent to this character as they had been to a 1960 variant by Lee and Kirby called Dr. Droom.

Stan enjoyed more success by collaborating with Jack again for another new team. In June 1963, DC Comics' attempt to apply the Lee-Kirby approach resulted in a series called *Doom Patrol*. Comprising Robotman (a race car driver who survived a crash and had his brain placed in a robot body), Elasti-girl (an actress who gained the power to shrink in a chemical accident), Negative Man (a pilot who wore bandages on his head and could turn into a dangerous radioactive being), and the Chief, a mysterious figure confined to a wheelchair, the Doom Patrol were feared and mistrusted by society and billed as "the World's Strangest Heroes."

What Stan told Jack now sounded almost the same: Originally called the Mutants, but retitled after Goodman demanded a revision for younger readers, the X-Men were outcasts and loners with strange powers united by another mysterious figure in a wheelchair. Three months after *Doom Patrol* debuted, the X-Men – Cyclops, whose visor contained potentially lethal blasts from his eyes, telekinetic Marvel Girl, the winged Angel, the ape-like Beast (who quoted Shakespeare), and Iceman, a reversal of the Human Torch – were promoted as "the Strangest Super Heroes of All."

Unlike DC's group, the X-Men were young and vibrant. They were born with their powers. They wore matching yellow-and-blue uniforms and trained at Professor Xavier's School for Gifted Youngsters, in a mansion in Westchester, New York. Their leader was bald and clean-shaven and nowhere near as demanding as the Doom Patrol's bearded Chief. And with Jack as artist, their villains and battles were more exciting (in the "sensational Fantastic Four style," the cover announced).

During this same period, Goodman told Stan, "Let's get a book and put them all together." So Stan and Jack created *The Avengers*, pitting Thor, Hulk (whose title had been canceled), Iron Man, Ant Man, and the Wasp against Thor's nemesis, Loki. Goodman finally had his version of the Justice League.

By now, Stan had successfully revived the Human Torch and the Sub-Mariner and was feeling nostalgic. When he first came to Timely in the 1940s, he thought Jack and Joe's *Captain America* was the most brilliant adventure superhero strip he'd ever seen. "The stories were clever, the artwork was wonderful, and now I was in a position to do almost anything I wanted," he explained. He wanted to bring Cap back but didn't quite know what twist to give him. The new Torch was a teenager, completely unlike Burgos's original android. The new Sub-Mariner was a destructive force with a modern reason to hate mankind (a nuclear weapons test had destroyed Atlantis). Before figuring something out, they decided to test the waters by including a version of Cap in *Strange Tales* No. 114's short Human Torch story. On its cover, Jack drew Torch throwing a fireball at a pointy-eared Cap, and Stan wrote, "From out of the Golden Age of comics into the Marvel Age, Captain America returns to challenge the Human Torch." "Impossible though it seems," the Torch thought, "one of the most fabulous super-heroes of the past is now my Enemy!"

In the story, Torch was shocked to learn that the old-time hero was committing crimes. After a fight, however, he discovered it was really his second-rate nemesis, the Acrobat, in the famous suit. The final scene showed Torch relaxing with a pile of old Captain America comics and a caption asking readers to write and let Stan know if they'd be interested in seeing the real Captain America return. Readers wrote in, asking for more.

While considering how to make Cap relevant to a new audience, they learned an assassin had killed President Kennedy while his motorcade traveled through Dallas, Texas. Jack, a Democrat who had drawn Kennedy in early Marvel Comics, was devastated, as was Stan. "It was the first time I ever saw everyone at the whole company just listening to the radio," recalled Flo Steinberg. "And everyone going home. It was a very sad time. Things changed."

Stan and Jack decided to ignore everything Stan wrote about Captain America since Jack left Timely in 1941. Steve Rogers never became a schoolteacher at Lee High School. Bucky didn't die of a gunshot wound in 1946. There never was a Golden Girl, and Cap was never the 1953 "Commie Smasher." Instead, they showed Cap and Bucky on a final mission right before the war ended. They leaped off motorbikes and onto a huge missile heading for a major city. Cap realized he couldn't deactivate it and told Bucky to let go. Bucky thought he could push a nearby button. Cap fell, and the missile blew up and killed Bucky. The twist would be that Cap was frozen in suspended animation and emerged with survivor's guilt and an inability to adapt to a changing, youth-driven society.

After including Captain America in March 1964's fourth issue of *The Avengers*, and showing Sub-Mariner freeing him (by destroying a huge iceberg Eskimos were worshipping), Stan and Jack had the Avengers induct him into their ranks. The new characterization, Cap blaming himself for Bucky's death, did the trick. Jack Kirby and Joe Simon's creation went from forgotten has-been to Marvel's most popular hero in years.

Stan then asked Jack to help with another character based on a 1940s idea. After the legal department told Goodman the name Daredevil was available, Goodman wanted to get something into print before any other company. The original Daredevil, published by Lev Gleason Publications in 1940, had worn a yellow-and-blue costume. He carried a boomerang and fought crooks after they killed his parents. He also suffered from a disability – he was mute until he changed into his costume. By the time Lev Gleason shut down in 1956, the hero had received a red-and-blue costume (divided down the middle), palled around with a kid gang, and was actually removed from *Daredevil Comics* in December 1950.

At home, after dinner with Roz and the kids, Jack drew a yellow-and-red uniform and gave this new Daredevil a red nightstick in a holster fixed to his left thigh. He was drawing more sketches when Bill Everett called. Everett, who had been working in advertising in Massachusetts, reported that Stan wanted *him* to draw the new series. Jack handed Everett his sketches and an idea for a cover – the new hero in midleap over the city, smiling and wielding his nightstick – and saw *Daredevil* become another flop.

Like the original version, this Daredevil had a disability – he was as blind as DC's 1940s hero Dr. Mid-Nite. But Stan had his blindness come from the same accident that gave him his powers. After pushing an old man out of the path of an oncoming truck, people in the truck – labeled "Ajax Atomic Labs Radio-Active Material" – tossed an "isotope" out of the burning vehicle. The glowing vial hit Murdock's eyes, blinding him. Though he couldn't see, Murdock could read by touching pages and use his "Radar Sense" to avoid walking into objects, gauge whether someone was lying, and "see" people's outlines – powers he used to fight crime.

Though the series included a few good ideas, readers were as unresponsive to Daredevil as they had been to Ant-Man. And though Stan tried to raise awareness by including him in *The Amazing Spider-Man* and *The Fantastic Four*, Daredevil never rose beyond being a midlist Spider-Man retread.

After years of hearing Goodman claim he'd close the company any day now, Jack could finally relax. Over the last three years, he and Stan had brought Goodman enough heroes to replace every monster in his titles. Goodman was now even willing to shove two heroes into some of these books in order to keep all of them in print. The reality was that Jack, Stan, and Steve Ditko were bringing in big money – and attracting different readers to comics. Instead of little girls mailing drawings of gowns for *Millie the Model* and *Patsy Walker*, older teens, college kids, and soldiers in Vietnam (some of whom would soon name their tanks "Captain America" and "Iron Man," scrawling these titles on the formidable barrels) were writing in to ask about a fan club. In 1965, Goodman, ever alert, began offering membership in his new Merry Marvel Marching Society (MMMS).

Stan made up cards and had production people Sol Brodsky and Marie Severin help create a pin, eight stickers prominently featuring the heroes, "a nutty new notepad," a minibook, a pencil, a certificate, and a membership card. Stan wanted his bullpen to join him in a special recording he'd include in the $1 membership kit. Most of the bullpen was willing, except for Ditko. But Stan was used to this: Steve never wanted anyone to take his picture and was unwilling to autograph comics young readers mailed in.

In the recording studio, Jack, stocky forearms, hair neat and short, stood near Stan and held the script he'd written. His parts were circled and the tape was rolling. "Okay, out there in Marvel land," Stan began. "Face front! This is Stan Lee speaking! You've probably never heard a record like this before, because no one would be nutty enough to make one with a bunch of offbeat artists, so anything is liable to happen!"

Jack leaned in to the microphone. "Hey, who made you a disc jockey, Lee?"

"Well, well! Jolly Jack Kirby! Say a few words to the fans."

"Okay. 'A few words.'"

"Look, pal: I'll take care of the humor around here."

"You?" he asked. "You've been using the same gags over and over for years!"

"Well, you can't accuse me of being fickle, can you? By the way, Jack, the readers have been complaining about Sue's hairdo again."

"What am I supposed to do, be a hairdresser? Next time I'll draw her bald-headed."

"Boy, I'm glad we caught you when you were in a good mood!" Stan replied.

The record was a smashing success. Fans loved their banter and the bullpen's Rat Pack image.

Once readers saw the ad for the fan club, they asserted their loyalty – just as an earlier generation of readers did when they learned there was a Miss America Club – by mailing fifty thousand $1 bills to Marvel's offices at 625 Madison Avenue. "We were working seven days a week just opening these envelopes," said Flo Steinberg, promoted to readers as "Fabulous Flo" and the recipient of numerous love letters from young fans. "This was before computers. Ugh! So I had to write down and type out their names and everything. And it was a huge success."

Soon, Goodman was selling even more products – a six-foot "life-size, full-color Spidey pin-up" made from a striking Ditko Spider-Man drawing, a $1.50 T-shirt with a sinister-looking Ditko-drawn Dr. Strange, a Thing drawing by Jack on "Official Swingin' Stationery," and a Jack-drawn Fantastic Four family portrait T-shirt – the clean-cut heroes facing out and smiling. "Order yours today!" the ad screamed. "Tomorrow we may keep 'em for ourselves!"

Chapter 9

By 1961, DC had been publishing comics for twenty-five years and had developed a very polished look. The only company that could deliver the same level of quality and polish during the late 1950s and early 1960s was Dell. Being beautiful and clean, however, was a double-edged sword, historian Greg Theakston explained. The books looked terrific, the house style appealed to a loyal readership, but DC became locked into a certain pattern. "DC was a machine at that point, punching out very similar-looking books, where on the flip side, Marvel Comics at that point was kind of a 'B' company, did not have the manpower, the huge staff; their offices were probably one-eighth the size of DC's when they were at 635 Madison Avenue; a core group of probably five people, where DC probably had a production staff of thirty."

For years, DC had been overconfident. Marvel, they felt, was handicapped because of a lack of production facilities or money to produce polished material. Marvel, under Goodman's direction, also kept churning out *Patsy Walker* and other mediocre comics for a female audience, a handful of war comics, a few western comics, and far too many horror and mystery comics. DC cornered the market on heroes and didn't take Marvel seriously when the tiny company decided to try its hand at the subgenre. DC was confident, despite the fact that its adherence to formula opened the door for a competitor willing to take chances and present outrageous stories. "Anybody that wanted to use Batman, Superman, or the

Flash was tied to what had come before and the expectations of the editor that you were using these characters from," Theakston said of DC back then. "At Marvel, it was an 'anything goes' scenario."

After twenty years of eight-page hit-and-run horror and western stories, Stan had filled *The Fantastic Four* No. 1 with some of the most jarring, visceral, gut-level writing the industry had ever seen. Yet DC viewed Marvel as a second-rate company – even as Stan and Jack continued to develop heroes, bending over backward to prevent them from being anything like DC's superhero line. "I suspect one of the reasons was that DC was distributing Marvel's books at the time, and there may have been a conflict of interest if all of a sudden Marvel began competing with the superhero line of DC, who had pretty much had a headlock on superhero comics of that time," Theakston speculated. "If DC had gotten irritated at this new rash of superheroes, they might have balked at renewing the contract when it came time for distribution. My theory is that Goodman and Lee decided to keep their superhero line looking as much like their horror line as they possibly could. Hence, you get the Fantastic Four in the first two issues without costumes, Spider-Man as a complete facial covering; in the context of everything that had come before, he looks like an alien. It was completely unknown for comics to have a face that was completely covered.

"The Hulk," he added, "no costume, he's just a big Frankenstein. Thor: Not really your superhero type, he's a god. So they were cutting this pattern, which kept their line from looking too much like DC's superhero line." It was evident even in the covers: The first two issues of *The Fantastic Four* featured monsters and aliens, with the new heroes barely noticeable – a pattern they followed with covers for Spidey's debut in *Amazing Fantasy* No. 15 and *The Incredible Hulk* No. 1. Only when DC failed to call and demand, "What the hell are you guys doing over there," Theakston explained, did they make the leap – give the Fantastic Four matching blue costumes and change the cover of the third issue, which would have featured yet another slightly misleading monster. That the company had to downplay the fact that it was now creating heroes, by hiding them behind covers with giant monsters, "forced them into deeper waters, where DC had never considered going," according to Theakston.

And unlike other companies, Marvel generated reader intimacy by crediting the people who actually created the comics – a move that greatly satisfied the creators, many of whom had toiled in the industry from the beginning, anonymously, of course, or with other people's names attached to their work. It helped the readers to feel they knew the creators and were part of an exclusive club, especially once Stan gave them all hip nicknames that evoked the Rat Pack; and it allowed him to move comics closer to the mainstream, where he thought they now belonged. The move to credit artists, thereby creating a star system, he said, was inspired by Hollywood. "The movies credit people. Why shouldn't the comic books? And little by little, I began writing these things for older readers, so I wasn't surprised that we had a coterie of college fans," he added. "But I was very gratified because it meant we were on the right track."

While DC continued to present the same old situations, Stan appealed to the audience that had followed the Beatles' every move since they'd disembarked from a plane in a New York City airport. Like the long-haired, suit-wearing Fab Four and some of pop art's biggest names, Stan's writing was irreverent and startlingly pro-youth, his interview comments were self-effacing, and the company, the comics, and the heroes were perceived as outsiders who refused to conform to societal expectations. Marvel was part of the enormous explosion that included the Beatles, former commercial artist Andy Warhol's Campbell's soup can paintings (created not as a grand statement on commercialism, but because he really liked soup), and the Little Orphan Annie dresses, shocking miniskirts, wigs, white boots, and topless bathing suits kids now wore to highlight how different they were from earlier generations. Madison Avenue had difficulty reaching these crazy-looking kids, getting them to spend money on their products, but Stan had no problem developing a rapport with them and selling them on products that reflected contemporary reality and recent cultural changes. He and Jack made everything louder, quicker, more colorful and exciting; he joked about "Jolly Jack" and "Swingin' Steve" in credits; his letters pages openly disparaged competitors and described Marvel as an outsider and underdog. Editorials and letter pages included hipster slang and insults about hipsters; cover blurbs would typically, and preposterously, describe a five-page story as "the greatest action-epic of all time"; dialogue referenced the hottest, most current trends; Jack drew heroes in the same outlandish Beatle wigs millions of readers had bought. Endless in-jokes, self-effacing humor, and recurrent team-ups among heroes helped Marvel shape its inimitable style as Stan drew even more readers. It was truly one of the greatest, most entertaining, and successful marketing campaigns his industry had ever seen.

Fans reacted and continued to respond to the amalgamation of Jack and Steve Ditko's unconventional art (Jack's bold pencil lines rendering everything – people, buildings, gadgets – with the same stonelike quality once applied to each month's Atlas monster; Ditko filling pages with panels that resembled photographs, cloaking his detailed backgrounds with shadows that evoked the Spirit's or Batman's earliest, grimmest adventures), Stan's over-the-top writing, praiseworthy plots (many incorporating faces or political battles torn from the day's headlines), and unremitting, self-belittling humor. And with Stan appearing in the media more frequently to promote Marvel, referred to constantly as tall, rangy, and dashing – and charming reporters with his jokes, anecdotes, flattery, and literary references – even fewer people were interested in DC's clean-cut, polished work.

In fact, unimaginable as it is today, there was a point when DC actually gave thought to canceling *Batman*. One Tuesday morning in 1964, editor Julius Schwartz called artist Carmine Infantino and told him Irwin Donenfeld – son of co-founder Harry Donenfeld and DC's editorial director – wanted to see him the next day. Infantino said he'd come in Friday when he dropped off the latest issues of *The Flash* and *Adam Strange*, but Schwartz said, "No, come in tomorrow." The next morning, in his spacious office, facing Schwartz and Infantino, Donenfeld told them, "Gentlemen, you two guys are going to take over *Batman*. The book is dying. I'll give you six months. If you don't bring it back, we'll kill it off."

After losing the impish alien villains and an extended Batman family that included yellow-clad Batwoman, a masked hound named Bat-Dog, and ludicrous extraterrestrial Bat-Mite, Schwartz and Infantino emphasized the caped crusader's crime-solving abilities. They killed off the prim butler Alfred and introduced matronly Aunt Harriet to counterbalance Wertham's claim that the dynamic duo were homosexual. Infantino also drew a physically fit Batman who operated at night (as opposed to the fat, smiling version Bob Kane and his staff usually showed in the daytime). They slapped a yellow oval around the bat emblem on his chest and added a younger, more curvaceous, and stylish Batgirl, a sleeker gadget-laden Batmobile, and newfangled villains like Blockbuster. Infantino also drew a series of haunting covers, Batman always in danger, about to be hurt or killed. "So that was a hell of a challenge," Infantino remembered. "We took it on, and about the fourth or fifth month, the books were starting to come back."

DC couldn't believe that Goodman's second-rate outfit – which they distributed – was actually making inroads into their sales. "I remember them having regular discussions," said John Romita, then working on DC's formulaic but reliable romance comics. Editors gathered in the bullpen to discuss why Stan Lee of all people was being noticed. "And they generally were missing the obvious, because he made no bones about how he was doing it – a lot of human interest and personal addressing of the readership."

DC held a meeting to analyze Marvel titles, but "some of the production people were pointing out that they thought the production values of Stan's books were crude and a little heavy-handed," Romita added. DC felt "their stuff was so much better," and Romita, part of the team, agreed. As the meeting continued, DC employees faced a display of Marvel and DC covers. One employee said Marvel's huge, jagged-edged cover blurbs were repulsive. Another:

"You know, it's possible that kids identify with cruder stuff." But many DC employees – including editorial director Irwin Donenfeld – disagreed. Marvel's covers were beautiful. By this point, Stan had Chic Stone, who had drawn *Batman* and covers for *Superboy*, working for them. And Chic was over there because of Jack Kirby. While visiting Stan's office, he'd seen some of Jack's pages. "Chic, would you like to ink this?" he asked. Chic said, "You're kidding." Since then, Stan had Jack and Stone working on "posterlike" covers that dominated the newsstands.

The irony was that DC had Jack working for them once but chased him off with complaints that his art wasn't clean or neat enough for the company. When he worked on DC westerns, one editor griped about him not showing the shoelaces on a cavalryman's boots. "What the hell does anybody care about shoes?" he asked. Another editor complained that he'd drawn an Indian mounting his horse from the wrong side. "You're out of your mind," Jack said. "You think the kids care about that?" DC stopped giving him assignments, and then Jack Schiff sued him over the *Sky Masters* strip, and now his presence at Marvel was inspiring some DC employees to sneak over there, work under fake names, and have Stan describe them in comical credits.

"The action was almost like everything was shot with a wide-angle lens," said artist Gene Colan, then drawing romance comics for DC. "All the action was heading in your direction and you'd better duck! And I loved [Jack's] anatomy. I didn't know from anatomy in those years, but I used to have his work as a model sheet and I was practicing at home, like how the heck to do this stuff. I learned a lot from Jack just by observation."

One of the first to defect to Marvel during this period was Roy Thomas. A former schoolteacher who was also involved with the early, influential fanzine *Alter Ego*, Thomas called to invite Stan for a drink. Stan had recently placed an ad in *The New York Times* for writers. Thomas had worked for DC for only two weeks but was already tired of his demanding boss. When Stan asked if he'd take their writing test, Thomas sneaked up to the office on his lunch hour and accepted four black-and-white pages from a *Fantastic Four* annual. He dropped it off during the following day's lunch hour. The next morning, Flo called him at DC to say Stan wanted to see him.

For ten minutes, Stan and Thomas chatted about everything but the test. Then Stan faced a window and asked what it'd take to hire him away from National. Thomas said $110 a week. DC had offered this initially, but when Thomas moved to New York, his superior had offered only $100. Stan agreed to $110. Thomas returned to DC and told his demanding boss he'd be working for Marvel. After calling him "a spy for Stan Lee," his boss kicked him out. That same afternoon, Thomas was back at Marvel, where Stan gave him an issue of *Modeling with Millie* to dialogue over the weekend.

Within days, Stan had John Romita back.

Next came Gene Colan, who, like Romita, had worked for Atlas and gone on to do romance comics for DC.

Quickly, more DC artists gravitated to Marvel. Werner Roth, who knew Stan from the Atlas days, sneaked over to draw *The Uncanny X-Men* under the pen name "Jay Gavin." So did DC artists Mike Esposito, who called himself "Mickey Demeo," and Gil Kane, who called himself "Scott Edwards." At DC, Kane had successfully helped revive Green Lantern and the Atom, but his tenure at Marvel was spottier. "I had a little trouble with Stan, who thought that all of my characters looked homosexual," Kane recalled. "He wanted me to imitate Jack Kirby."

Stan would also call John Buscema back. Buscema, who worked for Stan during the late 1940s, originally wanted to be a painter and left the industry for advertising when companies closed down during the 1950s. After an eight-year absence, he was lured back by Stan, who told him, "John, things are different today. We're making a big comeback. Things are picking up, we're making tremendous strides." Upon returning to Marvel and botching a Hulk job, Buscema said, "Stan thought I should study Jack's art and books, so he gave me a pile of Kirby's comics."

Soon he gave Buscema and some of the others more than that. Though Jack was drawing *The Fantastic Four* and *Thor* each month, he agreed to help Stan teach new artists how they did things at Marvel. By showing how to stretch short plots into full-length stories, he'd allow Stan to keep the entire line under his direction. The new artists would be able to work from short plots, Stan would be able to work with a number of artists at the same time, and Marvel would benefit by having Jack's ideas in more titles. While drawing rough storyboards for the new artists, Jack would leave notes in the margins that explained what was happening. If he'd never worked with an artist, he'd make his border notes longer and include a little dialogue. He handed Don Heck three issues of *The Avengers* and saw him flesh out his drawings. He did the same for Hulk, the Nick Fury series in *Strange Tales*, *The Uncanny X-Men* (creating classic villains like the Juggernaut and the Sentinels), *Tales to Astonish*, and the Captain America series in *Tales of Suspense*. In addition to helping to draw and plot everything but *Spider-Man* and *Daredevil*, he created two thirds of the company's covers.

Eventually he was called to help with *Daredevil*, too. Wally Wood was one of the first artists to request payment for plotting the story. When Stan refused to pay him, he left. Now in need of a new artist, Stan handed Dick Ayers a few pages as a test, but he didn't really like Dick's style on this title. At this point, Romita wanted only to ink, not to pencil. When he dropped off an *Avengers* cover, Stan handed him Ayers's *Daredevil* pages and asked, "Do you think you could handle it?"

Romita said he thought he could, though he really wanted to say, "No, remember our deal, I'm not gonna pencil." But he didn't. Resigned, he agreed to draw an issue of *Daredevil*. When Stan saw his first four pages, however, he felt the first was good but the rest were dull. "I'll tell you what," he said, reaching for the phone on his desk. "Just to get you rolling . . ." He dialed Jack's number in Long Island. "Jack, I got John Romita here," he began. "He's starting to do some *Daredevil* pages and he needs to get a quick pacing guide. How quick can you do ten pages of breakdowns?"

It took him two days. Jack drew blind lawyer Matt Murdock tearing open his dress shirt, soaring across his exercise room, and casually leaping out of a window. After swinging from a flagpole – inexplicably on the fifteenth floor – he performed a double flip in the air and landed on two taxicabs speeding on the East River Drive. He had a foot on each trunk as if trick riding on two ponies. Romita scanned the pages and said, "Say no more. I understand."

Stan nodded. "That'll get you started."

By 1965, the Vietnam War was starting up. High school students now had to worry about the military draft. At age eighteen, all males had to register with the local draft board. Every town had one. The draft board would send a notice asking them to report for a physical. If a young male didn't have any physical impairments, he could then be called upon, at any minute, to join the military and the war in Vietnam.

Herb Trimpe saw the war developing right before his eyes. A future artist for Marvel, he was then part of an air force weather team that provided the Eleventh Air Assault Battalion Experimental – the First Air Cavalry Division, shown in *We Were Soldiers* – with weather briefings at the base they'd cut out of the Central Highlands, near the tiny village of An Khe, or while everyone faced heavy mortar attacks in country. That year, the battle went from a small-scale attempt to eliminate Vietcong pockets entering the south to exert political influence in tiny villages to a full-blown military operation with troops sent over on a divisional scale. At this point, Trimpe recalled, there was still hope, and "an arrogant confidence that the United States would win. It hadn't gotten to the point where people said, 'Hey, these guys can really fight, and this is going to take a long time.'"

As days passed, young soldiers, new arrivals, some fervent anti-communists wanting to do their duty for their country, others dragged into the conflict because their number was called, realized that the Vietcong – some in black pajamas, others hidden among crowds of friendly villagers – would counterweigh limited resources with wily, unpredictable guerrilla tactics. “It wasn’t linear,” Trimpe explained. “In a linear war, the closer you got to the front, the more action there was. Here, you never knew where that would be. There was no predicting it.” The Vietcong launched mortar attacks in country; they hid in underground tunnels; they sprang elaborate booby traps. Soon, Trimpe heard that a friend of his, a helicopter door gunner, was shot dead. Then more soldiers died. Then young GIs began counting the days until they went home. All the while, the Vietcong kept changing the rules. “I mean, our airfield got overrun one night and they dropped satchel bombs and blew up some C130s and busted the Plexiglas on a lot of helicopters.” It was a long way from the easy victories depicted in *Iron Man* comics.

Stan continued trying to change how people perceived comics. He wrote up to his young audience and found college students writing back. Before he knew it, he learned people in other circles were also taking notice of his revolutionary approach. One afternoon at his desk, surrounded by the new comics in the racks on his walls, story ideas filling his mind, he heard the girl at the front desk say, “There’s Frank Felony or somebody to see you.” He didn’t know whom she meant and saw, without warning, film director Federico Fellini enter with an entourage close behind. Stan almost jumped out of his shoes.

“It was Fellini, and he was with four or five other people,” he recalled. “And it was funny because we had a narrow little corridor to come to my office. They were walking single file in the corridor in descending order of height . . . Fellini was the tallest and the next tallest was behind him and the next one behind him, and all were dressed in black. But Fellini was wearing a black raincoat thrown over his shoulders, because you probably know, no Italian director would be caught dead with his hands in the sleeves of the raincoat,” he quipped. “So I couldn’t believe it.”

He faced the world-famous art house favorite and asked, “What are you doing here, sir?” Fellini’s translator explained that he’d come to interview him. Stan was stunned. “It had turned out he was a fan. And I wanted to interview *him*!" He wanted to talk about the director and his work, but Fellini, through his translator, kept firing off a million questions. From this meeting, they developed an unlikely friendship, "and in fact, when my daughter went to Europe a few years later, she went to see him and he was very nice to her and showed her around, and he wrote me a few letters that somebody else had translated." It was, he explained, a very gratifying experience.

With Stan busy lecturing, working with other artists, editing, writing dialogue, and meeting with Goodman, Jack saw less of him and started contributing more to their stories. From writing margin notes for other artists, he now plotted 90 percent of the "Tales of Asgard" backup stories in *Thor* and moved the main feature away from the communist agents, shape-shifting aliens, Vietnamese warlords, Fidel Castro stand-ins, love triangles, and generic gangsters Stan threw into every other title, except *The Fantastic Four* (which Jack also worked on).

Instead, Jack wanted to show Thor meeting other gods. When Stan saw these stories, he'd add subplots that explored Thor's relationship with earth people. The collaboration resulted in fascinating stories, but Jack had more ambitious ideas. In "Tales of Asgard," he tried to present stories that evoked Prince Valiant. Instead of the standard captions and dialogue, Stan wrote the series in a storybook format. Though the original format returned, and Jack's epic tale of Odin battling the ice demon Ymir (and his ally the fire god Surtur) gave way to stories about Thor's childhood, Jack soon created an even bigger epic. Forgoing superheroes and love stories, he had Odin and the gods enter a flying ship and search for a magic sword. By the time this year-long story ended, readers saw the gods brave storms, cross the Sea of Fear, and battle monsters, dwarves, goddesses, and flying trolls – and Stan's dialogue had become a bit Shakespearean.

At the same time, Jack brought this large-scale approach to the *Fantastic Four Annual* No. 3, which featured the wedding of Reed

Richards and Susan Storm. In this giant-sized issue, he and Stan had every single Marvel character interact with one another. He filled panels with an unthinkable number of characters. One panel alone showed Sue chatting with Professor X in his wheelchair, Thing nursing a drink and talking with his girlfriend, the X-Men's Beast facing a record cover, the Angel and Marvel Girl gossiping with the Torch, and the entire Avengers (Wasp, Giant Man, Iron Man, Cap, and Rick Jones) watching Thor shake Reed's hand and tell him, "May the blessings of Asgard grace your coming marriage!" Then Jack showed Dr. Doom using a mind control machine to pit the Avengers, the X-Men, Spider-Man, Daredevil, Thor, Iron Man, Captain America – even Nick Fury and a few S.H.I.E.L.D. agents (the modern-day Sgt. Fury and other characters in a James Bond–like strip in *Strange Tales*) – against every single villain they'd created during the first half of the 1960s.

But some of Stan's changes irked Jack. The *Fantastic Four Annual* began with Doom reaching for the switch on his machine. Jack wanted him to use the apparatus to destroy the Fantastic Four because, in a recent issue, the Thing had nearly crushed Doom's hand. Stan overlooked Jack's margin notes. Stan also implied that Doom's face behind the mask was completely disfigured, when Jack felt that Doom had only a little scratch on his chin but was obsessive and paranoid. And he thought it was wrong that Stan showed Doom getting clobbered in *Spider-Man* or *Daredevil*, right after Jack had shown him nearly defeating the Fantastic Four. Eventually, instead of debating Stan, he decided to start plotting stories on his own. "Very often I didn't even know what the hell he was going to give me," Stan later said. "I'd get some pages of artwork, and I wrote the copy and turned it into whatever story I wanted it to be."

If they did plot together – as they did while Stan was driving him home after a story conference and his convertible got stuck in traffic – they wound up with weak villains like Diablo, featured in a recent *Fantastic Four*. At his home, feeling that Stan lost track of their plots, Jack continued to make stories last more than one issue.

He also began to cut up issues of *Life* and *Playboy* and paste the pieces directly onto his artwork. Though the production department griped about the printing process, he kept trying to change the look of comics.

He also kept doing layouts to teach other artists how to handle existing books, because Goodman planned to expand the line and wanted new heroes. By this point, Goodman had promised to cut him in on all the merchandising money, a good incentive. Goodman had also made similar promises to Steve Ditko, placing an arm around his shoulder, leading him down a corridor, and saying, "Don't worry, we'll take care of you once the book begins showing a profit."

With college students ordering every product and forming chapters of the MMMS at Harvard, Princeton, and Yale, and young producer Steve Krantz preparing a cartoon series that would feature Captain America, Iron Man, Thor, Sub-Mariner, and the Hulk (after Goodman let him have the rights to every hero and the proofs used to manufacture the original comic books), Kirby and Ditko stood to gain a lot once the money came in. Feeling the future was bright indeed, Jack drew up a modern version of Hercules that slightly resembled actor Steve Reeves in those sand-and-sandal epics coming from Italy and designed an entire Greco-Roman pantheon to oppose Thor.

Over another weekend, he designed the Inhumans. Stranger than the X-Men, this team lived in the futuristic "Hidden Refuge" located in the Himalayas and included Karnak, whose jujitsu chops could find the weakest point of any object (and a character who first appeared as a villain in *The Challengers*); Gorgon, whose foot stomps could rattle the earth; Medusa, whose long red hair could attack opponents; Black Bolt, a quiet leader whose whisper was like a bomb; scale-covered amphibian Triton; and Crystal, who controlled the four elements. Each member looked different.

That same weekend, Jack drew a hero in an all-black costume and a mask that covered his face completely and included cat ears. He called him the Black Panther and made him black, he said later, because he realized he had many minority readers. And while other comic creators were either racist or didn't care about black people, some of his first friends on the Lower East Side had been black. "And here I was ignoring them because I was associating with everyone else." As a leading cartoonist and a Democrat, he wanted to change this. He also created Native American hero Wyatt Wingfoot.

After bringing Stan these concepts, he learned that the expansion plans were on hold. DC's Independent News division wouldn't let Goodman add any more comics, so he introduced the Inhumans as supporting players in *The Fantastic Four* and went on to create new villains, which were always in demand.

He wanted, however, to move comics beyond stock villains. "I went to the Bible, and I came up with Galactus," Jack said later. For this giant world-killing villain he designed a costume so complicated that he had to refer to a nearby sketch to get it right. Then he remembered a newspaper story he'd seen about the latest trend. "There was a guy standing on a wooden plank out in California," riding a wave, he said. It struck him as fantastic and led him to wonder, what if there was a surfer who surfed the universe? He drew a bald, silver guy with the same eyes as his 1940s Vision (and Ditko's later Spider-Man) and rendered him naked except for glazed silver skin. He then drew this character into *The Fantastic Four* No. 48, surfing past a spaceship and trembling Skrulls.

When Stan saw the Surfer in his pages, he asked, "Who the hell's this?"

"I figured anybody as powerful as Galactus ought to have a herald who would go ahead of him and find planets," Jack replied.

"That's a great idea!"

Stan added dialogue, following some of Jack's suggestions in the margins, and *The Fantastic Four* No. 48 told the story of a bald, robe-wearing giant named the Watcher warning the team that the ultimate menace was on its way: Galactus, an alien who absorbed the life force of planets in order to survive. When the team saw the giant, they wanted to attack, but the Watcher blocked their path.

Jack wrote, "He says hold it – don't tackle." Stan revised this to, "Wait! You must reconsider! Your strength is not yet the equal of your courage! Before you press blindly forward, you must hear the words I speak!"

Jack wrote that Galactus was "a prospector of space – instead of gold – he mines energy." Stan had Reed say, "Think of Galactus as a gold miner – prospecting in space! But, instead of ore, he digs for energy!" In a panel that described how the earth would be consumed, Jack wrote, "The ocean beds will be bone dry in no time flat." Stan wrote: "Within a matter of minutes, Galactus' elemental converter will have dehydrated every sea . . . dried out every body of water known to man!" And near a close-up of the villain's impassive face, Jack wrote, "The awesome Galactus studies area – scouted it before – but now he sees nothing – except he feels waves of thought present." Stan wrote, "I have passed this way before . . . for naught remains . . . save silent desolation . . . and yet . . . I sense a subtle wave of thought . . ."

Though his dialogue and Jack's margin notes were identical in content, Stan subtly altered the Surfer. After giving him the fancier name Silver Surfer, he moved the character from being a noble-looking flunky for Galactus to becoming one of Marvel's most popular heroes to date. While Galactus and the team faced off, Jack drew the Surfer meeting the Thing's blind girlfriend, a sculptress named Alicia Masters. After she offered him a meal, he raised his hands, converted it to energy, and absorbed it. Later, when she begged him to save planet Earth, he turned with raised hands and looked as if he'd do the same to her. Stan wouldn't have it. This hero was too good to waste. He made him experience a sudden change of heart that implied the Surfer was more human than Jack knew.

When comic readers saw the Surfer, they were instantly hooked. Stan realized he had the makings of a hit on a par with Spider-Man and quickly decided to include the Surfer in more stories. And when Jack turned in the cover for the next issue, Stan asked in-house artists to change it at the last minute so as to emphasize the enigmatic new hero. Jack's cover figures were copied and cut and rearranged so that small head shots of the Fantastic Four surrounded an enormous drawing of Silver Surfer against an empty background. And to appeal to the growing college audience, the bottom corner showed a picture of Johnny "Human Torch" Storm arriving on campus for his first day of class. When Jack saw the credits for the Surfer issues, however, he shook his head. The credits read "Written by Stan Lee."

The twin issues of writing credit and Goodman reneging on promises continued to affect relationships at Marvel. Though producer Steve Krantz and the Grantray-Lawrence animation studio were turning Jack's and Steve Ditko's art into the series *Marvel Super Heroes*, and companies kept churning out licensed products, Jack had yet to see a penny. Ditko, who no longer spoke with Stan and plotted Spider-Man on his own, agreed to help producer Ralph Bakshi with the new cartoon but was still displeased. "I don't know if it was true or not, but they all hated comics," Bakshi said of Ditko, Wally Wood, and other comic artists he employed. "They all were ripped off, they all felt they hadn't gotten what they deserved, and they basically felt they had no future." To earn a standard of living, he added, "they realized that they had to keep knocking out those pages. And they realized that they were getting older and couldn't maintain it." Since they were artists, not hacks, they worked slower. "They were getting tired. And they would realize there was no future in any of this. I think that's the thing that scared them the most," Bakshi said, "that they were weakening in strength and the money wasn't going to be any better. There wasn't any sharing of royalties at all when I met these guys." They were easy to work with because "I'd pay ten times more for storyboards than they'd get for a comic page. Not because I wanted to. That was just what we paid in the animation business. I wasn't doing anything special for those guys."

What happened next contributed to Ditko's and Jack's dissatisfaction and worst fears about Stan, credit, and his relationship with the company owner. Jack traveled into the city on a snowy Friday morning in late December, passing all the Christmas shoppers and bundled-up executives rushing to their offices. He had an appointment for a story conference with Stan that would also be an interview with *New York Herald-Tribune* reporter Nat Freedland. "What happened was, he wanted to do an interview with me for the *Trib*, and I caused the whole problem because I said – and I said this innocently – 'Look, I've been getting all this publicity,'" Stan explained. "'Jack Kirby's doing such a great job, how about if you interview both of us? Jack deserves a little publicity himself.'"

During the meeting, Jack sat and listened to Stan's plot for *The Fantastic Four* No. 55. "The Silver Surfer has been somewhere out in space since he helped the FF stop Galactus from destroying the Earth," he began. "Why don't we bring him back?"

Actually, the Surfer had been wandering planet Earth since the end of their three-part story; and though college kids wanted more of him, Jack didn't want to use him again. "Ummh," he hummed.

On his feet, pacing, Stan added, "Suppose Alicia, the Thing's blind girlfriend, is in some kind of trouble. And the Silver Surfer comes to help her."

"I see," Jack said.

"But the Thing sees them together and he misunderstands. So he starts a big fight with the Silver Surfer." Hamming it up, throwing punches at the air, Stan added, "And meanwhile, the Fantastic Four is in lots of trouble. Dr. Doom has caught them again, and they need the Thing's help."

Lots of trouble: He'd have to come up with something. "Right."

"The Thing finally beats the Silver Surfer," Stan added. "But then Alicia makes him realize he has made a terrible mistake. This is what the Thing has always feared more than anything else, that he would lose control and really clobber somebody."

Jack nodded and noticed the reporter facing Stan in awe.

"The Thing is brokenhearted," Stan said in a lower voice. "He wanders off by himself. He's too ashamed to face Alicia or go back home to the Fantastic Four. He doesn't realize how he's failing for the second time . . . how much the FF needs him." When Stan finally sat down, Jack rose to his feet, pulled the cigar from his mouth, and said, "Great, great."

Freedland looked amazed at Stan's genius. Though Jack usually contributed many ideas, Stan did figure out a great way to bring the Surfer back and adhere to what Jack wanted for his creation (each adventure teaching the alien Surfer a new lesson about human nature). After shaking hands, Jack left the meeting and went home to start the story (which would actually fill four or so issues once he expanded this slim plot). "And I thought that the interview went very well," said Stan. "And Jack and his wife were thrilled, and he couldn't wait until the paper came out because that was a big thing in those days. We weren't getting that much publicity, and the *Herald-Tribune* was a paper on a par with *The New York Times*. The *Times* was the Democratic paper," he noted, "and the *Trib* was the Republican paper in New York. It was very big."

When Freedland was around, Stan had faced a page from *The Fantastic Four* No. 50, a scene where Galactus's big machine would suck the earth dry. "It's not clear that the rays are hitting now," he'd told production manager Sol Brodsky. He'd grabbed a pencil and scribbled in sound effects that read "Zik Zik Zik." Dressed in a crisp white shirt and dark tie, Stan had told Freedland about how he got his tan while he worked from his home on Tuesday, Thursday, and Saturday, writing three books a week. He bragged about director Federico Fellini dropping by ("He's my buddy now") and said he'd never expected that Marvel's circulation would rise to thirty-five million. "I just thought maybe it would be worth trying to upgrade the magazines a little bit," he said.

Freedland saw fans across the street from Stan's second-floor office, holding homemade signs as if Marvel were the Beatles, and he saw Stan meet with the Princeton-based fan club chapter, answering their complaints about *Spider-Man* by saying, "I don't plot *Spider-Man* anymore. Steve Ditko, the artist, has been doing the stories. I guess I'll leave him alone until sales start to slip. Since Spidey got so popular, Ditko thinks he's the genius of the world." Stan also said his three new assistants passed a writing test that two hundred other people failed but weren't ready for anything more demanding than *Millie the Model* and *Kid Colt*.

In the wee hours of January 9, 1966, Jack and Roz ventured out into the snow to buy an early edition of the *New York Herald-Tribune*'s Sunday magazine section. What they saw stunned them. "The King is a middle aged man with baggy eyes and a baggy Robert Hall-ish suit," Freedland wrote in the final paragraphs. "He is sucking a huge green cigar and if you stood next to him on the subway you would peg him for the assistant foreman in a girdle factory." Freedland described Stan as Marvel's guiding force and Jack as speaking up from time to time with "kind of a high-pitched voice." And when Stan ended his plot, he wrote that Jack "leaped out of the chair he was crumpled in" and said, "Great, great," with his "baggy eyes" aglow and a voice "young with enthusiasm." Freedland concluded, "You can bet Stan Lee hasn't lost the touch that won him three first prizes in the *Herald-Tribune*'s 'Biggest News of the Week' teen contest back at old DeWitt Clinton H.S."

"Yeah . . . well, Jack and I did manage to get friendly after that," Stan said. "It was a terrible, terrible, unfortunate, unforgivable incident. The writer who wrote that should be ashamed of himself." At three A.M. on Sunday morning, Roz dialed Stan's home number. "And she was almost hysterical, and she shouted, 'How could you do this? How could you have done this to Jack?' I didn't know what she was talking about. They must have run out the night before and gotten an early edition. So I went to get the paper and when I saw the write-up, I could understand why she made that call. She had every right to be upset. About four fifths of the article was about me, and made me out to be the most glamorous, wonderful human being that ever lived, and the very last few paragraphs were about Jack and made him sound like a jerk. And it was horrible! And Jack and Roz, who were lovely people, were not incredibly sophisticated, and there was no way that they could have understood that I had no control over what this guy wrote. And it took a long time before that hurt on their part subsided. Maybe it never fully went away. I mean, I spent months trying to explain to them how bad I felt and how terrible it was what that writer had done. But anyway, that's the story, and it was dreadful, and Jack had every reason to be terribly angry and offended.

"But I never knew that would –

"I would never have asked the guy to interview Jack if I –

"I don't know why he wrote it that way!"

Jack told Goodman he wanted writing credit. Since he was looking to sell the company and didn't want a potential buyer to feel a freelancer was creating these great heroes and stories, Goodman said he couldn't do it. He also said this because he knew Jack, a family man with kids to feed, wouldn't leave. But then again, maybe he would, so the next issue of *The Fantastic Four* ran a credit: "Produced by Stan Lee and Jack Kirby."

Ditko, however, was not as easily subdued. An intensely private person who wouldn't sign autographs, have his picture taken, or meet with groveling fans at conventions, he witnessed Stan include flawed heroes in *Spider-Man* and *Dr. Strange* and argued vehemently against them. For Ditko, *The Amazing Spider-Man* was more than a comic book. He invested a lot of himself into the series, made Parker sort of resemble him, and brought an attention to detail that included filling sketchbooks with practice drawings of heroes and curtains.

That he wasn't enthusiastic about young people rebelling against authority also led to terrible arguments with liberal artist Gil Kane. "He was the most archconservative I had ever met in my entire life!" Kane claimed. "But there was no moving him, so if you didn't argue with him, he turned out to be very pleasant." Publicly, Kane said Ditko was very nice and they got along, but they "just never discussed politics." Ditko's peers blamed what they felt was unsociable behavior on his reported enjoyment of Ayn Rand's novels *The Fountainhead* and *Atlas Shrugged* and overlooked that he was creating Spider-Man's plots and, in some cases, going without credit or payment for his work. Similarly, his refusal to let Goodman promote his name or likeness enhanced his reputation as unfriendly.

Since the eighteenth issue of *The Amazing Spider-Man* – an experimental work that didn't include a fight scene – Ditko had stopped talking with Stan. Then, in June 1965, he dropped by with No. 25 and demanded writing credit. Stan's "Marvel method" – artists co-plotting stories after Stan gave them brief verbal or written plots – allowed him to deal with many artists at once and keep everyone working, but it also, Ditko felt, let Stan receive credit for his plots. Though credits read "Written by Stan Lee," Ditko was drawing his own plots and sending them in. Stan added dialogue and captions, and someone lettered the pages, and then Ditko inked his drawings. Ditko's method was going fine: He changed Peter Parker from a bespectacled nerd to a nonconformist who refused to let the world trample on him – Parker treating his critics as dismissively as architect Howard Roark does his employers in Ayn Rand's *The Fountainhead* – and fans kept buying more and more copies of *The Amazing Spider-Man*. Stan agreed to share writing credit with Ditko – who also helped finish *Daredevil* No. 1 and brought Marvel its logo for every cover, a picture of the hero in a box near the trade name "Marvel Comics Group" – and though No. 25 announced, "Sturdy Stevey Ditko dreamed up the plot of this tantalizing tale," Ditko still wouldn't speak to Stan. Instead, he'd hand Sol Brodsky the pages for the latest issue of *The Amazing Spider-Man* and leave.

Apparently, Ditko didn't like what Stan was doing to his stories. In one issue, Ditko wanted to unmask a villain called the Crime Master. "Steve said in real life it would probably turn out to be somebody that nobody had ever seen," Stan explained, "and I said, 'I agree with you, Steve, but it wouldn't be dramatically good. It would frustrate and disappoint the reader. It would be like watching an Agatha Christie mystery where the butler gets ten people together and we're gonna find out in the last scene who is the murderer and suddenly we find out that the murderer is somebody we hadn't seen through the whole story.' I said, 'You just don't do that in a fictional story.'"

Ditko drew Crime Master sitting on a rooftop with a few cops facing him. Stan wrote, "He's the one we thought he was!" Then, when Crime Master died before revealing the identity of the Green Goblin, another masked villain, Stan had another cop say, "Boy! If I saw that happen in a mystery movie, I'd laugh at how corny it was!"

If Jack thought he had it bad with edits, a conversation with Ditko would have disabused him of that notion. When Ditko ended *The Amazing Spider-Man* No. 35 with a drawing of a new villain, Stan wrote, "Next Ish . . . a swingin' super-villain so different, so new, we can't even tell you his name yet! Let's meet him together in *Spider-Man* #36!" In that story, when small-time crook Norman G. Fester was banging a hammer against a meteor that gave him power, Stan had him think, "Just because I flunked science in school doesn't mean I can't discover the secret of the universe!" Then, in a separate caption: "You guessed it, friend! N.G.F. is a part-time nut!"

Ditko continued to resent the changes, and Stan felt he was becoming increasingly difficult to work with. "He could have replaced him," Roy Thomas explained, but it was simpler to keep him on the book as long as things were going well. "*Dr. Strange*, of course, wasn't really that terribly important, but *Spider-Man* certainly was," Thomas added. "It had already become the second best-selling Marvel comic."

Soon, however, Stan and Ditko got into it over Ditko's plan to show another strange face behind the Green Goblin's mask. Every time Ditko drew the unmasked villain, he had him lurking in shadows that hid his face. But he also kept including scenes of *Daily Bugle* publisher J. Jonah Jameson in a men's club and a man with curly hair standing in the background. Then this stranger, who never spoke, popped up in Jameson's office at the newspaper. Before the unmasking, Ditko reiterated, "It should be somebody they've never seen before, just some person."

"Every reader in America is going to think we're crazy," Stan answered. "They'll be angry. It's got to be somebody!" Stan's dialogue established that the stranger was Norman Osborn, father of Peter's college friend Harry.

Soon they got into it over another panel. Stan wanted Ditko to replace a villain with a picture of Spidey. While inking the issue, Ditko left the villain where he was.

He was also as adamant about not changing other things – especially the tone. Martin Goodman thought Spidey needed to make a few concessions for their new college readers. Though *The Fantastic Four* and *Spider-Man* both showed Human Torch and Parker enrolling at different universities, Goodman felt Ditko's depiction of youth was unflattering, and *Spider-Man* could benefit from returning to the original concept of Parker as a superpowered Archie caught between a brunette and a blonde and breezing through life on his motorcycle.

Goodman sent someone to tell Ditko to change the tone or else. It was the last straw. Believing that Goodman had reneged on a promise to give him and Jack some of the merchandising profits, Ditko entered the cramped office shared by Roy Thomas, Flo Steinberg, and Sol Brodsky, handed Brodsky his latest work, and said, "I'll finish these jobs I'm working on now, and that's it." While Brodsky ran to tell Stan, and Ditko walked out, Roy Thomas noticed a memo on Brodsky's desk that announced Ditko had just received a $5-a-page raise.

When Ditko asked Jack to leave with him, Jack considered the *Tribune* article and how Goodman had denied him writing credit. He told Steve they could form their own company and asked him to draw a two-page presentation for a new hero they could show investors. "It had that classic Ditko sixties look to it," Jack's good friend Mike Thibodeaux said of the drawing. "It was just jumping out at you."

While Ditko worked, Jack went to lunch with Gil Kane and complained about Stan. "I'm going to break this guy!" he yelled. "I'm gonna do some work for someone else! I'm gonna start a new company! I'm gonna see this guy run out of business!"

When they returned to the office, however, and Stan said, "Jack, I need you to change something," Kane recalled that he complied without question.

"That's the way it was," Kane told an interviewer, "and don't let anyone bullshit you about anything else."

Jack had a decision to make. If he stayed, he'd remain a freelancer while Stan was his superior and Goodman's relative. And by now, John Romita explained, "Roz was unhappy with Stan taking top billing and credit for creating all the stuff." At the same time, if he left, Goodman might not give him his share of merchandising profits. He didn't like or trust Goodman, but he had a wife and four kids to support, needed steady income, had been given some pretty hefty bonuses, and really couldn't start knocking on doors at age forty-eight.

He stayed with Marvel. Stan reported Ditko's departure in a column called "Bullpen Bulletins": "It's hail and farewell to sturdy Steve Ditko! *Spider-Man* #38 and *Strange Tales* #146 (both now on sale) will mark his final appearances in any Marvel mags! (Except for the numerous reprints you'll find in our king-size issues.) Steve recently told us he was leaving, for personal reasons. After all these years, we're sorry to see him go, and we wish the talented guy success with his future endeavors." And when reporters asked why Ditko left, Stan would say, "He never told us why."

Chapter 10

DC was riding high again. Since January 1966, when *Batman* debuted on ABC, a stream of articles called the show as vital a component of the pop art movement as aluminum wigs, geometric earrings, neon dresses, bell-bottoms, and the Carnaby Street regalia men wore in an effort to appear attractively nonthreatening to women. Despite fifty-eight-year-old producer William Dozier's approach – staging the show as a cliché-ridden spoof – *Batman*'s two weekly episodes continued to attract thirty million viewers and make the Nielsen top twenty. The media wanted to talk about *Batman* and pop art; the National Safety Council lauded the show for scenes in which Batman told Robin to fasten his seat belt; Marshall McLuhan, publishers, and anthropologists convened at the University of Pennsylvania to discuss "From Gutenberg to Batman"; actor Adam West, who played the hero, told *Newsweek*'s Peter Benchley (whose tale of a giant shark would later top the best-seller list), "Talking in art terms, I guess you could say that I am painting a new fresco."

Two years after it considered canceling Batman's comic, National/DC was on its way to earning $600 million from a thousand licensed products. It was the biggest demand the president of DC's in-house licensing firm had ever seen: Over 4.8 million mask-and-cape sets (priced at $1), Batman bubble bath, jewelry, cutout kits, Batarangs, model Batmobiles, $38 Batman clothing, $27 tricycles, pens and pencils, slippers, quilts, and over a million posters.

And even more companies wanted to be in the Batman business. While DC president Jack Liebowitz agreed to let them manufacture $50 Batman tuxedos and $125 Batman electric guitars, he swiftly vetoed Bat guns, Bat cigarettes, and Bat wine. Sales of the comic itself continued to soar; a recent issue sold an astounding 88 percent of its print run.

When Ditko left, Stan Lee tried to position old-hack Bill Everett as "another Steve Ditko – with an inimitable style all his own"; he had artist Dan Adkins take over Ditko's *Dr. Strange* strip ("I was actually told to swipe [copy] Ditko, and this was by Stan, up front," Adkins claimed); and he handed John Romita a stack of early *Spider-Man* issues, asking, "How would you like to try *Spider-Man*?"

Before reading the comics, Romita felt, "This is crazy, it looks like a young Clark Kent guy, a kid with glasses who turns into a superhero." Afterward, however, he liked the character, thought it was original, but worried that fans of Ditko's definitive Spidey – featured in thirty-eight issues and two annuals – might not accept his version. Since Stan was desperate and needed help, and Romita assumed Ditko's walkout would only be temporary, Romita agreed to do it, only to see Stan worry about fan response when he drew fewer creepy villains and dark alleys and more chic characters smiling at one another during sun-drenched afternoons. "Even the villains were starting to look good, and I was taking age away from Aunt May," Romita joked.

In the past, Goodman had been wrong about a few things – including the Hulk – but the romance element he requested did spice up the series. With Parker in college, and stuck between Mary Jane Watson, a curvy redhead who moved like a go-go dancer, and blond Gwen Stacy, who wore miniskirts, more readers were picking up each issue. But Romita soon complained about Stan's requests for Gwen. "Gwen's a lady," he said. "She's not the same kind of airhead that Mary Jane is. I can't have her smiling all the time." Stan insisted he draw her this way. "Pretty soon it was hard to tell Gwen and Mary Jane apart," Romita said. "They were like Betty and Veronica – the same girl except for the hair color." Then Stan asked why he kept drawing Parker in turtlenecks.

When lecturing, promoting the company, writing captions and dialogue for three books a day, editing the entire Marvel line, correcting artwork, and meeting with writers and artists began to take up most of his time, Stan shortened his story conferences with Romita. From three hours to one hour, he now gave Romita a quick beginning, middle, and end; a villain; and a setting. "Then it was up to me to fill in all the gaps," the artist explained. "Like the transitions from one scene to the next, we didn't always get to work those out in the verbal plots." Before he knew it, Romita decided the Kingpin would be bald and fat and *Daily Bugle* editor Robbie Robertson would be black and have a rebellious son and a long-suffering wife. And once Romita started working in the office, some story conferences consisted of Stan leaving a note on his desk that would say something like "Next Month: The Rhino." "That's all," Romita recalled. "He wouldn't tell me anything, how to handle it. Then he would say, 'The Kingpin.'" Romita didn't mind, but he did sometimes joke, "I do the work, and Stan cashes the checks."

Meanwhile, Jack continued to share Ditko's opinion that Stan wasn't telling his lecture audiences or reporters how involved he'd been with creating the heroes. In the "Bullpen Bulletins" column, Stan did explain that all he really did was provide a germ of an idea to artists who "make up all the details as they go along, drawing and plotting out the story" before "our leader simply takes the finished drawing and adds all the dialogue and captions!" But credits like "By Stan Lee & Jack Kirby," "Scripted by Stan Lee," "Panoramically Produced by Stan Lee and Jack Kirby" or "A Stan Lee–Jack Kirby Modern Day Masterwork" continued to imply that Stan was telling artists what to draw.

When Stan finally let Jack receive credit for a Nick Fury story, about the agency trying to get rid of its director, Marvel promoted it in the "Bullpen" column as "And, for the most unexpected surprise of all. Jumpin' Jack Kirby himself wrote the script – in addition to doing the layouts – for Nick Fury's S.H.I.E.L.D. thriller in *Strange Tales* #148!" The "Bullpen" column then followed this with another item that claimed Jack had left "an hour-long story conference with Stan" and told employees, "Well, we just polished off a few holocausts, and a cataclysm or two! Now, I'll go out and relax by dreaming up a few simple disasters!" The Lee-Kirby brand name was too lucrative an image to abandon.

With *The Fantastic Four*, Marvel's top-selling title, Jack kept doing pretty much what he wanted, plotting his own stories with the artwork and margin notes. He did the same for Thor, and stories in *Tales to Astonish*, *X-Men*, and *Tales of Suspense*, as well as the layouts he created for new arrivals to the Nick Fury series in *Strange Tales*. While layouts brought extra money, he felt he was doing too much of the work for a quarter of what he'd get just for drawing someone else's story. But Stan wouldn't let him stop, he said later, so he continued to teach new artists how to draw fight scenes that seemingly exploded from panels. "If you're at the business end of a fist, that's what you'd see," he explained, "or if you're involved with a blast, that would be your impression."

When Jack supplied layouts to John Buscema, who returned after an eight-year absence from comics, Buscema decided to erase some of the storyboards and submitted a terrible Fury story for *Strange Tales* No. 150. Stan assigned him a Hulk story. Buscema again ignored Jack's layouts and delivered more horrible work. Stan then gave him a few of Jack's old comics, which Buscema kept in front of him while drawing a Sub-Mariner story. "Every time I needed a panel," he said, "I'd look up at one of his panels and just rearrange it." Seeing that Buscema had included Jack's standby – a hero sending ten guys flying with one punch – he said, "You got it, John. Now tone it down."

For the next Fury story, Jack created layouts for newcomer Jim Steranko. They had met in 1964 when Jim had been a fan stopping by the house; Jack asked if he'd had lunch, then led him to the kitchen, buttered some bread, slapped bologna on it, and offered him a sandwich. While eating in Jack's studio that day, Jim had observed his art, model planes, old comics, and desk and complimented his work. Now, after meeting Joe Simon and doing a few comics for Harvey, Steranko was at Marvel, itching to bring something new to the field.

"When I came into Marvel, most of the people were old-timers," Steranko recalled. "They were vets who had been working there for decades, and the magic was gone. Maybe they had it somewhere along the way, but with a few exceptions, like Kirby, most of them just didn't give a damn." Steranko took to the layouts much quicker than Buscema had, and Stan let him stay on the book.

By now, the Vietnam War was dominating the news. Every night brought more scenes of soldiers running through the jungle or carrying rifles past reporters. Young people with long hair kept holding huge peace marches, and some of them were getting nasty. At one big event, Flo Steinberg recalled, someone announced the number of American soldiers who had been killed, and the audience clapped. "I just walked out and never went back. I certainly wanted the war to be over, but that applause just creeped me out."

At home, watching the nightly news with Roz, Jack would tell her he'd worked hard during World War II, had sweated it out, so that Neal and other people's sons wouldn't have to go to Vietnam. "I didn't like that war," he said later. "I thought it was crazy. And of course, that had an effect on a generation of young people who just couldn't understand it. They couldn't handle it; and they still have trouble today."

But young people in fringe vests, bell-bottoms, tie-dyed clothing, ragged jeans, and peace sign medallions continued to march in the streets and face cops with nightsticks and demand civil rights, black power, women's liberation, and an end to the war. And around the world, more young people were holding their own marches.

Many readers wanted Stan and Marvel to use comics to address Vietnam, civil rights, and riots, but Stan replied in print that he'd rather entertain than editorialize. When one reader urged others to write to soldiers care of Operation Mail Call Vietnam, Stan printed the letter but added, "This notice is not intended as an endorsement on our part of any specific policy regarding the war." Jack felt that behind the "hip" image, company management was as uptight as many other older people. These kids were the best thing his generation had ever done, and they had a right to complain.

When college students saw Galactus and the Silver Surfer feuding like father and son, intergalactic voyages that expanded consciousness, the Inhumans being as shunned and hated as the hippies, and a hero called the Black Panther (while a real-life group of young black men in berets were carrying shotguns in public), they sent two hundred to five hundred fan letters a day and told reporters from *Esquire* that Stan was their Homer, and Spider-Man and Hulk were more relevant than Sartre, Camus, Dostoevsky, and Marx. "All these grad students who decided it was so hip, so cool, to like comics would write him because they were sort of turned on by all his literary allusions and little quotes from Shakespeare that I bet he got out of *Bartlett's*," said Linda Fite, who worked in the office. "They would ask him to come speak at their school and knew they'd get press. 'Cause comics make people sit up and pay attention."

Meanwhile the Marvel bullpen was changing. Roy Thomas came to work with a Nehru jacket and goatee; other bullpen members grew beards – Stan didn't know what to make of it, although he did start wearing a hairpiece. "He experimented with one here and there, because at that time, that's what men did," Flo remembered. "I mean, now a bald head is wonderful. It's different. Then, it was embarrassing to lose your hair." Though he dressed more casually, however, some of the changes in youth culture confused him. "One of these days we'll find out what he's hiding under there," he wrote in "Bullpen Bulletins" about one writer's beard. Another guy's sideburns, meanwhile, were so long that he could probably tie them under his chin. One day he went to a meeting and noticed he was the only guy wearing shoes.

But when Bard College invited him to lecture, he gave it a try. Stepping onstage in his best suit and tie, he faced an audience of hippies in beads, ripped T-shirts, and army fatigues. He was self-conscious but started talking. This was the best way to promote Marvel and find out what readers liked or disliked about the books. After fifteen minutes, he turned it over to a question-and-answer session. "I could learn so much about our readers' tastes by the questions they asked and the comments they made."

Next Princeton called, and to avoid being seen as a square, Stan donned his oldest pair of jeans, a faded T-shirt, and a pair of worn sneakers. But this audience, he realized with embarrassment, was formally attired.

The more he lectured at colleges, the more the *New York Post*, the *Chicago Daily News*, the *Akron Beacon Journal*, the *Topeka State Journal*, the *Cleveland Press*, the *Altoona Mirror*, the *Milwaukee Journal*, and dozens more wanted to speak with him. "As far as what I talked about, it ran the gamut," he explained. "For example, one college might call me and say, 'We want you to speak about how comics are influenced by movies.' Another: 'We want you to speak about popular culture.' Another: 'We want you to speak about whether comics have a positive or negative effect on the reading public.' Or, 'We want you to speak about legends of the past and the future and how comic books affect them.' Or 'We want you to speak about creative writing.' It could be anything at all. It didn't bother me because I'm equally uninformed in any subject, so I could get up there and kill some time doing it," he joked. "I enjoyed it very much."

Soon, CBS Television's Tom Dunn and CBS Radio's Mike Wallace wanted him on their programs. Stan quipped about his high profile in "Bullpen Bulletins": "We just hope our leader doesn't start wearing a beret and sunglasses around the office."

Because of his promotional efforts, everyone was talking about, and buying, Marvel – not DC – and Goodman learned that during the last five years, sales had actually doubled. Now, Marvel was second only to DC and closing in fast. While TV's *Batman* dipped in ratings, *Marvel Super Heroes* debuted in syndication that September, aired five nights a week on over forty-nine television stations worldwide, and earned high ratings in key cities. Lancer was selling paperback reprints of early Fantastic Four, Spidey, Thor, and Hulk stories and phonograph record albums that came with actual comics. Other companies churned out Marvel Halloween costumes, Captain America and Hulk plastic models, baseball caps, buttons, toy rings, T-shirts, and sweatshirts. Goodman had also licensed the heroes for minibooks from gumball machines, trading cards, costumes for popular "action doll" toys, board games, jigsaw puzzles, and fan club materials. And more people were mailing $1.75 checks and money orders for twelve-issue subscriptions.

At the same time, Stan watched as other companies rushed to imitate the Lee-Kirby style. But DC and Charlton Comics' bizarre heroes and hipster dialogue weren't as egregious or as bad as John Goldwater having *Superman* co-creator Jerry Siegel write *The Mighty Crusaders* and call the book part of his Mighty Comics Group line, so he leveled most of his "Bullpen Bulletins" insults at MLJ. "To save them the trouble of trying to imitate our inimitable style, we're thinking of selling them some of our old scripts!" wrote Stan. "Then, they could be sure they finally have the same kind of stories as mighty Marvel!"

Marvel was so popular that soon DC's Carmine Infantino was interested in coming over. Once Stan learned that Irwin Donenfeld wanted Infantino to become DC's in-house cover artist in late 1966, Stan called Infantino to say, "Carmine, how about coming here and working for us?"

"Well, make me an offer," Carmine replied.

After Stan met with Goodman, describing how he helped revive *The Flash* and saved *Batman* from cancellation, Carmine was offered $22,000 (three grand more than what DC put on the table). At DC, Donenfeld told Carmine they couldn't meet that price. Carmine was ready to switch to Marvel. "But then Jack Liebowitz called and said, 'Come meet me for lunch,'" he explained.

Carmine liked and respected Liebowitz, who had been with the company for decades. Over lunch, Liebowitz said that DC couldn't meet Marvel's offer but would let him be art director.

"Chief, I don't know," he replied.

"What are you, afraid of the challenge?"

Carmine stayed with DC Comics, but Marvel sales continued to rise.

Marvel had the perfect setup. Jack and Stan created the heroes; Jack taught new artists how to draw like him and plot their own stories; and Stan came along to add his captivating characterization. As a result, even though both were burdened with other duties, they were able to spread their approach to every book Marvel published.

Thanks to Jack's layouts and plot ideas, Don Heck's three issues of *The Avengers*, DC artist Werner Roth's *X-Men*, old-timer George Tuska and John Romita's Captain America series in *Tales of Suspense*, and Buscema and Steranko's Nick Fury tales had been as explosive as Jack's own. But layouts meant plotting stories and drawing them out – 75 percent of the work – for a quarter of the pay, so Jack kept telling Marvel he didn't want to do them anymore. The company understood but would ask for just a few more to teach new guys "the Marvel method." Jack would comply, they'd quickly ask for just a few more, and these would also feature the credit "Written by Stan Lee."

After a while, Goodman began to complain about the money Jack earned. "He felt, 'Kirby's turning out so much work, let's cut his rate,'" Buscema explained. When Jack threatened to quit, Goodman backed off, and Jack finally refused to do any more layouts.

In the past, Jack and Stan's story conferences had been so loud that Flo had had to yell, "Keep it down." Three years later, Jack was handing Stan the next issue's plots in his drawings. Stan's copy was excellent at times, and his editorial input was invaluable, but Jack felt he should be receiving money and credit for his writing. And once Stan started to change a few of his stories, their relationship became more strained.

In *The Fantastic Four* No. 76, Jack wanted to introduce a new muscle-bound orange-skinned blond guy who resembled a recent villain on *Star Trek*. Through this character, he'd explore the downside of objectivism and possibly create stories for magazines geared toward mature readers. At his board, he drew a story about well-meaning scientists creating a self-sufficient, intellectual being. After ending the story with the creature emerging from a huge cocoon, he sent it in and considered the second part of the story: the being learning that the scientists were imperfect and destroying them. When Stan sent him the photostats with his dialogue, however, Jack saw that the scientists were bad guys and "Him" was innocent. Debating the issue would lead nowhere, so he changed the ending to conform to Stan's feel-good version but decided not to bring Marvel any of his latest ideas, including the Young Gods he'd introduced in Thor's backup series, "Tales of Asgard." If Stan hadn't changed this story, his margin notes for Thor would have continued leading up to Ragnarok, the final battle that would kill most of Thor's cast and showcase the debut of a younger, more ambitious pantheon. Now, he told Stan they'd done all they could with "Tales of Asgard" and should end the series.

During the period in which they celebrated their twenty-fifth wedding anniversary, Roz noticed how dissatisfied Jack had become. Because Goodman was now paying him a weekly check that amounted to his rate for fifteen pages, and bookkeepers determined what pages each payment covered, she tried to prevent Marvel from underpaying him by keeping a meticulous record of what he sent in and what he received.

Though Stan kept promoting him in the "Bullpen Bulletins" column, Jack still felt it wasn't enough. It didn't help to see the company credit newcomer Jim Steranko as writer of the *Nick Fury, Agent of S.H.I.E.L.D.* series, when the artist had only one or two inking jobs, a few stories from his layouts, and mediocre Harvey Comics series like *Spyman*, *Magicmaster*, and *The Gladiator* to his name. "I think Stan saw him as good press because Jim was really good at self-promotion," said Linda Fite. "That would make it easier for Stan. He didn't have to promote as much." Steranko *was* a true talent – his *S.H.I.E.L.D.* pages fused the Kirby style to pop art colors, collages, forceful layouts, and Ben Day dots that suggested Roy Lichtenstein. When Roy Thomas showed Jack some pages one day, he acknowledged this: "He's all right. He just needs somebody to kick him in the ass and make him turn out five pages a day." But Jack was disturbed that Steranko was receiving the credit he'd been denied for years, when he'd done more for the company.

Further aggravating Jack, Stan kept promoting himself as "Our Leader" in his monthly column, "Stan's Soapbox." He'd describe how Jack was guest of honor at a comics convention in Manhattan, then add that he went to one of his own and "talked and talked and talked and talked – and talked – for hours, in his usual capriciously confusing manner. . . ." Stan would follow a description of the list of concepts Jack brought to *The Fantastic Four* with the question "Now do you see why poor Stan and Jack even have trouble remembering their own names sometimes?" Then once Jack stopped calling or stopping by so much, or after one of their arguments, Stan would write that artists all respected him, adding, "Don't be embarrassed, Jack, this is just Stan's cornball way of telling you that it's been a ball all these years, pal – and the best is still ahead!"

During the summer of 1967, Jack worked on his usual titles as well as an Inhumans title that Stan soon changed. As Jack saw it, the Inhumans were created billions of years ago by the alien race the Kree and placed in a hidden city as part of a social experiment. The Inhumans knew the Kree wanted them to help cavemen evolve and knew their makers' armored robot the Sentry would visit to monitor their progress. In Jack's vision, the Sentry observed them staying in their hidden city, refusing to help anyone, and secretly creating forbidden weapons. After someone fired a laser at it, the robot cautioned that their poor attitude would cause humans to hate them and call them inhuman. The conclusion showed the Sentry warning he'd tell the Kree their experiment failed. Stan's version changed everything: The Inhumans didn't know the Sentry or that the Kree had created them until their visitor announced it;

they lived by themselves because the Kree didn't want them mixing with humans; the Sentry was shot at and said their weapon was pretty good work; the Sentry waved good-bye and said he'd tell the Kree they'd succeeded. The changes made Jack unhappy, but not as much as the news that his Inhumans stories would run as five-page replacements for "Tales of Asgard."

Then, when drawing Captain America again, Jack noticed someone had changed the face he'd drawn on Cap's love interest, blond S.H.I.E.L.D. agent Sharon Carter. "He says he hated it and that it was wrong," his friend Mark Evanier recalled. "It was one of those things that in hindsight most people wish had never been done." The faces were changed because Stan, while dialoguing, wanted to take a story in another direction. "So they'd give it to Romita and say, 'Make her do this and change her this way,' and he'd have to change a few heads to make it consistent."

That fall, Kinney National purchased DC, and editorial director Irwin Donenfeld stepped down. Jack's pal Carmine went to Jack Liebowitz and said, "Hey, Irwin's gone. Who is editor now? Who is the chief now?"

Liebowitz replied, "You."

As editorial director, Carmine replaced most of the editors – including Jack Schiff, who had sued Jack over the *Sky Masters* strip and triumphed – and, knowing that many of Marvel's hit titles were actually artist driven, promoted pencilers to top editorial positions. Carmine had once told Jack that if he ever got the top spot, he'd hire him. When asked if he'd like to come over, however, Jack said no, not quite yet. He was dissatisfied, but hopeful. . . . Goodman allegedly offered him a share of every penny of the merchandising money and promised that any corporation that bought Marvel – Goodman was busy trying to sell the company – wouldn't obtain rights to characters Jack created or co-created without his receiving a considerable sum from the deal. "If and when I have certain problems with Marvel," Jack told Carmine, "maybe I'll leave." But he added that Ditko could bring DC the Marvel style and good ideas, so Carmine soon had Ditko working on the inspired *The Hawk and the Dove* (two heroes, one conservative and one liberal, who bickered about politics and America's involvement overseas) and *Beware the Creeper* (a maniacal vigilante in an outrageous costume who prowled the city at night), as well as Ditko telling him that Charlton Comics' editor Dick Giordano might also be willing to come over.

Jack was waiting for Goodman to finally honor his pledge – during a time when the company was unwilling to give Flo Steinberg, the "Fabulous Flo" they promoted in columns and magazines, a meager raise. For whatever reason, despite the fact that he was earning more money and stood to earn even more by expanding the line, Goodman refused to do it. When she left, Stan wrote, "Face Front, Flo! The best of luck to you where'er you go."

Then he got back to working on Goodman's latest request: Captain Marvel, a spaceman hero rushed into print to capitalize on the legal availability of the name. Captain Marvel was followed by a *Sgt. Fury* spin-off, the forgettable *Captain Savage and His Leatherneck Raiders*. Goodman's next move, however, was a winner: He signed with a new distributor. The "Bullpen Bulletins" promised that 1968 would "go down in comicdom history as the year of big changes in the wonderful world of Marvel!"

It was a promise kept. In April, Captain America and the Hulk received their own titles. In May, Iron Man and Sub-Mariner did, too. Then in June, Marvel published first issues of *Nick Fury* and *Dr. Strange*. Though they were already publishing eighteen books, Stan announced that the bullpen was "busily creating full-length masterpieces featuring a whole *new* array of Marvel stars – power-packed sensations soon to be headlined in their own strips – all-time greats such as Dr. Doom – Ka-Zar – Silver Surfer – and others too startling to mention!"

Now that the Silver Surfer would be getting his own book, Jack brought him and Galactus back to *The Fantastic Four* and started to plot and draw the Surfer's origin.

He was doing this when he learned Stan wanted John Buscema

to draw the new *Silver Surfer* series. "I may have thought that John would be a little better for this," Stan explained. "I may have wanted it to look a little bit more illustrative. John had a certain quality in his artwork. Or it may have been simply that Jack was too busy."

At the time, Jack was drawing *The Fantastic Four*, *Thor*, and the new full-length *Captain America* book while also working on the Inhumans. But if Stan wanted him on the book, Jack felt, he could've made it happen. When he learned that Stan and Buscema would be starting the series with their own origin story, Jack set aside his origin pages, completed the end of the Surfer story in *The Fantastic Four*, and vowed he'd never draw the Surfer again.

Then he felt Marvel made a mockery of the character. Though the first cover showed a muscular, battle-ready Surfer flying toward the reader, inside, Stan stretched the plot by having him offer lengthy monologues, a loquacious pacifist running repeatedly from danger.

Worse than this was the origin. Jack had never wanted the Surfer to be human in any way. He was an energy-absorbing alien formed by Galactus for the sole purpose of finding new worlds for him to consume. Since December 1965, however, Jack had seen Stan's captions hint that Surfer was really a human covered in a silver coating. Now, the Surfer was shown to be human scientist Norrin Radd, who lived on a Flash Gordon–looking planet, Zenn-La, and stopped Galactus from destroying his world by offering himself as a herald. Jack shook his head. This origin removed everything readers had loved about the hero – the fact that he was as strange and cold as Mr. Spock and blasted targets with his hands. When he saw Stan's Surfer on his knees, begging humans to be peaceful, it reinforced his desire to never again have anything to do with the hero.

Stan, meanwhile, faced his own problems. Though a recent large-format, black-and-white *Spider-Man* magazine tanked, Goodman wanted the Surfer in a twenty-five-cent forty-page comic that presented stories that could easily be chopped in two and thrown into standard twenty-page issues (in case he changed the page count and price). With the entire industry looking to see if this higher-priced book would sell, and if Stan could actually handle the character without Jack, Buscema said, "The number one issue sold well, but each succeeding issue lost sales. It just went down, which was probably what was bothering Stan." Sales continued to plunge, Stan didn't know what to do, and Jack was upset that the series even existed. "This was his thing, his idea, his creation," Buscema explained, "and it's being taken away from him and given to me."

But Jack kept his feelings to himself, especially now that Goodman was about to sell Marvel to Perfect Film and Chemical Corporation, the same company that bought – and, some felt, destroyed – *The Saturday Evening Post*. By October 1968, Marvel had sold fifty million comics and become the best-selling publisher in comics. Add merchandising money, popular cartoons like *Spider-Man* and *Marvel Super Heroes*, and never-ending media coverage, and it explained why his friend Martin Ackerman, president of Perfect, urged the company to buy Marvel.

When he heard of the deal, Jack felt as though his hard work and silent acceptance of various policies might finally pay off. As he'd allegedly done to Ditko, Goodman had promised Jack a share of all merchandising money and pledged that the new owners wouldn't get rights to anything he created or co-created without paying him a sizable amount. But in recent months, he had begun to wonder. His contract had expired, and no one would renew it. Goodman kept reassuring him of another, better deal, but nothing was in writing.

Though Jack helped create Marvel's stories and heroes, reporters continually promoted Stan as sole creator of the Marvel universe, and Perfect refused to buy the company unless Stan signed a three-year contract with Marvel. Perfect believed the media coverage and didn't want the company without what they believed was its driving creative force. "I had never been under contract before and thought the notion was pretty damn flattering," Stan explained later. After signing the contract and receiving a raise, he visited Goodman's home, where Goodman put his arm around his shoulders and led him to the downstairs den. "Stan," he said, "I'll see to it that you and Joanie will never have to want for anything as long as you live."

Meanwhile, Jack couldn't get anyone at Marvel to discuss his new contract. "He was very unhappy with the way he was being treated," said Mark Evanier. "He found that the businesspeople wouldn't talk to him. He had this rotten deal that wasn't even properly committed to paper. His contract had expired. It was all kind of verbal. And he felt since Marvel had been taken over that he ought to have an actual contract that spelled out everything he was promised. He said, 'I want this,' and nobody would talk to him. He couldn't get his calls returned. He went over to the executive offices and heard people say, 'We're all too busy to talk to you. Go back and draw *The Fantastic Four*.'"

The company alienated him again just when he was working on another batch of new creations. When he told people, "I'm not going to give them another Silver Surfer," he meant it. Instead of including his new characters as villains or handing sketches to Stan, he sent them to Don Heck for inking and showed them to people who stopped by to express interest in publishing his work. Among the sketches were a red champion with a fearsome silver helmet, an insect man in green and yellow, a cold circuit-covered hero in a mechanical chair, and an old-fashioned caped green-and-yellow hero. "Some were for *The New Gods*, some for a new edition of *Thor* – a different approach – some were completely original characters, and some were variations of a few Marvel properties," Evanier recalled.

While he tested a few concepts in *Captain America* – the strange helmet on the villain Fourth Sleeper, the Sleeper becoming ghost-like and swimming through rock under the earth's surface, and characters in flying chairs – Jack didn't bring Stan the epic he'd been thinking about lately. Instead, his ideas went into the growing pile on his desk, which he would use either for another company or as leverage with Marvel. "There was no distinct game plan for these other than that he knew that if you show people new characters, their faces light up and they say, 'I want that,'" Evanier explained. "And that gives you clout if you're the creator."

With Marvel refusing to renew his contract, and his valuable original pages being stolen from the office by young employees or other artists, he asked his lawyer to write Marvel and request that they send him his work. By now, Linda Fite explained, the art was lying around the office or kept out in the open on shelves. "Each shelf had a different title of a book," she recalled. "And the art would just sit there when it came back from the printer." Though Marvel planned to ship the pages to a warehouse, one or two people stole even more pages and sold them at conventions. "Pages would be littering the floor," Steranko recalled. "In the hallway, for example, there'd be a foot-high stack of pages. They'd be all over the bullpen. They were never locked up. And these were comic pages now selling for ten to thirty thousand dollars."

Soon, Steranko asked for his original art, too. "And I had had many bitter battles with Stan about it, but the thing was he didn't own the art, so it wasn't his to give back. It belonged to Mr. Goodman." They reached an impasse, Steranko added, "and Stan was very tired of me talking about this. I think I gave him an ultimatum, because they were being stolen out of the offices and showing up on dealers' tables at conventions and I wasn't getting anything for them. I said, 'Unless I get my pages back, I'm gonna go to the IRS and tell them about the original art inventory. And it must be massive because it goes back through the Atlas and Timely periods. And it must be worth a fortune, even if it's just a dollar or five dollars a page. You have to pay taxes on your inventory, just like everybody.' And at that point, Stan had enough and said, 'Jim, you do whatever you have to do. But I never want to discuss this again, ever. Never bring it up again.' So I took care of it on my own. And when Stan saw I had my originals for display at conventions and shows and exhibitions sometime later, he never mentioned it, and I never mentioned it again." Jack, however, continued to see his pages turn up at conventions.

Chapter 11

Roz stood in the town house, facing the canyon right outside the window, where sheep grazed on grass. "Just beautiful," she said. During his twenty years in Long Island, Jack had barely left his own doorstep. But since a milder climate would help Roz's health, and Lisa his fourth child, couldn't take severe winters anymore, he moved the family out to California. They were in a development where every house looked the same, but their three-level rental rested on a mountain facing the view. They lived on one level with a swimming pool. The level below had room for a corral. The one underneath it was empty. Below that lay the valley, the stream, and the sheep.

In a way, it was a brand-new start. Jack wanted to spend more time with the kids and be outdoors a little more. After moving in their belongings, he and Roz started building the corral for a horse they promised to buy Lisa. Before actually buying the horse, Jack reminded her that he'd do it only if she fed and took care of it. She agreed. One day, however, she caught him cleaning up and said, "Dad, I thought I was supposed to do that."

"Girls are not supposed to do this kind of work," he answered. With a shrug she left. "It was like his little break from work," she explained, "to go out there and clean my corral."

Now, when he worked, he faced a window and the pool outside. Though they decided to leave the dining room set behind, he couldn't quite part with the weather-beaten old drawing table he'd used since he and Joe had an office in the early fifties. And though it didn't match, he liked sitting in his wooden, stiff-backed dining room chair while drawing. It was comfortable on the back, which was important since he was fifty-one years old and had to work all night to get Marvel fifteen pages a week. Every night until two, he'd draw one of the three monthly comics he was handling. After sleeping a little, he'd awaken, read the morning paper, and then get back to the desk by one or two in the afternoon. It was an odd schedule, but he also had a heavy workload: No sooner would he finish a *Fantastic Four* than Stan would ask for another or the next issue of *Thor*.

When Stan announced in the "Bullpen Bulletins" that Jack had moved away, he wrote, "Here's an announcement we make with mixed emotions. Jack (King) Kirby and family are leaving New York and moving to California. In fact, by the time you read this, the King will already be settled on the shores of the blue Pacific!" After joking that he'd be "spending most of his extra cabbage on air-mail stamps rather than those king-sized cigars he loves to sport," he added that it was "a terrific deal for the Great One, who certainly deserves his place in the sun."

The sentimental article, however, concealed that Stan might have preferred that Jack not be so close anymore, Roy Thomas opined. Their relationship was severely strained. Since Jack seemed upset with him, "He thought, Well, maybe talking over the phone once in a while would be okay." But the distance meant Stan would have to ask in-house artists to change, or correct, Jack's art before publication.

He'd also have to find someone to take over *Captain America*. Jack no longer wanted to draw the full-length series – or give Marvel any new creations. As a result, he populated *Captain America* with the Red Skull again and his band of generic human Exiles. Before starting an issue, Jack would be assured that a replacement was on the way. He'd fill Cap with listless fight scenes or another rehash of his origin, figuring he was out of there anyway, only to hear Marvel ask if he could do one or two more issues, since no one wanted to follow his run. When Steranko agreed to do a few issues, Jack could finally leave *Captain America*. But just as quickly, Marvel called him back: They needed a fill-in issue done in two days. After Jack rehashed Cap's origin one more time, Romita came on board as the regular artist, and the "Bullpen Bulletins" reported, "As for Jolly Jack Kirby, the only reason the King has abandoned Cap is to give himself time enough to work with Smiley on a new title – one which promises to become the biggest blockbuster of '69 – and we'll bet you can guess what it'll be."

It was the Inhumans, which Jack had wanted to do for three years now. He looked forward to finally presenting his epic story of two races at war. But Marvel once again delayed the long awaited title, claiming that the company had signed a deal with a new printer, which led to a new set of deadline dates. "Dates which require our mags to be produced even faster than before!" wrote Stan in the "Bullpen Bulletins." For now, there would be no Inhumans, he added. "However, we're starting to get on schedule again, so maybe *this* will some day be known as the Year of The Inhumans!"

Until that day arrived, Jack had to work on titles he was more than a little bored with. And soon he couldn't even concentrate. Day in and day out, while in his chair and facing his board, he heard *Vroooom! Vroooooom!* "All this noise!" Roz explained. "And these motorcycles were down there." Right under his studio window, people were riding motorbikes and kicking up dust. "These kids would drive him crazy because it just echoed through the canyon," said his friend Steve Sherman. The noise went right into his window.

Jack and Roz complained to MGM, which owned the lot, but the film studio said they couldn't do anything about it. "Then we called the newspapers, and they took a picture of Jack pointing down into the valley," Roz said later. "They called him Superman because they always said all the superheroes were Superman. So the headline read, 'Even Superman Can't Get Rid of Them.'"

When Jack and Roz told the kids they didn't mind them riding around down there if they put mufflers on their bikes, they refused, "and the police would go after them on their motorcycles, and we'd have double the noise!" At a community meeting, parents complained that because he and Roz had chased them off their bikes, their kids would turn to drugs. The noise continued. Roz said, "It's no use. We can't take it anymore. I'm not gonna have Jack get sick." They began to search for another home.

That April, during Passover, Jack's old friend Carmine called to say he'd be in town on business. Carmine had gone from being a free-lance artist at DC to art director and, now, editorial director. Until now, Carmine had been telling him that once a certain executive, perhaps Jack Schiff, was out, he'd have enough clout to make a solid offer. "Jack didn't put a lot of stock in that because throughout his life people had constantly said the same thing, but it never came true," said Mark Evanier. But now, while in town for a meeting about a cartoon project, Infantino called to say, "Want to have dinner some night?"

Roz invited him to the house for a Passover seder. After joking around, catching up on old times, Jack told Carmine, "Come up to the room. I wanna show you something."

In his office, Jack pulled out three enormous covers for books called *The Forever People*, *Orion of the New Gods*, and *Mister Miracle*. Carmine said, "Very impressive, Jack. You guys are gonna really come out with that?"

"I'm not," he answered. "I want to come to DC and put them out."

"Well, what do you want?"

A certain amount for each page and a three-year contract, Jack told him.

"You got it."

Back in New York, however, Carmine realized that while Schiff was gone, others still held a grudge. "They didn't want him because there was a problem with Jack Schiff and the *Sky Masters* thing," he recalled. "They had sued each other, and the heads of DC did not want Kirby back there." Carmine told the old-timers, "Well, I'm hiring him anyway. I think he's a terrific talent and a good friend, and I'm hiring him."

In May 1969, Neal Adams came to Marvel. While speaking with Jim Steranko, he'd asked about the Marvel method. "Because at DC Comics, of course, they write scripts and you follow the script," Adams explained. Steranko told him that at Marvel, artists could do their own stories, "and Stan will just dialogue them." They didn't even have scripts. You could sit at lunch and discuss a story and go off and do what you want. "And he said, the way he was doing it, he was just doing the stories and handing them in. He just put notes on the page." Adams said, "You know, that's an interesting way to do it. I'd really like to try that." By now, he'd written most of the revolutionary scripts for DC's *Deadman*, the only DC title read by employees at Marvel. Adams had also done innovative work with Jerry Siegel's *The Spectre*. He was used to telling stories and thought it'd be fun to try it this way, to create a story and "just hand in the pages and let some good dialoguer put in the dialogue, which is pretty much how Jack had worked with Stan."

After a warm reception, Adams was led into Stan's office.

"What do you want to do?" Stan said. "You can do any comic in the house."

"Well, you got people working on comics."

"Any comic you want to work on, you can do."

"Gee, that's really nice. What's your worst-selling title?"

"Well, our worst-selling title is *X-Men*. We're gonna cancel it in two issues."

"In that case, I'd like to do *X-Men*."

"So why do you want to do *X-Men*? I told you we're going to cancel it in two issues."

"Well, you know, Stan, I'm interested in this Marvel style of doing things, and if you give me *X-Men*, you're probably not going to pay much attention to what I'm doing, right? So I'll pretty much get to do what I want."

"That's true."

"Okay, then I'd like to do that."

"I'll tell you what. You do *X-Men* and then we cancel it, but then you have to do an important comic book like *The Avengers*."

"Okay, sounds like a deal."

By now Stan was doing much less writing. So he introduced Adams to Roy Thomas. "Roy Thomas was very flexible in those days and said, 'I'd be glad to do it,'" Adams recalled. "Told me where they were in the story and then just let me go and play with it."

Adams and Thomas wowed readers with their first issue, May 1969's *X-Men* No. 56, but after eleven or twelve issues, Goodman canceled the book. By the time he learned that these issues had sold far better than he thought, Adams and Thomas had used *The Avengers* to tell an intricate story called "The Kree-Skrull War," which lasted nine months and showed heroes and planet Earth caught between two alien races at war. Like many other writer-artist teams, however, Adams and Thomas experienced creative difficulties. "On a professional level, I got along with Roy Thomas," Adams said. "On a personal level, where he mixed his personal point of view with the work, I didn't really get along with him very well. We just sort of ended it."

Stan came out for Jack's son Neal's wedding and wrote about it in the "Bullpen Bulletins" (simultaneously congratulating Jack after he won an award as World's Best Comic Book Penciler). And when he mentioned the reprints in *Marvel Super Heroes*, Stan called them the "Lee-Kirby Avengers" or "Lee-Kirby's X-Men." But just as quickly, he wrote that fan mail said Jolly Jack's art was improving with each issue and that their *Fantastic Four* read "more like the memorable masterworks of the FF's early years."

Though Stan used another "Bullpen Bulletins" column to explain that pencilers helped plot stories (and to praise Jack's ability to turn out three pages a day), Jack's resentment only increased. By now, Stan accepted that people might be telling Jack that he did most of the work and received no credit. But this wasn't true, he explained.

"Every time I was interviewed, I would always say how great Jack was. Very often the interviewers just left that part out. I had no control over what was written about us. People also used to say, 'Stan made all the money and Jack didn't.' I was a freelance writer. Jack was a freelance artist. As an artist he got paid a lot more per page than I did. The only reason I made more money was that I was also getting a salary for being the editor and the art director. That's why my income was more than his."

Since Jack didn't want to bring Marvel any new characters, *The Fantastic Four* was reduced to imitating plots from popular TV shows: In one issue, Dr. Doom trapped them in the village from *The Prisoner*; four more issues emulated the *Star Trek* episode "City on the Edge of Forever" and showed the team – like the crew of the starship *Enterprise* – in pin-striped suits, dodging tommy gun blasts on old-time streets. In print, however, Stan claimed, "Suddenly, the fabulous Fantastic Four have become the talk of Marveldom!" Then: "Take a bow, Lee and Kirby. We don't know how you do it."

The longer he stayed, the more Jack signaled his displeasure by marring his work with haste and carelessness. Where he once felt a connection with Dr. Doom, he now drew his iron mask differently every time. Sometimes rivets were around his eyes, other times they were near his mouth. Then his mouth wouldn't have any: The rivets were on his nose. "You never knew where they were going to be," inker Joe Sinnott said later. The Thing had three fingers in one panel and four in the next. Jack also kept including collages made of photos even though his inker, and other people, felt he'd be better off penciling the stuff. And he stopped drawing big panoramic panels. Each board now contained up to twelve tiny scenes, which was bad, considering that Goodman had the company using smaller paper. Soon people were asking the Fantastic Four inker, Don't you think Kirby's not doing as well as he did? "Even before this period, many people felt Kirby was losing it somehow," Sinnott revealed. "But I thought he was getting better all the time." If the book lacked energy, he explained, it was because "the characters weren't as good as they were when the Silver Surfer and Galactus and the Inhumans came into being."

In one issue, he had the good Inhumans fight the bad ones, with the team trapped in the middle. When Jack presented an old-fashioned Creature from the Black Lagoon knockoff as villain, Stan claimed in print, "The title's enough to tell you that it's Lee and Kirby at their greatest! The Monster from the Lost Lagoon!" Another issue had the team on the moon, taking giant steps for mankind. For its cover, Jack sketched an atmospheric Thing whose rocks were covered with shadows. But Marvel saw the inked cover and had in-house artists reach for the correction fluid, paint over the shadowy chest, and draw their version of Thing's rocklike skin.

While he was still in early negotiations with DC, a number of new incidents further soured Jack's view of Marvel. First, the company didn't pay him for his help in a lawsuit about Captain America involving Joe Simon and Martin Goodman and his wife, Jean. In 1969, the first twenty-eight-year term of copyright for Captain America had expired and Joe had hired attorneys to apply for the copyright renewal for the first ten issues. The U.S. Copyright Office put the renewals in Simon's name, and Simon's lawyer, Edwin Reiskind, told Goodman and Krantz Films, currently planning a *Captain America* television series. Goodman hired his own lawyers to contest his claim and get the copyrights back.

It wasn't the first time Simon had tried for the copyright. In November 1966, while filing suit in the New York State Supreme Court, he wanted a judge to rule that Marvel and Grantray-Lawrence's use of Cap was unfair competition, that he had the right to renew the copyright, and that he was entitled to royalties from Captain America. A year later, he filed a second lawsuit in the southern district of New York for the copyright; it dragged on for two years, angering Goodman to the point where he reprinted the earliest Captain America stories in *Fantasy Masterpieces*, but without Simon's name in the credits. This was when Goodman told Jack, "Simon said he created Captain America. He wants the copyright, and it looks like you're out." Jack reacted by siding with Marvel against Joe. After Goodman promised to pay him whatever Simon got for a settlement, Jack signed a document that handed Marvel his rights to Captain America. "What he didn't know was that a coauthor is entitled to half ownership of any copyright awarded to the designated 'author,'" Simon later explained.

After Simon sued for Cap, Carl Burgos tried for the copyright on the Human Torch. Burgos, who had drawn a few recent Giant Man stories, witnessed the original Torch's reappearance and death in a *Fantastic Four* annual. "Stan had no personal involvement," Roy Thomas said. "Of course, it would have crippled him a little if they'd lost the characters, but I don't think he was terribly involved unless he had to give some sort of deposition." After Marvel settled with Burgos for undisclosed terms, Goodman approached Bill Everett, who was drinking heavily and experiencing money problems. Everett's wife had been sick and living in Connecticut while Everett lived and worked in Manhattan. When she died, debts piled up and Everett kept blowing deadlines, "so they'd just pile up some more," said Roy Thomas. Goodman offered to pay off some of his debts "if Bill would basically sign something that would sort of decrease or eliminate the threat of any, uh, potential lawsuit in the future. And Bill, who I don't think had any intention of suing anyway, just looked on this found money and signed on the dotted line and that was the end of that."

As Simon's lawsuit against Marvel continued, an interviewer asked what part Jack had played in creating Captain America. "Well, I can't tell you how it came about for my own reasons, and there are legal reasons involved," Jack replied. "I can't talk about it. Except that we were both involved in it."

On November 5, 1969, Jack learned that Joe Simon had signed a settlement agreement that handed Marvel the copyright to Captain America and acknowledged he was working for Goodman when he created him. In exchange, Simon reportedly received $7,500. "You just don't have the money to fight a machine like Marvel," his son Jim explained. "My father was not a rich man. My father and Jack Kirby should have been rich men."

Though he wondered where his payment was, Jack was still willing to work for Marvel – and for Marvelmania. Marvelmania was created after Goodman ended the Merry Marvel Marching Society, which he felt was too expensive to maintain, especially since some members were buying an expanded membership kit for the same fifty cents it cost to manufacture. Though Stan had argued that it was great public relations, Goodman's son Chip told him an executive in California was willing to pay $10,000 to license every Marvel character and slap them onto products he'd sell through a mail-order company called Marvelmania. "I think he paid five thousand and never paid the rest," recalled former Marvelmania employee Steve Sherman.

But shortly after opening its doors, Marvelmania International removed the captions from one of Jack's recent *Captain America* covers, enlarged it, and offered it for sale as a poster. Then the company asked him for an illustration to accompany a bio it planned to run in its Marvelmania fanzine. After drawing a self-portrait – Jack at the drawing board with trademark cigar in mouth and Marvel heroes leaping off the page – he decided to try using a new inker. He called Mike Royer, recommended to him by legendary artist Alex Toth, and the next day, Royer stopped by the house. After showing Royer the drawing, Jack asked if he'd like to ink it. Royer said yes; then Jack – noting he'd brought his tools – pointed at the table and said, "Why don't you do it here?" When Jack entered the office later to check in on him, Royer seemed nervous. Jack left the room, spent the morning with Roz, then went and told Royer they'd break for lunch. After he and his two daughters ate with Royer, the inker returned to the office and completed the job. When he saw the finished page, Jack was pleased. Marvelmania would get their artwork, and Jack had found a new embellisher.

But Marvelmania itself was becoming a problem. By now, Goodman had given Marvelmania original pages for twenty or so classic comics Jack had drawn, so it could create posters, envelopes, stationery, and fanzine issues. And Jack was doing most of the artwork for other products. Whenever he and his son, Neal, dropped by for meetings or to deliver work, Jack ran into some kids from a comic book club whom he had met at a sci-fi convention and who were now working at Marvelmania. One day some of these kids visited him in his office, and Jack met a young guy named Steve Sherman. In the empty bedroom that held his old drawing table, Jack sat and started a Thor story without any research. "Just a piece of paper and a pencil and a couple of issues so he could see what was going on," Sherman recalled. After Jack told them about his troubles with Marvel, showed them a few new heroes, and said, "I'm not going to give Marvel another Silver Surfer," he heard Sherman, and Mark Evanier, the comic book club president who had gotten his job thanks to Jack, tell him things didn't look good at Marvelmania. He might want to come and get his artwork before the place closed up.

Evanier said when he arrived at the tiny office, he saw local comic fans accepting pages of Jack's original art as payment for rolling posters, filling envelopes, and licking stamps. "Just about everything about the Marvelmania operation was sleazy," he said. After Evanier bought some art from other employees, or sneaked some out (since Marvel never gave this company the right to give the art away), he returned pages to Jack and inker Joe Sinnott. Jack let him keep a few for himself, then appeared at Marvelmania with Neal to pick up the rest of his pages. "These were huge, black-and-white pencil-and-ink drawings for the posters," Sherman recalled. "So he came, took all of his art back, and left."

Though Marvel didn't pay him his part of the Simon settlement, and still hadn't renewed his contract, Jack tried to bring his new characters to Stan anyway. He figured they could be featured in new books, but Stan turned him down. "He preferred to have Jack just keep doing what he was doing," said Roy Thomas, which was drawing *Thor* and *The Fantastic Four*.

By now, Jack wanted to get moving on the Inhumans. He was tired of the company stalling. Stan let readers decide. After mentioning that Jack was ahead of schedule and might have time to handle another series, Stan asked, "Which strip is most worthy of the Master's touch? Should we finally launch the Inhumans? Dr. Doom? Ka-Zar? Or, do you have some other oldie or newie you'd like him to bring to life? Sock it to us, sweetie, and we'll let you know how the mail keeps coming in!" After three months, Stan wrote, "The votes have been counted! A united Marveldom wants Stan and Jack to come up with an Inhumans mag for 1970, or they'll sic [the team's huge dog] Lockjaw on 'em!"

Jack started working on his idea of two groups at war, only to learn that Goodman wanted to improve sales by reviving the split format with new books *Astonishing Tales* and *Amazing Adventures*, which would include different heroes, like DC's *Showcase*, and see which, if any, were profitable enough to support their own titles. The Inhumans would share one of these titles with another hero. Jack was displeased, but Stan said he felt the Inhumans would do well enough to merit a title. Jack stopped doing *Thor* and worked on the Inhumans for *Amazing Adventures* and another revival of Ka-Zar in *Astonishing Tales*.

Once Jack sent his pages to Stan, however, Stan claimed he was too busy to write the *Inhumans* series. Jack told Stan he wouldn't work with another writer. By now Roy Thomas had been credited for an Iron Man and Sub-Mariner plot Jack had created for *Tales to Astonish* No. 82. "He didn't want to put somebody else's name on the thing or above his as a writer, so he talked Stan into writing it," Thomas remembered.

In print, Stan claimed that during a trip to New York to discuss the new *Inhumans* series, "sly ol' Stan not only conned Jack into doing two yarns at once but even cajoled the King into doing the script as well as the penciling for this great new series."

His first ten-page episode, "The Inhumans," revolved around sales-boosting guest stars the Fantastic Four attacking the group and ended with their leader, Black Bolt, deciding to go to war. The second part, "Friend Against Friend," showed both teams learning that Black Bolt's insane brother, Maximus, was responsible for the fight. The final two episodes included Stan-like titles ("With These Rings I Thee Kill") and mediocre Iron Man villain the Mandarin. As editor, Stan had his work cut out for him: Jack drew their way-out hidden city and the wild creatures that lived there, but he neglected to include subplots, humor, drama, or suspense. The dialogue was wooden, stilted, and heavy on exclamation points. Everyone seemed to be describing events readers could see for themselves. "While Jack may have felt Stan just edited his notes and his dialogue, Stan did rather more than that," Roy Thomas avowed.

They worked together on the first Ka-Zar story for *Astonishing Tales*, and then Stan had Roy Thomas write the second one. After telling Thomas he didn't want to draw his new comic based on Robert E. Howard's Conan novels, Jack saw Thomas again receive credit for a plot he had created with his artwork. This was just how things were done at Marvel, Thomas explained, "and we didn't question it at the time. Neither did Jack or Ditko."

One afternoon in early February 1970, Jack and Roz stopped by Marvelmania and took Mark Evanier and Steve Sherman out to Cantor's Delicatessen. By now, Jack had been negotiating with DC for close to eighteen months. Also, he was still working for Marvel despite the fact that his contract had expired and no one had bothered to renew it. He didn't even try to speak with the new owners about it. Whatever they offered would include terms he couldn't agree to. At the table, after ordering potato latkes, he said, "I'm pledging you to secrecy. I'm leaving Marvel. I'm going to DC. I'm gonna be an editor there. I'm gonna try to put together an operation that will produce comics out of L.A.

"I need some assistants," he continued. "I need some guys who can help me put this stuff together. Would you like to be my assistants?"

They immediately said yes, and he swore them to secrecy again. "Because the deal with DC is not signed yet and I don't want anybody to know about it until I have a signed contract in hand."

Meanwhile, things at Marvelmania continued to fall apart. The guy who ran the place had overextended himself. He had great ideas for full-color catalogs and posters, but just as many outstanding bills from printers. Sherman quit working there. Three weeks later, after completing the next Marvelmania fanzine, Evanier also left. Soon, creditors came after the guy who ran the place, the sheriff shut him down, and the police sat there and took the funds as they came in the door. Employees who left work on a Friday arrived on Monday to find the guy had "cleaned the place out and disappeared."

Then Stan called Jack to help with *The Silver Surfer*. While college students might ask about Surfer during Stan's glib lectures, they weren't buying enough copies to make up for younger readers who weren't. And with the entire industry in a slump – partly because Goodman had raised prices from twelve to fifteen cents – Goodman was dropping titles like *Not Brand Ecch* and *Dr. Strange* and telling Stan, "We ought to downgrade the stories a little. Let's make them a little simpler. Stop using thirty-syllable words, Stan. Let's get more action and fighting and stuff, and then it'll sell better."

The *Surfer* book was in trouble. Every issue since the first had dipped in sales, and nothing Stan did revived them. When Buscema tried to get away from the Kirby style for the fourth issue, a well-rendered tale of Loki tricking the Surfer into having a slugfest with Thor, people in the office congratulated him, but Stan looked through the pages and said one wasn't bad, the next was, the one after that was all right, but the next needed work. After being urged to "think like Kirby," Buscema left Stan's office completely demoralized and wandered into Romita's room next door. When Romita asked what was wrong, Buscema said, "John, how the hell do you do comics?" At home Buscema told himself, "Screw it, I'll go right back to the same old crap," and made his work even more Kirby-like, to no avail. The book just wasn't clicking. Even when Stan claimed it was "probably the biggest smash hit in comic mag publishing since the still supreme FF," sales stayed the same. Nothing worked. Fans were unaffected by Stan's stories about a modern-day Frankenstein monster, the ghost of a pirate, and the Satan-like Mephisto and his claim that the book was unquestionably the year's biggest hit and had been topping the best-seller lists since its debut. Readers ignored the book even after the page count was cut, the price was reduced to fifteen cents, it became a monthly title ("because you demanded it"), and Stan threw in Spider-Man and the Human Torch (claiming it was part of a new policy of guest star appearances).

Instead of inviting Jack to draw the series, Stan kept telling Buscema to draw more like him and had inker Chic Stone apply heavy lines that made it look Kirbyesque. He even had Barry Smith – an English artist skillfully emulating and adding to Jack's style – draw a cover, but sales of *The Silver Surfer* No. 17 were just as dismal. If he didn't do something quick, Goodman would kill the book.

He decided Buscema could handle *Thor* for a month – interrupting an epic Jack was working on – and Jack could draw the Surfer.

But Jack was offended. "He had a certain proprietary interest in that character and felt it should have been offered to him first but wasn't for reasons that seem to have been kind of arbitrary," Mark Evanier recalled. Stan hoped he could do something to get the book back on track before another Kirby imitator, Herb Trimpe, started as new artist with No. 19. At the same time, Stan was testing Buscema on *Thor*, seeing if he could put Jack to work on reviving sales of other titles. "And Jack was not too thrilled with this," said Evanier. "First of all, he didn't like having his continuity in *Thor* interrupted. Second, he didn't like coming in and doing a rescue job, from his standpoint, on *The Silver Surfer*. Third, he didn't really want to do any new characters for Marvel until he got a deal. So all of sudden he's being steamrollered into salvaging a book he should have been doing in the first place."

Even so, he agreed to do the issue. Trimpe, who would take over as artist in one month, did the cover while Stan worked to change the Surfer. "They were gonna actually call the book *The Savage Silver Surfer* because they felt the Surfer was too much the pacifist and that kids didn't buy the comic because he didn't have the power, he wasn't smashing things like the Hulk, and he wasn't as forceful a character." At the same time, they were using the word *savage* for a specific reason. "Martin Goodman used to keep these lists of words he felt could boost sales if they were included in the title of a comic or on a cover, and 'savage' was a big one. That's why they did *Savage Tales*, *Savage Sword of Conan*, and *Captain Savage*. So the word *savage* was stuck in there to make Goodman not lose faith in *The Silver Surfer*. And Stan had this concept of making the Surfer angry and savage and fierce, and Jack didn't really agree with that approach. He felt he already had one foot out the door – he was very unhappy with Marvel – and figured, 'Okay, I'll give Stan what he wants.'"

While doing the issue, however, he got into a number of disagreements with Marvel's businesspeople over a new contract. He couldn't sign what Marvel offered. "The wording was very offensive, and he felt he could not deal with the environment," Evanier recalled. "They were treating him like cattle. They were being enormously rude and insensitive to his needs, and he said, 'I can't sign these documents: I can't do what they want me to do. I wouldn't be able to shave. I couldn't look at myself in the mirror afterward.'" The Silver Surfer story he submitted reflected that he'd encountered arguments, slights, legal problems, threats, and someone at the company so insulting to him that he finally said, "That's it." After the Surfer battles the Inhumans, he escapes into space, lands on a meteor, faces the reader, and threatens to fight mankind on its own terms. "You can just speculate how much of that came out of the fact that Jack was just very unhappy that month."

The "Bullpen Bulletins" found Stan trying to draw readers by claiming Trimpe's "unique, hard-hitting style" would bring a brand-new majesty to the book. "Not to mention the fact that Stan the Man promises a totally different image for the Surfer, as he reaches a fateful turning point in his own fabled career!" When Goodman received discouraging sales figures for previous issues, he killed the book before Jack's work reached stands and Trimpe had drawn one panel. Poor sales of *Astonishing Tales* and *Amazing Adventures* also ended Goodman's plan to feature the Inhumans, Ka-Zar, Dr. Doom, and the Black Widow in their own titles.

Meanwhile, Jack finally signed a five-year deal with DC: a three-year contract with an option for two more.

"Jack did not want to leave Marvel," Evanier revealed. "He just felt he had no choice. Throughout his career, he frequently found himself in these situations where he had to move one way or another, without choices."

At his board, drawing the first half of *The Fantastic Four* No. 102 with guest star Sub-Mariner, Jack felt as though a huge weight had been lifted from his shoulders. After completing the pages, he shipped his final *Fantastic Four* issue to Stan in New York. He knew the pages would arrive on Friday, so he waited until then, called the company, and asked for Stan.

At his desk, Stan was opening the package when the secretary announced, "Jack's on line two." Jack got on the line and told him that after this issue he was leaving. "I felt terrible," Stan said. "I never wanted him to leave." He had planned, he claimed, to entice Jack to stay by offering him the position of art director and letting him share everything equally. "Whatever my salary was, he would have the same, and he could run the company creatively with me. But he didn't want to do that. It may have been just as well." They were both strong-willed, "and if we disagreed on art, it would have been tragic. But I really never wanted him to leave. I would have done anything if he'd stayed."

Jack hung up and started drawing his first comic for DC.

Back in New York, Stan was stunned by the call. He knew Jack was angry but didn't know why. Jack had kept everything bottled up inside. He considered how abruptly Jack had left and got angry. But by the time production man Sol Brodsky and Roy Thomas entered his office, he was somewhat depressed. He told them Jack had called to quit and was already working for DC, so there was nothing negotiable about it. Even worse, the *Fantastic Four* story he submitted needed work. When John Romita arrived that morning, everyone asked, "Did you hear that Jack is gone?" He thought, My God, we're gonna have to drop *The Fantastic Four*, *Thor*, and God knows what other titles. In Stan's office, Romita asked, "What are we gonna do? Who the hell can do *The Fantastic Four*?"

"You're gonna do it."

"You're crazy!"

Romita received a stack of Jack's *Fantastic Four* comics that had been marked up with comments like "Swipe this machinery" and "Do Thing head like this," said Mark Evanier. While drawing the next issue, Romita kept them on his desk in an attempt to make it a seamless transition.

John Buscema also thought they were going to close up. "As far as I was concerned, Jack was the backbone of Marvel," he said.

Joe Sinnott told someone, "They'll never replace Jack Kirby. The FF will never be the same."

A day or two after he left, Jack called Romita. "John, here's the story," he began. "You know I'm going to DC."

"Yeah."

"Here's what I'd like you to do: I would like you to come over with me and help me. What I want to do is, I want to write more than I draw."

Like Stan, he wanted to oversee a staff that produced books. He said he'd love for Romita to pencil books and help organize a stable of artists. "I got some great inkers ready to work on your stuff," he continued. "It would be great for me, and I think I can make it worth your while. It would be a terrific idea."

Romita said, "You know, I got to think it over, Jack." When his wife, Virginia, heard about the offer, she was stunned. "First of all, if you go with Jack, you're going to be a Jack Kirby clone," she said.

"Well, I don't know how," he answered. "I'm not going to be working on his artwork. He's going to be writing and I'm going to be penciling."

"No, you're going to end up working for Kirby," she said. "Your personality will be buried and nobody will know anything about you."

Romita told Jack he couldn't do it. "Frankly, if I were a single guy, I think I would have," he said today. "If I had been struggling, I would have jumped."

With Kirby gone, Marvel invited its freelance artists to a meeting in the office, held up all of Jack's covers, and analyzed why his designs worked. And when Romita stopped doing *The Fantastic Four* after four issues, Carmine Infantino claimed, "Jimmy Steranko was offered *The Fantastic Four* and he turned it down. He said he wouldn't presume to follow Kirby."

Instead, Stan told Buscema, "We're going to put you on *The Fantastic Four*."

Buscema asked, "Stan, you sure you want me to do it?" Jack, he said later, scared everyone. "I said it before, I will say it again: He approached genius as far as I'm concerned. He revolutionized the way we did comics."

Ultimately, Buscema told Stan he'd do his best and kept dozens of Jack's comics on his desk while drawing *Thor* and *The Fantastic Four*. If he needed a panel, he'd face Jack's drawings, change things around, and include them in his stories. ("I still use those books," he said decades later. "I still have Jack Kirby's books.")

Though he had artists filling the void, Stan was still stunned by Jack's departure. "Because I always felt that Jack and I would be working there forever and doing everything," he said. In a reflective "Stan's Soapbox!" column, he reminded readers of how Ditko left, then reported that Jack had unexpectedly announced his resignation. "That's where we're at – understaffed, undermanned, and underfed," he added, "but as bushy-tailed and bewildered as ever! So watch for the fireworks, friend, as we turn ourselves on, knock ourselves out, and do ourselves in to prove once again that while we may not be the biggest, we're still the boldest and the best!"

Chapter 12

At Marvel, Stan had told reporters DC wasn't any competition. Jack had to agree. Conservative editors were sitting on great characters, not letting writers and artists explore their other sides. Since they were never portrayed as people in trouble, DC's heroes were bland, sterile, and unimaginative. The few changes DC did make were like the *Batman* program, which murdered the character and made him look ridiculous. "Someone up at DC once told me, 'Jack, watch what we're doing now, we're coming out with something really good, and wait until you see this.'" He was still waiting. The irony was that he and Stan had helped create a generation of readers that hated DC and didn't react to Carmine's changes to *Green Lantern/Green Arrow*, *Aquaman*, and *The Atom*. Even when Ditko did *The Hawk and the Dove* and *Beware the Creeper*, both books were canceled after a handful of issues.

DC's conservative policies were helping Marvel to run them over. And though nothing was working, DC employees were perpetually optimistic about new books – until top-level executives saw sales figures for the first issues and canceled them after their fifth or sixth editions. Then DC employees became optimistic about other new titles. "And since Jack was such a big superstar, there was more optimism when he walked in the door," Mark Evanier explained. "Everybody was running around, saying, 'This is the one that's gonna change the entire dynamic of the industry, it's gonna change everything.'" Since Jack co-created the Marvel

Universe, DC felt he'd come up with something to put Marvel out of business in a week. "When he started at DC," Steve Sherman remembered, "he told Mark and me, 'I'm basically competing against myself.' At the time it seemed like 'Oh yeah, right.' But he was right. He'd created all these characters for Marvel, and these books were doing extremely well. Now he was going to quit, go to another company, and try to start all over again, competing with everything he'd done before."

While he discussed what he'd actually do for the company, Jack saw Carmine include his photo in DC comics near the slogans "Kirby is coming" or "The Great One is coming." Neal Adams explained, "Everybody thought, Boy, the millennium's here!"

Carmine wanted Jack to do Superman, Batman, and all the DC characters, but Jack said, "I don't want to do that. I don't want to take work away from guys who have been doing it. I've done that."

Since editor Mort Weisinger had left DC, *Superman* sales had plunged. Carmine wanted to see what Jack could bring to DC's biggest icon. But Jack refused to take *Superman.*

"What's the worst-selling book?" Jack asked.

Carmine replied, *"Jimmy Olsen."*

If he could turn it around and speed up sales, Jack would prove himself. And with the *Olsen* title lacking a regular artist, no one would lose work or income. At the same time, *Jimmy Olsen* would be a good forum for the Newsboy Legion revival many editors kept pushing for. Jack said he'd take the book and started thinking of how to tie *Olsen* into the epic he'd present in other books.

By now, at his home, he had Evanier typing up proposals for other books while he pitched ideas over the telephone and sent Carmine drawings of new characters. One idea was a Captain Marvel revival called *Shazam!* DC liked the idea but didn't want Evanier to write it or C. C. Beck, who'd drawn the hero in previous decades, to handle the art. Instead, the company cut Jack out of the project and had editor Julius Schwartz, writer Denny O'Neil, and artist

Bob Oskner develop the concept in New York (until editor Nelson Bridwell convinced them to have Beck draw it).

While going through his pile of sketches, Jack put some heroes in one team, some in another, and some back on the desk. Villain Granny Goodness was based on comedienne Phyllis Diller. Female warrior Barda, Mister Miracle's armor-coated independent love interest, resembled buxom brunette chanteuse Lainie Kazan, who had recently appeared topless in *Playboy*. Gray-haired mystic Himon looked like convention promoter Shel Dorf and would be Miracle's mentor, an old guy who returned to life after villains killed him. Virman Vundabar, drawn like Benito Mussolini, and Kanto, patterned after Errol Flynn in a film still, were bad guys, while Metron, based on Leonard Nimoy as Spock, would frequently change sides.

The idea of the New Gods had come to Jack years earlier, when he was plotting 90 percent of the "Tales of Asgard" stories in *Thor*. He wanted to have two planets at war and end with Ragnarok, the battle that would kill Thor's lucrative pantheon. Instead, he tried the idea in his Inhumans stories. Now he was presenting it in its original context. Though he wouldn't ever say it publicly, the *New Gods* books started right after the gods in *Thor* killed one another. The first page of *Orion of the New Gods* showed the same scenes from *Thor* – a planet torn in half and armored gods holding swords and dying on a fiery battleground.

The *New Gods* epic would involve Darkseid, Jack's attempt to bring DC a powerful, first-rate villain. Darkseid would rule a planet and lead armored troops in search of the Anti-Life Equation, a way to control people's minds and essentially render a person dead. "The idea of the Anti-Life Equation is that all Darkseid has to do is say a word and you become a slave," Jack said. "That's what he's after."

New Gods started with war between peaceful world New Genesis and its evil counterpart, Apokolips. On New Genesis, gods lived in a futuristic city teeming with statues, green pastures, and flowers, led by Highfather, a gray-haired, staff-wielding Moses type who frequently asked harp-strumming youth for their opinions. Upon learning that stone-faced Darkseid, ruler of the smoke-covered industrial planet Apokolips, wanted the Anti-Life Equation, Highfather called Orion for help. Born on Apokolips, but raised on New Genesis because of a baby-switching pact that kept the peace, Orion had no idea he was really Darkseid's son. Highfather led him to the Source, a fiery wall and vague cosmic essence that held their universe together, and both watched a disembodied hand write that Orion had to battle Darkseid's men on earth, then meet his father for a final battle. From here, *New Gods* showed Orion and his idealistic partner, Lightray, fighting on earth and Orion hiding his real face behind one that resembled "Him."

The Forever People also showed young people caught up in this cosmic Vietnam, but Mark Moonrider, shaggy Big Bear, Vykin the Black, space cowboy Serifan, and Beautiful Dreamer were nonviolent. "The nearest they come to fighting is this fella, Big Bear, who is just so strong that he could lean against a pole and that's it. The Forever People are a challenge to see how nonviolence can work in comics." After they placed their hands on their Mother Box computer, yelled, "Taaru!" and vanished, the heroic Infinity Man would take their place and handle their opponents. Like Orion, they also wanted to stop Darkseid from finding the Anti-Life Equation.

The third book, *Mister Miracle*, showed aimless drifter Scott Free trying to stay out of the war. The son of Highfather, raised on Apokolips after the baby-switching pact, Free met an old-time escape artist, saw mobsters gun him down, and donned the old man's costume, cape, and mask and flew after the bad guys on flying disks under his boot soles. After trouncing them, he stayed on earth to use his gadgets, escape skills, and Mother Box computer to battle Darkseid's troops.

Jack wanted to get *Orion of the New Gods*, *The Forever People*, and *Mister Miracle* off the ground and then hand them to other artists. If all went well, Mark Evanier and Steve Sherman would dialogue his plots and Wally Wood would draw *Orion*, Don Heck would handle *The Forever People*, and Steve Ditko would illustrate *Mister Miracle*. Jack himself would work on a second wave of books, including *Big Barda and Her Female Furies* and the horse-riding *Lonar*, and try to move past the standard comic book format. "He wanted to do what they're doing now, a big novel using the comic book format," Steve Sherman recalled. "And they just weren't ready for that."

After waking up at noon and reading the paper until two or three, Jack would work until dinnertime. He'd spend some time with Roz and his daughters and then work until five in the morning. At the drawing table, he had a TV on with the volume down and a radio playing. Or the TV volume was up but tuned to the Spanish station. Though he couldn't understand a word, he liked the way the voices sounded. "It provides a little company for a lonely job, I guess," he said. "So it's like a little world in itself." He'd hit the sack at dawn, wake up at noon, and repeat the cycle. "He'd do that seven days a week," said Sherman.

Since DC asked him to redesign Superman, Jack planned to include him in *The Forever People* No. 1. Superman's costume was perfect. What needed to change was the type of story he appeared in. After calling his good friend Superman co-creator Jerry Siegel and receiving his blessing, Jack re-created the Man of Steel.

The issue started with the young team arriving on planet Earth in their flying car and reporter Clark Kent interviewing a boxing champ in his office at the *Daily Planet* newspaper. The fighter uttered a few self-pitying remarks and left, then Kent faced his window and the street below, wondering if mankind hated him because he was stronger. Then he admitted that he was lonely. Borrowing a page from *Thor*, Jack showed the all-powerful hero in costume, sitting by himself and coping with emotions. For him, Superman wasn't a robot; he was a guy with superpowers who felt lonely, fell in love, and disliked people. But someone at DC hated what he did to the character and vetoed his Superman.

Once he finished drawing *The Forever People* No. 1, Jack rested for an hour, then started on *New Gods* No. 1. He sent DC the original Orion sketch he'd hand colored and inked so that the company would know what colors were on his costume while preparing the cover. He also sent them the actual art for the cover, an Orion drawing pasted onto a collage of space photos. The finished cover contained the Orion drawing and one photo of a planet. Someone had drawn in a background. Usually, changes would upset Jack. But he was happy. The image was a striking introduction to a Kirby who wrote, drew, and edited his own ideas. When he asked DC for the original Don Heck–inked sketch, however, someone claimed it was lost. Jack kept calling and yelling until someone said they'd found it hidden in the back of a drawer. When Jack got it back, it was folded and wrinkled.

He leaped right into working on *Mister Miracle* No. 1 after finishing *New Gods* No. 1, only to learn DC didn't like Mister Miracle's green-and-yellow costume. On the cover of *Mister Miracle* No. 1, DC had colored it red, while inside it was purple. Jack asked DC to let him change it, then handed Evanier and Sherman sketches of Mister Miracle to experiment with color schemes. When they held up their coloring, he said he liked Evanier's version best but changed the green parts to blue, telling them about how a printer once said a hero's costume should be red, yellow, or blue. Green, orange, brown, or purple would give them trouble and look horrible, he added.

Evanier asked when he had heard this, and Jack answered, In 1941.

A week after Jack left Marvel, Wally Wood brought Roy Thomas new art pages. Thanks to Thomas, Wood had been able to return, and there was talk of having him ink Jack's pencils for a new series. When Thomas told him Jack had quit and was at DC, Wood quickly called DC editor Joe Orlando to set up a meeting and then pleaded for the assignment to ink Jack's new books. Orlando told him Vince Colletta already had the assignment.

Colletta, who inked Jack's work on *Thor* and the classic "Tales of Asgard," had a bit of a reputation. If Dick Ayers drew seven trees in a panel, Colletta inked one and erased the other six. "When I penciled the romance stories, I used to tell myself, Vince wrecked what I did," said Joe Sinnott. "He would eliminate people from the strip and use silhouettes, everything to cut corners and make the work easier for himself."

But he also charged less and could bring an innocent Marvel Age look to Jack's new heroes. Still, since he was receiving $15 to $18 a page, less than what Stan paid, Colletta started replacing Jack's intricate buildings with easy-to-ink "checkerboard" patterns of straight lines and erasing background characters who didn't figure into the story. Bustling crowd scenes became easier silhouettes, and the books looked a little dull and bland. Though Sherman, Evanier, Wally Wood, and fans who stopped by the house and saw his uninked work urged Jack to fire Colletta, he didn't view Vinnie as a problem. Also, he didn't want him to lose work – until Evanier showed him a page where Colletta had erased an entire crowd scene. Jack nodded and muttered, "Yeah, now, that's not right." But when Jack told Carmine he wanted another inker, Evanier recalled, Carmine convinced him to let Colletta stay on.

After turning in first issues of *Orion*, *The Forever People*, *Mister Miracle*, and the magazine-format old-time gangster anthology *In the Days of the Mob*, Jack worried that someone might tell Marvel what they were about. Since they wouldn't be published for months, and so many artists worked for both companies, he felt someone would describe what he'd seen and that Marvel would rush a similar work into print before his own reached stores. One day, DC production man Sol Harrison called to reassure him the books were being kept under wraps. "Nobody here's seen them. Don't worry, Jack. Nobody's going to rip off your ideas. We have total security."

Besides Carmine and editors Dick Giordano and Joe Orlando, no one at DC knew what the comics were about. When Sherman and Evanier stopped by, Carmine rushed them into his office and locked the door behind him. After Julius Schwartz asked what the comics were about while they were leaving, they called Jack that night to say DC was doing a great job with keeping his ideas classified. Jack was relieved, until they called the next day to say that they'd dropped by Marvel's offices and seen his DC pages hanging on almost every door. Colletta, they explained, had made copies and showed them around. He had distributed them so widely that, once, when Jack needed a page from *The Forever People* No. 2 for reference and DC couldn't send it back, Evanier obtained a copy by calling Marvel, where the receptionist pulled the page off the wall, made a photocopy, and mailed it to him.

Initially, DC didn't have any concrete plan about how to publish Jack's new books. When he heard they wanted to shove the New Gods in one issue of *Showcase*, the Forever People in the next, and then publish *New Gods* No. 1, he complained that this would throw him off schedule and force the story he had created for *New Gods* No. 2 to appear as a first issue. Besides, his deal called for him to have his own titles. If readers saw Orion in *Showcase*, they'd think DC wasn't sure about the concept and his entire saga would be affected. After DC axed *Showcase*, a book called *New Gods* appeared on the schedule. He wanted it to be called *Orion*, and for DC to promote his three books under the umbrella title *The New Gods*, but someone eventually decided to call the book *Orion of the New Gods*, then shortened it to *New Gods*. And soon they were calling all of them *The Fourth World*.

After shipping DC the first two issues of *Jimmy Olsen* and the first *Forever People*, Jack heard DC say they'd done a few minor touch-ups. He figured that they had changed a few lines here and there but learned that a fanzine quoted hostile DC employees saying his Superman was so abysmal that DC had to have another artist completely redraw every panel. He called the company and discovered the touch-ups were significant. When the photostats arrived, he was shocked to see that every single Superman he had drawn now sported an all-new head. It looked as if he'd drawn everything but the last son of Krypton. "I didn't hurt Superman," he explained. "I made him powerful."

But DC's production people felt his Superman face interfered with continuity and didn't resemble the model guides sent to toy manufacturers. His version didn't make for a consistent image to slap on licensed products. When Jack called to complain, Carmine said, "Jack, the Superman heads are very special, like Mickey Mouse. You can't fool with those heads."

Despite the jarring revisions by old-timer Al Plastino, Jack's debut on *Superman's Pal Jimmy Olsen* – the struggling title's 133rd issue, which included the Newsboy Legion – experienced a record-breaking leap in sales. He laughed. "DC couldn't believe it."

When his assistants arrived, he'd tell them ideas for different formats and ask for input on titles. "He would show us stuff and say, 'What do you think?' or, 'Here's the story I'm gonna do,'" Sherman gushed. "We'd go, 'Yeah, that's great.'" Then he'd send presentations to DC with notes about what he wanted to work on next. Soon, writing, editing, and drawing a complete book each week, he had his assistants begin suggesting story ideas, plots, and characters for *Jimmy Olsen.* When they brought up the corny idea of including comedian Don Rickles, he said, "Oh, yeah, let's do that." They asked Rickles's agent for a publicity photo for the cover while he drew the comedian into July 1971's absurd *Jimmy Olsen* No. 139. And though he'd escaped the noisy young bikers in the canyon by buying a home on Lynn Road in Thousand Oaks, California, he stuck a few riders into *Jimmy Olsen* as villains terrorizing superpowered hippies.

Once Carmine had published his *In the Days of the Mob* and *Spirit World* magazines in black and white ("what DC felt it could sell at that moment," Evanier said) and rejected his romance comic with black characters ("Not good!" Carmine snapped. "I wouldn't publish it"), Jack hoped to draw a vampire. Originally, he thought of creating a magazine called *Dracula* that showed the vampire during different time periods (an astronaut in one story, a pirate in the next). Hearing Marvel announce that its new *Dracula Lives* magazine would soon publish the same idea, and with Carmine still delaying, Jack tried to beat them to the punch by sticking a superpowered vampire into October 1971's *Jimmy Olsen.* Since the code banned vampires, Carmine waited to hear if it would let them publish the book, while Stan Lee had his writers and artists throw their own superheroic vampire, Morbius, in the latest *Spider-Man.* Morbius appeared first, fanzines accused Jack of stealing Marvel's idea, and Carmine felt Jack had to leave the title. "Jack took it over and the book died," he said. "The reason it died is that *Jimmy Olsen* was written for little kiddies: Jack was too sophisticated for them, so we moved him off of there."

DC started publishing the titles in the order Jack submitted them, and his life became an endless loop of work. Once the latest *Mister Miracle* was done, he'd start the next *New Gods*, then get to *The Forever People.* If someone asked what he'd done in a story completed a few hours ago, he'd have to consult photocopies for an answer. Only when DC called to say they needed a cover immediately did he stop work. And once he finished whatever DC needed, he got right back to it. Since he didn't use an outline, he placed completed pages that didn't fit into a current story into a pile near his desk, only to reach for them later and stick them into other comics.

At one point, he showed Roz a drawing of his new hero, the Black Racer, a black guy who wore a red-and-blue medieval-style suit of armor and skis. "It's crazy," she said. "It'll never go over. What kind of crazy name is that?"

"Don't worry," he answered, "it'll catch on."

The Racer was Jack's version of the Grim Reaper. But after he met Sgt. Willie Walker, a completely paralyzed black Vietnam vet who was stuck in his bed in the ghetto, the Racer turned to dust and Walker miraculously stood up and put on the armor. Jack wasn't really keen on writing about death, but Carmine seemed to like this sort of stuff, and other editors encouraged him to put as many new characters as possible into his books. Figuring that DC might get behind his work a little more and that kids might see the skis and remember Surfer's board – and enjoy this sports tie-in just as much – he sent DC the sketch, planning to introduce the Black Racer in *New Gods*. And if readers liked him – the way they had liked the Surfer in *The Fantastic Four* – maybe he'd give him his own title.

But Evanier urged him to hold off. Already the books were all over the place. Assuming that others would take over, Jack had spent early issues introducing dozens of characters, their weapons and powers, and the fact that their planets were using the Earth as a battlefield. The costs of his ambitions, however, were nonlinear plots, awkward dialogue, and too many creations. When Evanier noted that readers still didn't know who Orion, Lightray, or Metron were, Jack agreed to set the Racer aside for now. But once Evanier left, Jack worried that someone at DC would show Marvel his sketch and that Marvel would rush a knockoff into print. That night, at his board, he ignored everyone and drew the Black Racer into *New Gods* No. 3.

By now, he and Carmine were promoting an image of unity that rivaled the one he'd had with Stan Lee, but Jack was secretly wondering if Carmine would ever let him hand over the Fourth World books to others. He suspected that Carmine was keeping them on a bimonthly schedule so he'd have time to do them, and once, as he sat near Carmine during an interview, he heard him tell a young comic fan that he wouldn't let anyone else touch Jack's characters. "He knows what he's doing with them," Carmine added.

There might have been other reasons. He was working on the fourth issues of his new books; DC, meanwhile, would just be receiving sales figures for their inaugural editions. If he handed the books off to Ditko, Heck, and Wood, and sales figures reported that the debuts were hits, new creators might cause the books to lose momentum. On the other hand, if they flopped, they'd be axed. Since he'd be staying, Jack stopped drawing the three titles as individual stories that introduced characters and worked to expand the scope and make them one sweeping epic.

In the meantime, he had to deal with another Colletta-related problem: Vinnie kept letting one DC editor change some of the writing on uninked pages. The editor had good intentions, but he went from fixing legitimate grammatical errors to rewriting entire sentences and pages. If he fired Colletta, he'd be able to prevent this. He also considered how Colletta kept diluting his work.

After flying to New York, Jack met with the Inker and asked him to stop erasing things. "This is what I have to do to meet my daily quota," Colletta replied. He insisted he'd keep doing it and suggested that Jack consider drawing simpler pictures so they could both get things done a lot quicker. Enraged by the conversation, Jack told Carmine that Colletta was out. He thought of Mike Royer, one of the first people he'd told about the deal with DC. Previously, Royer had brought Carmine his inking samples and said, "I can do a better, truer job to Jack's pencils than Vince Colletta is doing, for the same money." DC editor Dick Giordano had warned Royer over lunch to be careful. "I was getting a reputation for being cocky," Royer explained, "because I walked in and said that to Carmine."

Jack insisted that Royer was in. "Jack, you can do anything you want, you know that," Carmine answered.

"Well, what are you going to do with Colletta?"

"I'll give him work, don't worry about it."

Until then, Carmine had wanted him to continue inking *Jimmy Olsen*. "Vince was very upset, of course," he said, "but Jack had the right to do that." Jack then called Royer to say: "You're inking and lettering the books now, Mike."

Soon, however, DC beseeched Jack to bring Vinnie back or try other inkers in New York; readers wrote to denounce him for replacing "Vince the Prince" and abandoning the Marvel-style look. At home, he and Roz wondered if they'd made a mistake. Though he was a bit lazy at times, Vinnie Colletta was still an esteemed inker, and firing him had alienated a few readers, especially those who enjoyed Vinnie's work on *Thor* or "Tales of Asgard" and had followed Jack over to DC. Jack exploded and condemned Evanier for convincing him to boot Vinnie. Ultimately, he apologized to Evanier and stuck with Royer, realizing that having him ink and letter the comics in California prevented New York editors from making changes. And since Royer had given up other work to take the job, he didn't want to leave him hanging.

Unfortunately, DC started publishing *Jimmy Olsen* and *New Gods* when Martin Goodman decided to go from publishing fewer than twenty comics to sixty regular titles. In addition to superheroes, sword and sorcery, horror, romance, and western books, Goodman was flooding the market with comics that reprinted Jack's old work. With retail outlets selling fewer comics, and Marvel pumping out more, the market was more competitive than ever. From the time Jack left to when DC published first issues of *New Gods* and *The Forever People*, comic readers had already seen Marvel publish twenty-five of his old stories and ten old covers and Goodman go from showcasing his old work in two reprint books (*Where Creatures Roam* and *Where Monsters Dwell*) to publishing nine monthly titles (*Roam*, *Dwell*, a revived *Marvel's Greatest Comics*, new titles *Fear* and *Special Marvel Edition*, *The X-Men*, *Nick Fury, Agent of S.H.I.E.L.D.*, *Monsters on the Prowl* and *Creatures on the Loose*). Goodman also planned to print Jack's old work and three old covers in double-size *Fantastic Four*, *Thor*, *Hulk*, *Avengers*, *X-Men*, *Iron Man*, and *Captain America* annuals. During the next sixty days, DC published *Mister Miracle*'s debut and second issues of *New Gods* and *The Forever People*, while Goodman published thirteen more old stories and six covers of Jack's.

And he was just getting started. For comic books dated October 1971, Goodman went from selling thirty-two pages for fifteen cents to offering forty-eight for a quarter. DC responded by offering sixty-four pages for twenty-five cents and padding October 1971's *New Gods* No. 4 with cost-effective reprints. "It cost us both money, but I wouldn't let them take the shelf space," Carmine explained. "Many years before, I had heard the story of how DC did that to Gold Key and knocked them off the stands. So Marvel was going to try the same thing with us, but I wouldn't fall for it."

During a time when Jack's new books had to compete with long-time hits *The Amazing Spider-Man*, *Batman*, *The Fantastic Four*, and *Superman* in a shrinking market, DC insisted that his books include reprints. Though Jack wanted Jack Cole's ingenious *Plastic Man* stories – Cole, who later made his name away from comics by drawing cartoons for men's magazines, presented the stretchable, shades-wearing sleuth becoming everything from a race car to a butterfly net – Carmine went with old Simon & Kirby tales, which alienated readers. A month after DC imitated his price and page hike, Goodman then cut Marvel books back down to thirty-two pages and lowered prices to twenty cents. And since the price represented a 25 percent price increase from the original fifteen cents, for the same number of pages, he could let wholesalers have the books for a 50 percent discount. Since DC offered only 40 percent off the cover price, retailers stocked more Marvel titles. "Very slick," Carmine explained. "He did a good job. He was a sharp cookie."

DC stuck with the larger size and higher price despite the fact that comic readers rarely bought the more expensive comic – even if the comic was better and gave more for the money. "Martin Goodman was killing them," Carmine added. Though DC eventually lowered prices, Marvel ended DC's thirty-five-year reign and remained the industry leader.

At the bottom of the final page of *Mister Miracle* No. 5, Jack wrote, "Next Issue: You know him! I know him! Everybody gets to know a FUNKY FLASHMAN!!! The question is – do we need him? This can become a desperate issue – if a 'Funky Flashman' can decide your fate!"

What came next shocked the entire industry. Jack had a file that contained at least one hundred articles in which Stan was described as sole creator of the Marvel Universe. He would now use *Mister Miracle* No. 6 to send a message Stan and the industry would never forget. "Jack was sitting around and he had to come up with another story idea and we had been talking about Stan and the Marvel stuff and he had been telling us stories about Stan," Steve Sherman explained. "And it hit him that here was a way to get it out of his system, so he came up with these characters."

January 1972's "Funky Flashman" started with a bald caricature of Stan in a bathrobe, cloaked in shadows, checking his wristwatch while his short Roy Thomas–like butler Houseroy awaited his latest orders. "In the shadow world between success and failure, there lives the driven little man who dreams of having it all!" he wrote. "The opportunistic spoiler without character or values, who preys on all things like a cannibal! Like death and taxes, we all must deal with him!"

From here, haggard old Flashman told his toadying butler to scratch his back for him. Then he sifted through a staggering and somewhat pathetic array of wigs and fake beards, slipping at last into a pair that resembled Stan's current haircut and beard. At Mister Miracle's house, Flashman appeared in a con man's gaudy hat, coat, and scarf. He wanted to be Miracle's manager, he explained, after he watched him perform an escape, then reappeared a few panels later in a hippie-style hat, shades, and a flamboyant polka-dot scarf. Holding a long cigarette holder, he yelled, "Say no more! Your act is sensational! Glad I wore my 'uneasy rider' outfit today!" By the finale, Big Barda and her Female Furies learned Flashman was responsible for all of this issue's mayhem and advanced to attack. Standing behind Funky, subservient Houseroy tried to warn him. But Funk, now clad in a conservative suit and tie, put his nose in the air, shushed him, and said, "I'm preparing for my establishment stage!" When he did see the ladies approaching, he grabbed Houseroy by the seat of his pants and the back of his collar. "Master Funky! My leader! What are you doing?" He literally threw his loyal servant at his attackers, yelling, "Worry not, noble warrior! I know your valor will stem the tide until the local fuzz arrive!"

Jack ended the scathing attack with Funky running out on faithful Houseroy, leaving the decaying mansion just as it exploded. Watching it burn, flames reflected in his eyes, casting shadows on his haggard face – with his bald head revealed and fake beard dangling from one sideburn – he none too subtly referred to the inferno as "a marvel of contrast!" Jack then drew Flashman walking away from the mess he'd created, both hands straightening the tie on his ragged suit, with the caption "Whistling, with rising new spirits, like all his endless kind, Funky Flashman strides with new hopes – new schemes – into the night!"

The story's acrimonious tone inspired Jack's former assistant and friend Steve Sherman, after he read it, to say, "Oh man, Jack, you're not really gonna do that, are you?"

With a laugh, Jack said, "Oh yeah! Oh yeah! This is gonna go out!"

"Okay, if you think they'll do it. . . ."

"Ahh," he said dismissively. "It's funny!"

While inking the issue, Royer asked, "This is Stan, isn't it?"

Shrugging: "Whatever do you mean?"

"He thought it was great," Sherman explained. "And he was right. It was damn funny. It wasn't that mean, and you could read between the lines, but I think Jack was just sort of kicking their ass, saying, 'Well, if this is the only way I can get at you guys, then this is what I'm gonna do.'"

Chapter 13

At the house on Sapra Road, two miles from the one on Lynn, fans continued to show up unannounced. Sometimes Jack invited them to one of the pool parties he and Roz threw for artists and friends. But sometimes they kept him from relaxing with the television news or his favorite Charles Bronson and Clint Eastwood action movies. One day someone knocked, and Jack saw two conservative, clean-shaven men with short haircuts standing outside. After introducing themselves as "the Sun" and "the Moon," they explained that they'd abandoned their wives, sold their businesses, and were headed for Oregon because the mother ship was coming to pick them up. They wanted him to accompany them. "Come on in," he said, "have a cup of coffee!"

In the kitchen, Roz asked, "What are you talking about? Why did you let these people in?"

"Well, they looked decent."

She gave them a few oranges and a couple of bucks and pointed them toward the freeway, where they could hitch a ride. Lisa couldn't believe it. If Charles Manson knocked on the door, she joked, he'd probably let him in. When Jack went to her school for parties, he'd draw pictures for the kids, turning the first letters of their names into superheroes and helping her transform from a shy, self-conscious wallflower to one of the popular kids. Classmates were always asking, "What's your dad going to draw next issue?" During the Jewish High Holidays, he'd accompany Roz to temple.

Though his father, Ben, had gone every day and on weekends, Jack didn't feel he had to do the same to prove he was a good person. "Don't you think we ought to go more often?" Roz asked one day.

"I love God, and I believe in God," he replied. "And I'm still a good person, even though I don't go into the temple."

He kept reading his Bible, throwing more "gods" into his comics – and receiving fans. One day, a couple arrived and the woman fell into the pool with her brand-new camera. Then, when thirty people from Europe arrived, Roz sent someone down to McDonald's for thirty meals. One day, guests kept them so busy they couldn't pick Lisa up from school. And when her friends stopped by, they'd exclaim, "Wow, this is what your dad does? Can I see the studio? Can I meet your dad?"

Until now, DC had told Jack his Fourth World books were spectacular hits. "The first printing was three hundred fifty thousand and cleared a fifty percent sales," Carmine said. "That's livable." With Marvel outselling their books, however, DC stopped telling him *New Gods* was successful. Worrying that the books would be canceled, Jack spent a day at his drawing board, knocking out sketches of characters like Lonar, Lightray, and Infinity Man in an effort to convince them that the Fourth World series could, with more support, birth other successful titles. DC didn't respond to the sketches.

While Jack was building up to a climactic battle between Orion and his father, Darkseid (and planning to throw readers a curveball by having Darkseid refuse to fight him), Carmine asked him to raise sales by including his character Deadman.

Deadman was a circus acrobat named Boston Brand, murdered while swinging on a trapeze, who returned to life as a ghost in a red Daredevil-like costume with a big D on the chest and hunted for his killer, a man with a hook on his left hand. Carmine asked for Deadman despite the fact that, in his own defunct series, the hero had already caught the killer. He wanted Deadman included because people at DC felt the Fourth World needed to be part of the mainstream DC Universe. They wanted the New Gods to interact with Superman, Batman, and Wonder Woman and for Jack to draw more like Neal Adams. By now, Carmine had sent him a copy of Adams's cover for *World's Greatest Superheroes* No. 6, a one-hundred-page "superspectacular" that starred the combined members of the Justice League and their 1940s counterparts, the Justice Society. Carmine told him that the front and back covers – which showed thirty-four heroes facing the reader – was one of the best he'd ever seen. Jack disagreed. Adams had drawn most of these heroes with the same body and in the same one or two poses. He told Carmine the cover was horrible, that all these heroes standing around with their hands on their hips should've been fighting, flying, and punching: "All your characters look alike!" But many at DC felt *he* was the lousy artist, and one old-timer – harboring a grudge from the Schiff debacle – openly told people, "Neal Adams represents the future of comic art. Jack Kirby represents the past."

If Carmine expected Jack to deliver a successful Marvel-style take on Deadman and make it a hit, it wasn't going to happen. "The timing or the era wasn't right," said Sherman. "It wasn't going to work." Besides, if he'd wanted to rehash themes, he wouldn't have created the Fourth World. He could've made Mister Miracle a standard hero, turned the Challengers of the Unknown into another Fantastic Four or created a monster hero like the Hulk. "Maybe that would have been more successful. Maybe that's what the readers wanted to see. But that's not what he wanted to do. He wanted to do the Fourth World. That was the next step for him. And if it was successful, fine. If it wasn't, well, at least he'd tried."

Though he didn't like the character, the name Deadman, or the fact that this death-obsessed hero didn't belong with his life-affirming hippies, Jack tried to live up to his reputation of being able to make anything work, even an idea as rotten as this. Over dinner, he and Mark Evanier discussed ideas for the Deadman revival. Evanier felt Deadman was weak because DC let him catch his killer when readers were starting to buy the book. They should create a loophole and show Deadman caught the wrong guy. They'd be able to do it, he explained, since DC printed a few issues with the killer having his hook on the wrong hand. By exploiting this, he could reopen the case and give readers what they liked best with their character.

Jack was open to the idea but ignored most of the outline Sherman and Evanier submitted. Instead he delivered "Monster in the Morgue," an old-fashioned *Forever People* story that found the guest star battling a modern-day Frankenstein monster and meeting an "old ex-carny gal" named Trixie Magruder who tells him during a séance, "He wasn't the killer! The hook was on his left hand! The man who killed Boston Brand had a hook on his right hand!" Jack ended *The Forever People* No. 9 with Deadman defeating the monster and the team handing him a space cartridge that would give him a new body and let him "become a being of New Genesis!"

At DC, executives expected him to give Deadman a new costume and make him a huge success. When they saw what he'd done, some ran around the office yelling, "Oh, my God, Kirby has changed Deadman! We can't have this!" Jack also felt it'd been a bad match. "He didn't like losers, he didn't like dead people, and he chose not to dwell on failure and defeat and death in his work," Evanier recalled. But when DC started telling him what to do, "some combination of personal pride and a desire to be a compliant employee caused him to tackle them, and I don't think he was very happy with how Deadman came out." Fortunately, after two issues, this new Deadman was put to rest.

Since DC was griping about low sales, Jack tried to present ideas he felt were more commercial. He worked with Mark Evanier on a presentation for Kamandi, an idea he'd developed when he was trying to land a newspaper strip during the 1950s. Back then he called it *Kamandi of the Animals* and hoped to draw an older guy in a postapocalyptic world inhabited by weird mutants and a few talking animals. In the new proposal, Kamandi was younger but went through the same story beats. Jack asked Evanier who he thought should draw the book. Evanier suggested local artist Dan

Spiegle. Spiegle came by the house, and they got along, so Jack promised to mention him to Carmine.

A day after he received the proposal, Carmine asked for another new comic with a monster in it. By now, Warren Publishing was selling lots of black-and-white horror magazines, Marvel was churning out *Ghost Rider*, *Dracula*, *Werewolf by Night*, *Tales of the Zombie*, and *Brother Voodoo*, and the industry wondered if superheroes were passé. At Howard Johnson's over dinner, Roz, his kids Lisa and Barbara, and his assistants Sherman and Evanier chatted and waited for their turkey sandwiches to arrive. Jack sat quietly and thought about what to bring Carmine. Soon he started telling them a story about a man named Jason Blood and his ability to transform into a fiend from hell.

During the final days of Camelot, he said, Merlin changed his sidekick, the yellow-skinned, red-eyed demon Etrigan, into the bewildered, troubled young human Jason Blood. And today Blood didn't know this until Morgaine Le Fey turned up and tried to force him to lead her to her enemy Merlin's tomb, where he kept the secret for eternal youth. To force him to lead her there, she turned Blood back into his demon self.

Rehashing a name he'd used with Joe Simon, Jack called the book *The Demon*. And at home, he rushed to his table and started jotting down ideas. Then he opened a hardcover book that included drawings from Hal Foster's old Prince Valiant stories and found the page where Valiant disguised himself with a terrifying mask. He drew the same face on his Demon, gave him pale yellow green skin and a dark-blue-and-green costume, and sent it in.

But a DC colorist gave the hero the same yellow skin Foster put on the mask and changed the costume to yellow and red. Jack felt the colors were too bright, but he didn't protest. He figured his involvement would end after the first issue: Evanier and Sherman would write it, and someone else would handle the art. And though he originally wanted to make it a continuation of the Fourth World, he'd include the Demon and Merlin in the August 1972 debut issue but make it more like *Batman*, with each adventure offering a separate story and new villain. Doing this, he hoped, would prevent DC from canceling it.

Once he finished *The Demon* No. 1, Jack heard DC reject Dan Spiegle for *Kamandi*. He suggested other artists, but DC vetoed them as well. "In both cases, Jack was trying to come up with something new that he could preferably edit and not write or draw," said Evanier. "He wanted to work with other writers and artists, including myself as a writer, and created Kamandi and the Demon for that purpose." DC considered hiring inexpensive Filipino artists for *Kamandi* and *The Demon* – with Jack handling the layouts – then decided Jack should draw both books himself.

First, though, Carmine wanted to add a few ideas to Kamandi. He had just seen the Charlton Heston movie *Planet of the Apes* and said, "Jack, how about a book something like that?"

Based on Pierre Boulle's novella, *Planet of the Apes* broke ratings records when it aired on network television. Viewers loved the idea of astronauts crash-landing on a primitive planet where talking apes enslaved humans.

Jack hadn't watched the movie, but he knew the story. He had Kamandi mix it up with talking animals. But Carmine supposedly wanted to make it closer to the movie and asked for its most famous image, a damaged Statue of Liberty, to be included on the cover and in the first issue. Some readers saw it and accused Jack of copying *Planet of the Apes*, but October 1972's *Kamandi* No. 1 emerged as his most successful DC title to date. And the series continued to outperform Marvel's consequent *Planet of the Apes* magazine.

Even with Jack's cumbersome dialogue and strange punctuation marks (three exclamation points and "quotes" around inappropriate words), readers continued to buy his Fourth World books. But when sales of *The Demon* No. 1 and *Kamandi* No. 1 were encouraging, DC altered the plan again.

Jack was working on the eleventh issue of *The Forever People* (the October–November edition) when Evanier remembered Carmine calling to say, "We are so hot on *Demon* and *Kamandi* that we want to launch them as monthly books. So I'm suspending *New Gods* and *The Forever People* so you don't have to turn *Kamandi* and *Demon* over to others for a while."

Suspending a title, Jack knew, was the same as killing it. In addition to resenting DC for giving up on his books too quickly, he was stung by the realization that people at Marvel would now be saying that this showed he was nothing without Stan.

At his table, he drew a final adventure of his experimental nonviolent work. But Carmine pulled the plug so quickly that Jack wasn't able to get Orion and Darkseid into the same room, let alone to their long-promised battle. Said Mike Thibodeaux, "When *New Gods* was canceled, he was crushed."

With two thirds of his epic canceled by October, Jack had to find a way to keep *Mister Miracle* going. After the tenth issue, DC suggested he abandon the Fourth World plot, which they felt detracted from more commercial superhero elements. He agreed to deliver simpler stories but worried that each issue would be the last. To buoy his spirits, one of his young friends arranged a telephone conversation with Roy Thomas, now editor in chief at Marvel (while Stan was publisher and president and Martin Goodman and his son Chip were gone). "An intermediary went to Roy and said, 'We'd like you to call Jack and just tell him that the door is open,'" Evanier explained. "And Roy called Jack and said, 'Hey, you know, if you ever want to come back, we'll make you an offer.'"

Since there was no firm offer, however, Jack continued with his remaining title, filling *Mister Miracle* with generic villains Dr. Bedlam (a minion of Darkseid turned average villain), Mystivac (a robot whose knuckles sprouted long claws, with the sound effect "snik"), and King Komodo, an Asian man in an iron mask who kept a statue of Hitler in his cave.

Following a story about a satanic cult in a haunted house, he tried to boost sales by throwing in black teen sidekick Shilo Norman, who sported a big, somewhat outdated Jimi Hendrix hairdo. But by fall, after a few more Scooby-Doo-style adventures (villains using tricks and gadgets to convince others that ghouls and goblins exist, then being unceremoniously unmasked during the closing panels), DC had had enough. "Each issue that came out went downhill, and then it went as far as forty-two percent, which was losing about five hundred dollars a month," Carmine explained. "It was a lot of money then. They just weren't making money anymore. I had to tell him, 'Jack, the books are not doing well.'"

Jack was facing more serious problems than low sales. For one, Kinney's purchase of DC caused infighting between the licensing and distribution divisions. And since *MAD* and *Playboy*, which Independent distributed, outsold anything DC published, and comic book circulation was declining, people in the Independent News division asked, Why are we even bothering with comic books? "They were very negative about everything DC came out with," Evanier recalled. "The more enthused the comic book division was about something, the more the distribution people said, 'This will never sell.' And when the distribution division says this, it's a very self-fulfilling prophecy."

Then there were people in the company who worried that because of the potential success of the New Gods, and Jack's friendship with Jack Liebowitz – which stretched back to the 1940s – they might lose their jobs to him. Carmine was a friend but was also said to be a bit overprotective of his new position as DC publisher. After Carmine fired editor Dick Giordano without warning, Neal Adams said Carmine publicly accused him of trying to become publisher. This was untrue, he added. But once this happened, "it became very clear to some of us that there were people who were perhaps more capable of doing the job than Carmine. And Jack under the right conditions would have been one of those."

If *New Gods* succeeded when every other DC comic was tanking, Liebowitz might have tapped Jack to be publisher. What his critics didn't know was that DC had already offered him the position, Steve Sherman recalled. And Jack had turned it down. "He didn't want to move back to New York. For health reasons, for Roz and his daughter Lisa, he liked it here. He didn't want the hassle of being a publisher, especially of DC."

Then there were employees who had worked at DC since the 1940s and would resent having him, of all people, as the company's would-be savior. During most of the previous decade, DC's management had openly expressed their contempt for Marvel Comics. During meetings, they'd called the Lee-Kirby books badly drawn and written and DC titles superior. "I tried to read them," Julius Schwartz said of the Fourth World. "Jack Kirby was a very good friend of mine – we adored each other – but when I thought of him as a writer, and so on . . . as an artist, he was terrific . . . Let's put it this way: He was not nearly as good a writer as he was an artist." Some employees resented that the guy they all agreed had created inferior comics was now receiving the best deal at the company.

With his entire saga gone, Jack didn't know what to do with the stack of ideas on his desk. Everyone in the industry saw DC ax his books; some of his readers felt cheated out of a proper ending and shunned his new work. DC let him handle *The Demon* and *Kamandi*, but his critics pointed to the Fourth World cancellations as proof that he was really worthless to the company. DC gave him so much freedom because they wanted him to create a new comic book universe for them, Neal Adams explained. "Then the guy goes ahead and does it, and he's got nothing to fetter him, calm him down, back him off, or say, 'Okay, Jack, you know, you're doing too much. Let some writers go over your work. The writing is minimal. It needs to be enhanced a little bit. You need to work with some people.'" When things got bad, he continued, "They basically blamed Jack and turned on him like dogs. And suddenly, it was Jack's fault." They created the situation and then ignored "that there wasn't enough time in his life to write and draw all this stuff and maintain a professional level of quality."

When Miracle was killed, Jack once again felt trapped, without options. Carmine would want him to work with other writers, while Marvel would deprive him of credit. After debating Carmine about how DC regarded him and what he'd do next, Jack threatened to quit. "If you ask Infantino or anyone at DC, they'll say, 'No, Jack never threatened to leave, he never quit,'" Evanier explained. But he did ask Marvel what they'd offer if he broke his contract, and Marvel did leak the news to fanzines *The Comic Reader* and *Rocket's Blast Comic Collector*. "They both had people at Marvel call them and say, 'Jack's coming over.'" Though the fanzines even mentioned tentative ideas about what Marvel books he'd handle, including *The X-Men*, the stories were premature. What they didn't know was that a DC editor traveled to California to tell Jack Kinney executives wouldn't let him go and might take legal action if he tried to break his contract. Kinney was willing to compromise, but Marvel wasn't offering anything great, so he stayed where he was.

Since *The Demon* was axed after sixteen issues, and *Kamandi* sold well – and he had to give DC fifteen pages a week – Jack agreed to bring them something else set in the future: OMAC, an acronym for "One-Man Army Corps." After dressing up Captain America's origin with futurology – Professor Myron Forest choosing meek, unassuming office worker Buddy Blank to become the Global Peace Agency's supersoldier – Jack spent each issue predicting what life would be like in "the world that's coming." In addition to lifelike robots, floating cars, and telephones you could actually take outside with you, he showed a device that let people wear goggles and interact with computerized images and surgeries performed with lasers, without sedatives. In *OMAC*, scientists could actually grow new bodies with DNA research, a worldwide organization was trying to keep the peace, and a huge satellite housing a computer named Brother Eye orbited planet Earth and communicated with people below. The world that's coming, *OMAC* told readers, would be violent, run by world-spanning corporations and freethinking computers. The September 1974 debut issue came with a disquieting cover – a hero with a strange Mohawk haircut – and even stranger ideas. In one issue, a rich criminal rented a city for a night and stocked it with killer street gangs. In another, OMAC was killed and resurrected by the satellite. In a third, he received test parents and watched a captured terrorist hold a tiny black sign and pose for a standard police mug shot.

Before he knew it, Carmine asked Jack to work with Joe Simon again. Though Simon had been writing for the company on and off for a few years, he hadn't really scored any big hits on his own. Simon's *Brother Power the Geek* was an intriguing attempt to fuse superheroes to hippie culture, but in 1968, executives felt it was subversive, too different from DC's other clean-cut, law-and-order books, and told Carmine to cancel it. Then Simon's *Prez* – another unusual, pro-youth title, this one about a turtleneck-wearing teenage president of the United States – also died. Simon's *The Green Team* and *Championship Sports* flopped as well. "It's funny," Carmine recalled. "He was great with Jack and without Jack, his books . . . Jack was the same without Joe!" By reuniting them, Carmine hoped to see sales as high as those of their 1940s Captain America and Sandman work.

Simon showed Carmine a new character with the old name Sandman. Said Evanier, "I believe somebody else actually drew an issue of *Sandman* and DC wasn't happy with it, so he discarded it and said, 'What if Jack did it?' Figuring that somehow there would be some new chemistry with Simon and Kirby reuniting."

Carmine called him at home. "Jack, I'd like to do a book with you and Joe again, and I'd like to do the Sandman."

By now, Jack and Joe had been on opposite sides of the battle for Captain America's copyright. When asked about Captain America, Jack told reporters other people actually created work signed by Simon & Kirby. Eddie Herron, he added, created the Red Skull, and while Joe might claim he wrote every story, Jack said, "I wrote them and I penciled them . . . and I inked them half the time!" Jack stiffly rejected the idea of Sandman and a reunion. "I'm not going back to the past."

"You guys are so great together," Carmine countered. "Do me a favor. Do one issue and we'll see what happens. Is that fair?"

The reality was that Jack wanted to write, draw, and edit his own books. "Anything else, he felt, Okay, I'll do it, 'cause they're paying me, but if I had my choice, I really wouldn't," Sherman explained. He told Carmine, "Okay."

When *Sandman* No. 1 became an improbable hit, Carmine called him again. "I said, 'Jack, Joe will even leave his name off the book so you two can keep working together.' He wouldn't do it, just refused."

After this, Jack's relationship with DC deteriorated even more. Though his deal called for Jack to do what he liked in his own titles, Carmine stuck what Jack thought was *Atlas* No. 1 – about a muscle-bound Greek god – into a new tryout book called *First Issue Special.* The title existed because Independent News told Carmine that most new series, after high-selling first issues, dipped in sales. "So he said, 'Okay, let's just do first issues,'" Sherman explained. "Which didn't sit well with Jack, because not only did he have to come up with an original character every time, but once he came up with a story and a character, he had to walk away from it. He felt that wasn't fair to the reader, to come up with this stuff and just drop it."

Instead of initiating new titles, Jack was kept filling the tryout books with a revival of Manhunter and another kid gang called Dingbats of Danger Street, none of which led to an ongoing series. DC also had him working on a lesser-known war series called *Our Fighting Forces.* In order to fulfill his contract, Jack worked on whatever they assigned – even if it was the hackneyed *Super Friends* – but he was unhappy. DC had ruined his reputation, he believed. All he wanted at this point was to be allowed to produce stories he could view with pride. And though DC might quickly cancel anything he put together, he tried again. "I remember the thing that really put the icing on the cake was when we did *King Kobra,*" said Sherman, who had dropped by the house with a new hero called King Kobra. Jack sat at his kitchen table and read the script. The name and title were fine. But the story . . . "Boy, does this stink," he told Sherman. After cutting them slices of chocolate cake, he sat and lit a cigar, smoked in silence for a few minutes, then said, "The Corsican Brothers."

"What?"

"The Corsican Brothers by Dumas. Identical twins, one good, one bad."

The rest of the afternoon was spent hashing out ideas for two issues, forgetting that *King Kobra* would be only a one-shot in *First Issue Special.* Then Sherman went home to write, while Jack, pleased, felt this could finally be the start of the line he'd wanted to produce since his arrival at DC years ago.

A week later, Sherman brought over the new story. Since then, Jack had already started drawing the comic, dividing it into panels. After incorporating what Sherman had written, he shipped the comic to DC.

Six weeks later, Sherman stopped by to pick up fan mail for *Kamandi*'s letters page. Jack showed Sherman the completed *King Kobra* book. Sherman opened it with astonishment. DC had changed the title to *Kobra* – and almost everything about the main character; DC had pasted Jack's art in a different order, added beards and new hairstyles to the characters, and credited the story to another writer. "Whoa," Sherman said. "What's this?"

"Yeah, I know," he answered. "I'm quitting. I'm not gonna renew my contract with DC."

It became apparent that DC wanted Jack to do nothing but draw. His latest assignments entailed working from some pedestrian writer's comprehensive script. Slowly he was stripped of his editor duties on *Kamandi.* Where he once wrote, drew, and edited the title, now someone else took the finished comic and rewrote the dialogue, and another letterer placed these alterations onto each board. DC knew he'd soon renew his contract or leave and tried to mollify him by claiming the New Gods would be revived in a new series. But he suspected what a new contract would call for. "Essentially, it would have reduced his editorial powers and forced him to do more of other people's projects, which he was not enjoying," Evanier said.

Jack no longer regarded writing and drawing as separate from each other and didn't want to stay at DC and illustrate other people's scripts or characters. When he spotted Roy Thomas at the San Diego Comic Convention in 1974, a year earlier, he'd approached the bespectacled editor to say he might be willing to come back – if Marvel would make him a decent offer. Thomas was receptive but mentioned that "Stan had been kind of hurt by that Funky Flashman."

He laughed. "Well, you know, it was all in fun."

Since that meeting, Thomas had resigned as editor in chief, so the same young conciliator who contacted him earlier now called Stan to say, "I think that Jack is ready to come back if you'll make him an offer." The telephone calls between them had to be brokered and negotiated, Evanier explained. "'Well, I'll call Jack if he promises not to hang up on me.' And, 'Jack, you'll promise not to hang up on Stan, fine.' So the call was arranged, and he got to tender an offer, and it was not a great offer, but it was better than what he'd get out of DC."

Soon after the offer, Stan invited Roy – who continued to write for the company as a contracted writer-editor – into his office and asked, "What would you think about Jack Kirby coming back?"

"I think that's great!" Roy answered. "I just got one piece of advice."

"What's that?"

"Don't let him write."

"Well, the deal is that he's gotta write," Stan told him. "He'll come back, but he's gotta write his own stuff."

"Well, if you gotta have him, then bring him back anyway," Thomas said.

Stan said he was pleased to hear this, because other people in the office weren't happy about Jack's homecoming.

"Well, they're crazy," Thomas said. "The idea of getting Jack back from DC will simply vindicate you to some extent, and vindicate Marvel, and even if you have to let him write and you can't edit much of it, just find someplace where he will be able to do the most good and put him up."

After speaking to Stan, Jack ended his forward-looking action-packed *OMAC* series on a decidedly gloomy note: Buddy Blank lost his power and returned to being a faceless nobody, leaving the orbiting satellite Brother Eye to battle an ocean-stealing villain alone. Then he looked at the telephone. He and Roz had already talked everything over – now he had to tell Carmine.

Carmine had tried. He didn't want to cancel the Fourth World. But the distributors in Independent News kept saying that for what DC was paying Jack, sales were meager. "Carmine didn't want to admit defeat," former editor Dick Giordano remembered. "It cost him a lot in pride and honor to have gone out and gotten Kirby and then have to say, 'I'm sorry, we can't go ahead with them.'" As publisher since 1974, Carmine was answerable to other people. He had to work with dozens of creators and titles and somehow compete with Marvel's endless reprints, price changes, retailer discounts, and two-to-one market share.

Jack called his old friend and told him, "Carmine, I want to move on."

"No problem. But we're still friends."

"Absolutely."

"Take care and good luck. And if you want to come back, don't hesitate."

Jack thanked him, hung up, and began to prepare for his trip to New York. It would be his first visit to Marvel's offices in years. "I think by then Jack was pretty much tired," Sherman opined. "He had finished with DC and that didn't work out, so now here he was back at Marvel. He still didn't have the rights to his characters, but he had to make a living. There wasn't anyplace else to go. If you were going to do comics, you worked for DC or Marvel. Those were the only ones who would pay him the rate he needed to live on."

While Jack sat in Stan's spacious office discussing his return, artist Marie Severin walked in. "When he left Marvel, Stan nearly had a heart attack," she recalled. "It was supposed to be a big secret." Stan showed her a page Jack had drawn and told her, "You did not see any of this!"

"Okay, I did not see any of this," she answered. But as soon as she left the office, she yelled, "Kirby's back!"

From here, Jack and Stan traveled to the local hotel that would host the three-day Mighty Marvel Comic Convention inker Vince Colletta had organized. All around him, Jack saw long-haired kids in button-up shirts, plaid slacks, thick eyeglasses, floral print outfits, polyester slacks, and dirty jeans. There were kids in superhero outfits holding a parade and a contest, where one guy won first prize for his homemade Thing costume. Jack had the chance to meet with Romita, Buscema, Heck, Dick Ayers, and Roy Thomas. Then Marie Severin led Joe Sinnott over to him. He'd never met or spoken with him, but they got along well and spent much of March 24, 1975, talking about World War II and the Fantastic Four and posing beside each other while fans took pictures.

Then Jack stood outside of the room where Stan and Roy were holding a Fantastic Four panel. He heard Stan tell the audience he had a special guest. The doors opened, and Jack stepped inside. The entire audience leaped to its feet and gave a standing ovation. Surrounded by screaming, cheering fans, Jack walked down the aisle and made his way to the podium. He stood near Stan Lee, and for a brief moment, fans felt the magic was back. After Stan announced that he was coming home where he belonged, fans pressed forward to ask Jack what books he'd work on. "Whatever I do at Marvel," he said, "I can assure you that it'll electrocute you in the mind!"

To which Stan replied, "Electrify, Jack! Electrify!"

Chapter 14

Over the last four years, Stan hadn't really created anything to match the success of the earlier Lee-Kirby co-creations. His Spider-Man story – someone leaping off a roof after taking pills – paved the way for the revision of the Comics Code (he published it without the seal of approval) but came to be only after a government agency sent a letter. He told Roy to put "a super-villain vampire" in the series, but Morbius flopped. Goodman canceled his black-and-white magazine *Savage Tales* and the hero Black Brother after one issue. He gave Roy a one- or two-sentence prompt for a swamp hero named Man-Thing, but this was when DC was using the same idea (based on a long-gone hero, the Heap) in their *Swamp Thing* story. *Conan the Barbarian* was the only new comic making real money, and Stan had had nothing to do with it. In fact, when Roy brought him the idea, Stan, a little wary, told him to write a proposal for Goodman.

Where people like Jack created new gimmicks for every comic, Roy Thomas and other former comic fans based their creations on what Lee and Kirby had done. The Valkyrie was a sword-wielding female Thor; longhaired Doc Samson gained his powers from the same gamma rays as the Hulk. While riding whatever trend came along, the young writers rehashed many of Stan and Jack's old origins (having black ex-con Luke Cage undergo an experiment and emerge as a low-selling *Hero for Hire*). Though *Warlock*'s "cosmic" pretension and pseudointellectual dialogue intrigued hard-core fans, the new hero was nothing but Stan and Jack's old "Him" character crossed with Roy's attempt to emulate Jack's Fourth World and the Broadway play *Jesus Christ Superstar.*

Stan continued to have less to do with the comics but wanted more control at the company. When he stepped down in 1972, Goodman appointed his son Chip, a chubby, balding hipster in rose-colored glasses, as his successor. By now, Stan's relationship with his distant relative was strained. Since Martin Goodman felt Stan hogged credit during interviews and issued a stream of backhanded compliments in the "Bullpen Bulletins" column, his son wasn't going out of his way to help Stan get even more credit. After Stan and John Romita created two weeks of sample *Spider-Man* strips for a newspaper syndicate and gave it to Chip, who ostensibly would contact the company and close the deal, Chip didn't even bother taking the pages off his desk. "So, we missed the boat on the first go-round," Romita said. "Chip Goodman single-handedly screwed up the whole deal." Another day, facing the cover of a western reprint title, Chip told Stan and Roy to put animal masks on the villains. When asked why, he said, "I don't know, maybe it'll sell better." "While Chip tried hard, he certainly didn't know anything about comics," Roy claimed. "I think it rankled Stan, which is why he went after and finally got the control of the company by sort of backdoor means."

Stan's strategy involved implying that he'd leave, going so far as to meet with DC to discuss working for them. But a corporate shake-up at Perfect led new chief Sheldon Feinberg to change the company's name to Cadence Industries and ease Chip out the door, "causing a lot of family friction," Romita explained. As president and publisher, Stan immediately promoted Roy Thomas to editor in chief. And just as immediately, every Marvel comic now came with "Stan Lee Presents" on its opening page. Thomas claimed Stan was reluctant to use this phrase but that he, Thomas, pushed for it because "'Stan Lee Presents' just seemed to sound right. 'Stan Lee publisher or president' doesn't have any pizzazz. That sounds too much like 'business stuff.'"

The phrase made Stan the company figurehead – the Walt to their Disney – and had him present things he had nothing to do with. "I guess businessmen figure don't tamper with success," Romita felt. "If it was used in the sixties, why not in the seventies?" But it made sense, he added, because "he was such an integral part of the relationship with the readers."

After his promotion, Stan stopped writing *The Fantastic Four* and *Spider-Man* and told editors, "The Surfer is my baby, and I don't want anybody to use him." He let Roy include him in a story about the Defenders, an antisocial group that included Hulk and Sub-Mariner, but not in their ongoing series. When another writer asked to feature Surfer in a few more issues, Stan agreed – temporarily. "You can't have him forever, but you can do that."

Eschewing heroes, Stan developed the black-and-white magazines *Savage Tales*, *Dracula Lives*, *Monsters Unleashed*, *Vampire Tales*, and *Tales of the Zombie*. He helped develop comics like *Werewolf by Night*, tryout books *Marvel Premiere*, *Marvel Spotlight*, and *Marvel Feature*, the Spidey-driven *Marvel Team-Up*, *Tomb of Dracula*, *The Living Mummy*, and the pseudofeminist *Claws of the Cat* – most of which sold poorly and were quickly canceled. He worked with Kirby-like artist Rich Buckler on *Man-Wolf*, which turned J. Jonah Jameson's astronaut son into a werewolf, but this also tanked.

By 1974, Stan was no longer president of Marvel. "I gave it up because I realized I was spending most of my time going to financial meetings," Stan explained. Instead, he developed horror heroes like Brother Voodoo, and Son of Satan, persuaded *The Electric Company* to include Spidey in their educational children's television program, and wrote essays for *Origins of Marvel Comics*, a Fireside/Simon & Schuster trade paperback that reprinted his old work with Jack but came with a cover that read "By Stan Lee." Roy Thomas felt Stan left Jack's name off the cover because Jack was at DC, and he didn't want to praise a competitor. He also said Marvel downplayed Jack's contributions because they wanted to play it safe after Simon and Burgos sued for Captain America and the Human Torch. Either way, Stan was accused of hogging credit, a charge that had plagued him since the 1940s and 1950s "because he was the only writer who slapped his name on credits. He had a 'precredit' credit."

Stan's image continued to suffer. At Phil Seuling's huge comic convention in New York, held on the July Fourth weekend, he sat on a panel with Joe Simon, who explained that they only let him write the text page because no one, including the editors, ever read it. When asked what spirit held Timely together back then, Simon said it was "the spirit of nepotism. Almost everybody there was a member of the Goodman family, and we were all good friends and we had a nice spirit about it." Roy's wife, Jean (once hired as Marvel's receptionist), asked the panel about Captain America. After describing an article that called the hero a fascist, Joe asked, "Did you read that, Stan?" Simon opined that Cap's flag-colored uniform was "a camp thing now" and gestured to Stan. "But the uniform's valuable, isn't it, Stan?"

Stan struck back by implying that Jack did all the work for Simon & Kirby. He didn't see Jack for the first three weeks, he recalled, because Jack was busy working and ignoring the orders Joe gave him. "And it didn't matter because Joe changed everything he did anyhow," Stan said. "And Jack used to smoke, I think, Joe's left-over cigars or castoffs. Jack had to smoke a smaller cigar than Joe. And this was the mighty Timely staff for quite a while, while I worked there." They were great bosses, Stan said, but when he faced a Simon & Kirby page, "I never knew whether Joe gave Jack the idea and Jack drew it, or Jack gave Joe the idea and Joe had Jack draw it, or Joe drew it first and Jack copied it. I sometimes suspect that they didn't know, but that was a real good example of two guys –"

"Usually we stole the idea," Joe interrupted.

"I'd like to say, from me," Stan countered. "But they didn't, because I was just learning at the time."

Next, Stan saw Martin Goodman try to put Marvel out of business by forming a rival company called Atlas Comics. "Because they did that to his son, Martin Goodman decided to try to disrupt their successful role," Romita explained. Goodman offered Marvel talents the highest page rates ever, the return of their original art, and rights to whatever they created. "He lured quite a few people, starting with Larry," Roy remembered. "But that was more amiable. Stan sort of understood that, after all, Larry was a relative of Goodman's, too, by marriage, and that his brother might need to get out from under his shadow." Once Goodman began to imitate Spider-Man and the Hulk with Tiger-Man and the Brute, however, Stan became upset. "It's bound to leave a bad taste in your mouth, even though there was nothing illegal or even unethical about anything," said Roy.

At Marvel, Stan continued to meet with younger writers who pitched ideas for new books and heroes. During one meeting, writer Steve Gerber described a talking duck named Howard. "Great! Do it!" When he wasn't conferring with writers, perusing covers, developing new magazines, or lecturing about Marvel and the viability of comics, he was off on one-day trips to Hollywood, checking into hotels and pitching Marvel properties to executives at film and television studios. "I remember him coming back to the office, trying to figure out who the hell Howard the Duck was," said artist Jim Starlin. "He disconnected pretty well, despite the fact that his name was on the books for a long time."

Jack – hair graying at the temples, a few lines etched into his face, now favoring sweaters and plaid slacks – and Stan – youthful, rangy, mustached, longer hair combed to the side – discussed what Jack would do for the company this time around. "Anytime Jack was there I was delighted," Stan said. "He was a guy I could give anything to." He listened to Jack say he wouldn't do *The Incredible Hulk*, *Thor*, or *The Fantastic Four*. During these preliminary discussions, Jack's former assistant Mark Evanier suggested a wartime version of *Captain America* or *Sgt. Fury* so his dialogue wouldn't seem as dated and editors wouldn't ask him to include their heroes in his stories; but Marvel was indifferent to *Sgt. Fury*, and Roy was already including the old Cap in the action-packed World War II series *The Invaders*. Besides, Stan wanted Jack on a noteworthy book like *Captain America*. Though he had helped bring the character to life decades ago, and helped breathe new life into him during the 1960s, "he didn't particularly want to do *Captain America* again," Evanier said. "He didn't want to do characters that other people had handled. In fact, he would always say, 'If you give me a character, I'm going to do my version, not anybody else's. If you want somebody else's version, give it to somebody else.' He didn't even want to read other people's versions of his characters," Evanier continued. "It was not a question of not respecting or liking them, although I don't think he liked much of what he read at Marvel at that point; it was simply how he had to work."

Even so, he agreed to write and draw Cap's adventures, and the book's current writer Tony Isabella, a longtime Kirby fan, called to wish him luck and say he'd gladly provide information about recent events in the increasingly complicated, politically charged series. By now, writer Steve Englehart had reflected the nation's disillusionment about Watergate and Vietnam through an extended story in which Cap uncovered corruption in the highest branches of the government, resigned from his post as America's supersoldier, removed his famous flag-colored costume, dressed himself in a black costume, cape, and domino mask, adopted the name "the Nomad," and spent months traveling the country as in *Easy Rider*, encountering other young people who reacted to the tumult of the previous decade by withdrawing, turning their backs on politics and society. Isabella's offer was gracious, kind, but unnecessary: He wouldn't be reading any of the issues, Jack told him. If anything, he'd be starting over. Bringing the hero back to his roots, losing the identity crisis, and making him heroic again. "And quite frankly, I thought that was a good approach," Isabella said.

Marvel also wanted him to adapt the eight-year-old movie *2001: A Space Odyssey* in one of their enormous ten-by-fourteen treasury editions. For his seventy-page adaptation, Jack covered his desk with still photos from the classic film but alienated fans by drawing heroes with stock character faces – strong, square jaws, furrowed brows, whatever hairdo he had in mind at the moment – rather than the likenesses of actors like Keir Dullea. And instead of director Stanley Kubrick's extended silent sequences, he filled panels with extravagant scenes of outer space, hackneyed dialogue, and anti-climactic captions.

When he traveled to another convention, Stan spent much of his time behind a podium onstage heavily promoting the fact that Jack was back with the company. He trumpeted Jack's return despite the fact that his DC work left him cold. "I looked at it," said Stan. "I wasn't the world's biggest fan of Jack's writing. I think his story-telling sense was superb. I don't think he was a great wordsmith, but his artwork, his concepts, and his imagination were magnificent. So I would look at what he did and it always *looked* great."

After the oversize treasury edition of *2001* came out, Marvel decided to publish an ongoing series. The licensing fee for the tabloid gave them the right to do this for a certain amount of time, so "they said, 'Well, let's use the name since it's free,'" Evanier recalled.

Jack wasn't thrilled with the assignment, but publicly he did his part to talk it up, filling letters pages with kooky upbeat essays. He drew and wrote stories that followed the film's three-act structure: A hero is introduced; the hero is in peril; the floating humming black stone, a galactic mystery called the Monolith, appears, bathes the hero in otherworldly light, transports him on a faster-than-light, sight-filled journey across various dimensions, and transforms him into the glowing, highly evolved infant life form. Everything would have been fine – the series played to a few of his strengths, and his characters were compelling (including the comic fan in one issue who somehow became a hero in another world and learned everything he believed about heroes and comics was false) – but behind the scenes, he was caught between Marvel's businesspeople, the publisher's editorial office, and the film studio itself. The three could not agree on whether the *2001* comic should feature a recurring character. One side would call to tell Jack to include returning characters, and he'd set his thoughts on creating one. Then another side would call to say, "No, it has to be an anthology." During the months he spent trying to please everyone, the book developed an uneven, inconsistent tone. He'd bring a two-part adventure to an abrupt end, following with a self-contained tale of a hero, the eerie black stone, and the transformation. "Finally, all of a sudden, the people got in sync, and said, 'Quick! We want a recurring character in the next issue,' and Jack had already started this thing about this robot character, so he gave him a fancier name like Mr. Machine and said, 'That's our recurring character,'" recalled Evanier. "People at Marvel said, 'Hey, that's great, but Mr. Machine is the trademarked name of a toy by Ideal Toys,' so he changed it to Machine Man." Jack was just getting used to the idea of drawing his purple robot with red-and-yellow eyes, and human emotions locked in a battle with a ghastly stand-in for Satan – trying to rob him of his plastic human face mask, his identity, and his free will – when the licensing contract expired and Marvel changed the plan again. "They said, 'Well, this book isn't selling well enough to warrant paying for another term of using the name, so let's drop the book and just keep this Machine Man character going on his own so we don't have to pay a licensing fee for the title to MGM.'" With a shrug, Jack began working on a Machine Man title.

Captain America was just as tumultuous. Publicly, he told reporters – including one from Marvel's in-house fanzine *FOOM* – he was delighted to be reunited with the character. But his approach to the title – removing Cap from Marvel's sixty-five other titles and its universe and having him battle Latin American dictator the Swine, who physically resembled John Lennon – caused a few employees in the office to openly insult his work. "It just seemed as if the combination of Jack's writing and drawing didn't grab the Marvel readers as much as the combination of Stan and Jack had before," Roy Thomas later said. "Times had changed, and Jack had been in the field a long time, and maybe he was slowly winding down, even though certainly the work looked great."

When Jim Shooter, a young, seven-foot-tall associate editor who began his career at age thirteen with popular stories for DC's *Legion of Super-Heroes*, received some of Jack's pages, he said later, "I would gently edit them. If what he said in a balloon made sense at all, I left it alone, except for punctuation. If I figured out what he was trying to say and he wasn't really saying that, I would suggest that maybe he change it, and he always did. He didn't have a problem with it. He was a joy."

Jack, however, told his friends and associates a different story. His deal called for him to be his own editor. And he didn't see the changes made by the office until his books were on sale on the newsstand. The more changes they made, the more he resented Marvel for reneging on a promise. Archie Goodwin, Shooter's superior, a well-loved editor with experience working for Warren Publishing, honored the agreement, even if Jack's stories didn't always seem to make sense. One month, when he sent Goodwin an issue, Jack forgot to include a page. Rather than asking in-house artists to fill the void and repair the story with new material, Goodwin took the pages to Stan. That night, Goodwin called Jack at home to delicately address the issue; Jack calmly explained that he forgot to include a page and quickly sent it in. Even when it appeared something was wrong, Stan and Goodwin didn't change anything; they gave Jack the benefit of the doubt and had faith that he would, as his own editor, provide whatever solution was needed.

Jack's grievances were legion, however. He was especially plagued by a problematic assistant editor – never named by Evanier – who kept telling anyone who'd listen, including some of Jack's closest friends, that he should be writing Jack's dialogue. Young, supercilious, contemptuous of Jack's writing, but dying to have his name listed alongside Jack's in a "Lee and Kirby"–type credit, he also ignored that Jack's contract called for no one to alter his work. He changed a Captain America story to the point where Jack's blood boiled, and Jack gave Goodwin an earful of more complaints.

"Jack was not getting along with certain people on the Marvel editorial staff," Evanier explained. "And there were some arguments back and forth. He felt gratuitous changes had been made and appealed first to Archie Goodwin. Archie agreed that someone in the office was changing material that didn't need changing. Then Archie left as editor and Jim Shooter took over, and again, there was some rewriting. At this point, Jack went to Stan Lee and sent Stan 'before and after' photocopies and said, 'Look what they changed here.' And I have a memo someplace in Jack's files where Stan wrote back and says, 'You're right. I'm gonna see what I can do about stopping this.'" Once Stan intervened – he was working in Hollywood but still exercised considerable influence on the comics and authority in the office – "the process was cut back on, but it was never stopped."

Though Stan did what he could to ensure that Jack's work experience was as easygoing as possible, the irony was that, for Jack, his defender and advocate was partly responsible for the controversy between him and a few of the kids in the office. Jack knew the score. Many of these assistant editors wanted to be his new Stan Lee; they'd achieve this by working with him on stories that recaptured the feel of the tales he and Stan had told during the 1960s. But Jack never forgot how the media had credited Stan as sole creator – a file Jack started contained one hundred articles that claimed Stan did it all himself (including creating *Captain America* and drawing many of the stories) – and how the Fireside Books reprints of their early collaborations had included the credit "By Stan Lee" on their covers, and this made him unwilling to work with any other writer. If he did, Jack worried, this person would wind up getting full credit for plots or characters he'd create with his artwork. After refusing anyone who asked, he felt this assistant-turned-editor should take the hint already. But to his surprise, the editor kept pushing to have someone take over his dialogue. And one day, the contentious relationship reached a disrespectful new low when the guy called to say he'd received the new issue of *Captain America* in the mail and felt the artwork was breathtaking, but "everyone here in the office agrees that the writing is shit."

Soon, Jack learned that indignant employees were telling fanzines, in anonymous phone interviews, that his writing was responsible for the dip in the book's sales. Then someone called Evanier to warn that unless Jack had the caller or Evanier write his dialogue, he'd wreck his career. The fact that he wouldn't give in and include recognized guest stars in *Captain America* only added to Jack's growing image as someone who wasn't a team player.

The same unalleviated complaints followed him to another new book he brought Marvel. Titled *The Celestials*, the series expanded on the aliens-perceived-as-gods theme he'd sprinkled throughout his work since the old Simon & Kirby days. With author Erich von Daniken's *Chariots of the Gods?* topping the best-seller lists, Jack felt the idea was timely again and pitched it to Marvel. Someone at Marvel felt the new series could piggyback off the nonfiction book's success and changed the title from *The Celestials* to *Return of the Gods* (during a period in which DC was moving forward with plans to revive the Fourth World pantheon in *Showcase* as "Return of the New Gods"). In their enthusiasm to cash in, Marvel also created a cover with the new title presented in the same font as the logo on Daniken's celebrated work. Once someone in the legal department saw the cover, the title, and the same font published in a few comics, however, he told the editors, "Wait a minute, we're going to get our rear ends sued off here." The title changed again, to *The Eternals*.

Chapter 15

When Universal executive Frank Price expressed interest in optioning the television rights to enduring Lee-Kirby creations Hulk, the Mighty Thor, Nick Fury, Agent of S.H.I.E.L.D., and the Invincible Iron Man, as well as Jack's co-creation Captain America, Everett's Sub-Mariner, Burgos's the Human Torch, and Ditko's Dr. Strange, Jack Kirby suddenly saw Marvel executives heavily promote Stan as sole creator of the properties and again describe him as just another penciler who followed orders and drew what he was told. This seemed to be the pattern whenever Hollywood expressed interest in the heroes, and while it saddened him, there was nothing he could do but accept it. He was under contract; he couldn't start knocking on doors at his age; he and Roz were facing intermittent health problems, and – after toiling in comics for decades, bouncing from one company to the other and back again, without any sort of pension – they needed the money. So he gritted his teeth and dealt with it as he always did, internalizing his rage, frustration, and despair and moving on to the next character or story. Gripping his pencil, facing the upper-left-hand corner of the empty white Bristol Board on his battered old desk, he let the pencil in his quick-moving right hand fill its blank surface with more of his disheveled, stonelike heroes, maddened wide-eyed villains, strange new worlds, and futuristic technological wonders, weapons, spacecraft, and gadgets. Roz, his loving wife of decades, the sounding board for new ideas, an off-the-record, unbendable business manager, and Jack's staunch defender against exploitative fans, was angrier about Marvel playing down his contributions "because she wanted to leave a lot to her kids, her family," Mike Thibodeaux recalled. "And if things had worked out differently, she could have."

Too old to redefine himself, or to begin anew in another industry, Jack agreed to pitch in when Stan asked for help with a new *Fantastic Four* cartoon. In Hollywood, working with Hanna-Barbera on the project, Stan faced an interesting dilemma: Since Price held the rights to the Human Torch, and they didn't want anyone using the character, this second Hanna-Barbera adaptation of the comic would have to offer the team with a new member. Stan first asked *The New X-Men's* co-creator, Dave Cockrum, a gifted artist with a flair for costume design, to conceive a miniature R2-D2-like robot. Privately opposed to the thought of replacing the Torch, and unaware of the deal with Universal, Cockrum submitted one impractical idea after another. "One of them looked like a trash can on wheels with a 4 on it," he said later. "Another was a lamp on wheels with a 4 on it." After six of these, Stan finally told him, "You know, you're really hard to work with!" Jack, on the other hand, quickly presented a streamlined little robot named ZZ-123, who could fly and wound foes with fitted lasers and other devices. After changing the name to H.E.R.B.I.E., Stan downplayed the silver robot's combat capabilities and included him in the group as comic relief.

During the first season, which basically updated many of his old collaborations with Stan, Jack was happy to see his designs on television and his name included in the final credits, though he was irked about not being paid for the second use of this material. When Hanna-Barbera wanted to move the show to NBC for its second series, and after Alex Toth and animator Doug Wildey both said they were too busy to do it (at the time, Wildey was helping competing studio DePatie-Freleng sell a *Godzilla* series to the same network), Evanier stepped in to propose that the studio bring Jack in to help create a presentation. By this point, Jack was miserable at Marvel, thinking that when his contract came up for renewal in a year or two, he would finally leave. The problem was that only two companies could pay what he needed to support his family. Since he viewed DC, where he'd seen the Fourth World fail, as a step down, and he refused to stay at Marvel, "he was just getting very nervous," said Mark Evanier. "Once again, this feeling of 'I'm a prisoner; I gotta find an escape route.'"

Jack met with Iwao Takamoto, the animation legend who designed *Scooby-Doo*, and left the Hanna-Barbera building with an assignment to deliver huge drawings of the Fantastic Four within two weeks. Forty-eight hours later, he brought Hanna-Barbera the giant pictures; Joe Barbera, bowled over, asked him to design things for other non-Marvel shows. When NBC, equally impressed with the art, wanted to buy the show, Evanier added, "Our old friend Lee Gunther moved in and locked up the rights to *The Fantastic Four* so that it would be produced by DePatie-Freleng instead." Hanna-Barbera objected, so the studios and NBC struck a deal: Hanna-Barbera would get the *Godzilla* series with Doug Wildey as producer; DePatie-Freleng would handle *The Fantastic Four*; and NBC would purchase and air both programs on Saturday mornings.

Where people at Marvel called him "Jack the Hack," covering his art pages with invective and hanging them on walls, where he'd worried about where to work when he left, Jack now had major animation studios DePatie-Freleng and Hanna-Barbera both trying to lure him to their shows with decent salaries and the ability to work from home. Since DePatie-Freleng and Marvel would, owing to NBC's deal, produce *The Fantastic Four*, and he didn't like or trust the publishing company anymore – and didn't want to do anything to make the company think he forgave past slights – Jack considered staying with Hanna-Barbera. At the same time, he wanted finally to be involved with a TV adaptation of the groundbreaking superteam. If he didn't go with DePatie-Freleng and Marvel, others would reap the benefits. And his workload would be even harder to support. His contract with Marvel called for him to deliver a set number of pages each week, and the company would count his animation work as part of the quota. At Hanna-Barbera, he'd have to do their work, then find time to create the fifteen pages Marvel expected each week. At age sixty, with health problems, he didn't have the energy. He chose DePatie-Freleng and Marvel's *Fantastic Four* cartoon.

Stan soon called artist John Romita in New York to complain about the animators. In the past, they'd grumbled about having to put so many lines on Spider-Man's web-covered costume and limited the detail to his mask, gloves, and boots. "Now they were going to have to do a lot of lines for the Thing, who looks like a lot of broken rocks," said Romita. "So they were cheating on it, and Stan was asking me to simplify the characters so they wouldn't leave blank spaces. They were just taking the cheap way out." He added, "They always simplified to the point where it didn't look like the characters."

Then Marvel president Jim Galton told Stan he'd convinced CBS to purchase a live-action *Spider-Man* show. During filming of a two-hour pilot, Stan called Romita to ask for an opinion and discuss changes. At one point, Stan said, "You can't believe what they're asking me to do." The producers claimed they couldn't make Spider-Man blue and red. "Can you believe it? They can't make him blue."

"Why not?"

"Well, they tell me that to get the action scenes, they need a matte, and they need to film him against a matte and the matte board, and the background is blue." If Spidey was the same color, people would be able to view the background through him, so producers wanted to make his costume red and black.

"You know, there's nothing wrong with Spider-Man being black," Romita told him. He was actually supposed to be red and black in the comics. The blue appeared on his costume as highlights because artists didn't want him to resemble a cardboard cutout. But over the years, artists started leaving him "open for color," which led to zealous colorists filling these empty spaces with lots of blue. "So it evolved into a blue-and-red costume, but he was supposed to be black and red originally," Romita explained.

During their call, he told Stan, "Now that he's known as a

red-and-blue character, it's a crime that they have to make him black on the screen." After noting that it wouldn't be the end of the world, he asked, "Why don't they paint the matte a different color?"

"What do you mean?"

"If they make the matte green, and make him blue, it wouldn't matter."

"And he got so mad," Romita remembered. "They were constantly taking advantage of him. They always gave him this line that he almost engraved on his desk: 'We know movies and you know comics; we know television and you know comics, so let us do our business, and we're telling you this is the way it has to be.' And a lot of times they bluffed him out." Later, while helping to develop a new *Spider-Man* cartoon, Stan foresaw a few potential problems and called to ask Romita to provide sketches for characterization. "This is the way I want the animators to make Peter Parker look," he said. "This is the way I want them to make the Scorpion look." Romita handed over beginner's versions of the characters to pass on to animators.

After the September 1977 live-action *Spider-Man* pilot scored extraordinary ratings, CBS ordered a series, and Stan watched in frustration as producers further altered Spidey's appearance. In addition to outsize silver wristbands (the web-shooters in the comic version were usually concealed under gloves), they fitted him with a bulky, matching "utility belt" (à la *Batman*) and replaced his silver eyes with black lenses. Within a month, however, CBS unceremoniously yanked the show from its regular schedule and opted instead to air episodes as infrequent specials. "I felt they had lost all the qualities that made Spider-Man popular in the comic books," Stan lamented. "There wasn't enough human interest and characterization, not enough humor, and I tried to tell them that, but in those days they didn't particularly listen to me. The show didn't do very well, it only lasted a short time, and then it was off the air." *The Incredible Hulk*, however, also part of the deal with Price and Universal, was another story.

CBS wanted to add Stan and Jack's raging green giant to its

lineup. After producer Kenneth Johnson finished *The Bionic Woman* (a spin-off of the hit *The Six Million Dollar Man*), Universal's Frank Price told the esteemed producer that he'd bought the rights to Marvel heroes. When he asked Johnson which he wanted to work on, the producer answered, "Gee, none of them, thanks."

Once he saw he could replace Stan's formula with a chase theme that evoked Victor Hugo's *Les Misérables* – and, simultaneously, earlier television series like the long-running *The Fugitive* – Johnson's zest for the character and project grew. In his effort to reorganize the basic concept, he wound up asking Stan why the Hulk's irradiated skin was green and not red ("the color of rage"). He also decided the name Bruce Banner was inane and revised it to the more masculine David Banner.

Bill Bixby, the soft-spoken dramatic actor who appeared in the popular dramedy *The Courtship of Eddie's Father*, was also initially indifferent to the show; his enthusiasm for the role of Banner, Hulk's alter ego (who traveled cross-country, tried to elude a meddlesome reporter, and became embroiled in and then solved various guest stars' personal problems), soared once he read Johnson's radical revision. After producers filmed and rejected Richard Kiel (a physical giant best known for his role as the iron-fanged villain Jaws in the James Bond installments) and instead cast bodybuilder Lou Ferrigno as the creature, *The Incredible Hulk* pilot debuted to condescending reviews and remarkably high ratings. "Oh, now that was excellent," said Stan. "I was more than satisfied. Because Ken did it in a very intelligent way and made all the right decisions." Johnson didn't have the Hulk utter the dialogue Stan once penciled into his comic book captions (monosyllabic statements like "Hulk smash!"). Johnson also emphasized Bill Bixby's character, role, and quiet vulnerability, limiting the Hulk's appearances to four minutes in the beginning and four or five destructive moments during each episode's finale. "And you'd wait for those few minutes when he became the Hulk, but most of the show was a quite intelligent human-interest program involving Bill Bixby and his problems," Stan recalled. "I think that's what made the show so successful.

Adults could watch it and not feel they were just watching the story of a silly green giant running around hurting people."

When he wasn't working on animation designs or rough pencil storyboards for *The Fantastic Four* series, Jack continued to create comics for Marvel. His heroes were as bulky as ever, with etched faces that spoke of complex inner lives and weary eyes that had seen too much, but his stories were grander, more ambitious, unlike anything the company was doing in other titles.

Roy Thomas supposedly suggested that he draw and write Black Panther. Though Panther's series and the title *Jungle Action* had just been canceled, Thomas figured his co-creator, who also worked on the earlier Coal Tiger, could make something of the character in a new decade. "I think he was slowing down a little, and he just wanted to do those couple of books," Thomas explained.

In the "Bullpen Bulletins" column, someone claimed, "What Jack came up with was so different, exciting, and inimitably his own, we just had to start it as its own title." Despite the grand send-off and subject matter – a costumed hero facing all manner of supervillains – Jack refused to repeat himself. It would have been easy; other artists did it all the time, rehashing the same theme ad infinitum, for higher pay, compliments, and more assignments. And while presenting standard superhero fare would have worked to repair fractured relationships with some staff members, after a lifetime of drawing other people's stories, after years of having to compromise, and most important, after having to promote values that he didn't agree with or believe to be true – and with the freedom, at last, to write, draw, edit, and control the creative side of his books – Jack delivered the stories he wanted to tell. They led, however, to yet more complaints from editors. Instead of race and politics, and the disillusioned tone then fashionable in comics and other media – with protagonists turning their backs on society and the idealistic goals of the 1960s to look out for number one – Jack showed the Panther and his comical sidekick, Abner Little, on archaeological missions, battling enemies for possession of religious artifacts like the Brass Frog. In years to come, a similar fusion of top-secret jungle hideouts, antagonistic tribes, lost maps, old-school gangsters, and condescending princesses would make a worldwide phenomenon of George Lucas and Steven Spielberg's *Raiders of the Lost Ark*. But when Jack did it, as usual a few years ahead of his time, the young editors at Marvel felt *Black Panther*'s pulp elements would alienate their audience. Even so, Jack stuck to his guns and presented stories that, while not his most memorable, and nowhere near as ambitious or daring as the Fourth World, did manage to please a small, loyal, somewhat older and nostalgic audience.

Before he knew it, Stan asked Jack to make another foray into the animation business. Once he heard that DC was working with Filmation to pitch *Kamandi* to CBS, and that CBS was interested, DePatie-Freleng's head of development, Lee Gunther, told Stan, "Hey, we've got the guy who created Kamandi here, we've got his services. . . ."

Stan asked Jack to create something that could sell as a Saturday morning cartoon. By May 20, 1977, he had completed a pencil drawing of a man riding a stone-textured *Tyrannosaurus rex*, firing a gun at tiny, costumed aliens. He titled it *Devil Dinosaur of the Phantom Continent*, drew two smiling stock faces at the bottom with old-fashioned hairdos – heavy on the midwest bangs – then wrote, "Featuring Rokki and Krayg." After shortening the title to *Devil Dinosaur*, replacing the humans with Moon Boy, and making it comprehensible for young readers (achieved by having characters utter dialogue like "Don't lose courage, stone-hand! Cling to the devil-beast!"), Marvel published April 1978's *Devil Dinosaur* No. 1. When some readers saw this new work and considered a few of the goofy antics in *Black Panther* (the hero and his buddy searching for Samurai City), and considered also how so many of his works were canceled pretty quickly – and, if they really followed his career, remembered how the "Kirby Is Coming" campaign led to an anticlimactic New Gods saga that vanished, before officially concluding, in just two years – they assumed that what anonymous editors were implying in interviews was true, that Jack, after decades, was finally all washed up. Many people in the office shared this impression, even though Jack's assignment hadn't been to create a standard Marvel comic. "It was to come up with something that Marvel could sell as a Saturday morning show," Evanier clarified. For nine issues, hoping *Devil Dinosaur* could become a Saturday morning hit, Jack delivered simple but action-packed stories, teeming with richly detailed panoramic views of prehistoric earth, enormous dinosaurs in battle, alien invaders emerging from spacecraft and posing as gods, cavewomen in peril, and simple but expressive captions and dialogue. In the end, *Kamandi* never sold; *Devil Dinosaur* didn't, either. Editors quickly canceled the title, convincing some fans that Jack was rushing headlong to obsolescence with his eccentric, noncommercial concepts.

He was getting used to the idea that yet another book had been killed when editors began to complain about *The Eternals*. In addition to disliking his dialogue (which was sometimes ludicrous but always earnest, as in the scene when an innocent bystander ran through the crowded metropolitan streets yelling, "Run! Run! The Devil's come back from space with an army of Demons!"), they wanted more renowned Marvel heroes in the book. And with it, of course, more superhero fights, more morals about great power and great responsibility, and less downbeat, fatalistic scenes of villains teaching deluded, self-righteous heroes that the bad guys sometimes – in fact, usually – won. To appease them, Jack included a few S.H.I.E.L.D. agents and the Thing – only to reveal that the hero was actually a man in a Thing Halloween mask. When he threw the Hulk into August 1977's issue, he later revealed that it was merely a cosmic-powered robot. Frustrated editors reacted by claiming in his letters page that a "controversy" was brewing about whether he should write his own dialogue and include other Marvel characters. Tony Isabella, who wrote letters pages for Marvel, said, "That was my first inkling that people at Marvel had a problem with Jack's deal."

His dialogue *was* stilted and filled with odd punctuation. One issue of *Captain America*, for instance, found the Red Skull addressing a female captive, the hero's love interest, with, "Oh, to have the confidence of youth! Exercise one's fantasies – and to reach for the stars! Foolish snip of a girl! You won't bring me to heel! Time may do it – but never one such as yourself! I am of a kind that dares to seize the throat of a world!"

Once again, his critics contacted fanzines, anonymously, to claim that his writing was killing sales. They made the claim despite the fact that besides top-selling *Spider-Man* and *Hulk*, every Marvel comic – including the ones they wrote or edited – experienced similar erratic, inexplicable sales dips. Even so, Jim Shooter would later explain, "it wasn't selling. We had single-digit sales figures for *Captain America*, and at that time the Marvel line average was up near fifty percent."

Though he was busy in Hollywood, Stan once again became involved. Evanier claimed that Stan asked him to start writing Jack's dialogue. Evanier, who also disliked Jack's dialogue at this point, said he'd help with the writing only if Jack agreed. Marvel called Jack to say *Captain America*'s sales were down and that he'd have to work with the editorial staff and a dialogue writer; Jack answered, "In that case, I'd rather leave the book." When he learned Evanier and Marvel had been discussing this without his knowledge, he also wrongly suspected Evanier of trying to undermine his position.

As with *The Eternals*, the letters page in *Captain America*, "Let's Rap with Cap," turned slowly against him. Letters noted that his art was superb, but the writing was appalling. With more editors griping, Stan soon came to agree that *Captain America* needed to be closer to the shared Marvel Universe, especially since Hollywood was beginning to express interest in bringing the hero to television. But when Stan asked Jack to use villains from other books – a compromise that would let both sides win and hopefully inspire readers of other titles to see their favorite characters and begin buying *Captain America* – Jack refused. Stan then told amiable editor Archie Goodwin they should have Jack do something else. Jack told Stan this was fine. At the time, he was in the middle of a story about Cap and his Stan-created African American sidekick, the Falcon, battling a goggle-eyed, wing-wearing villain called Night Flyer. The Night Flyer had somehow blinded Cap. In his final issue, Jack had Cap miraculously regain his sight, without explanation, then showed his usual final panel for a series that had been canceled prematurely, newly healed Cap and the Falcon turning their backs on readers and walking away. "Perhaps the Night Flyer deserves the credit," he had Cap say. "When he fired that early shot close to my eyes, he must have . . . ah . . . jogged the proper nerve into action!" The letters page ended this chapter of his life and career by noting that "the celebrated Mr. K" had ended a two-year stint that had been "one big roller-coaster ride of incredible encounters and fantastic folks."

The irony was that Marvel told him his ideas were old-fashioned just when a new movie, including identical elements, was about to forever change everything about the Hollywood film industry. The movie was *Star Wars*. With Marvel sales at an all-new low, Roy Thomas went to dinner with Ed Summer, owner of the Supersnipe Comic Emporium on Manhattan's Upper East Side. Accompanying Summer was film director George Lucas, Summer's old film school classmate, a silent partner in the store, and creator of *American Graffiti*, one of Roy's favorite movies. During the meal, Thomas didn't pay much attention to Lucas's discussion of a movie called *The Star Wars* but did feel Lucas had been reading a few Jack Kirby comics. "I don't know if George Lucas ever quite admitted it," he said later, "but I got the impression in my conversations with him that there was a little influence there."

Within months, Lucas's people contacted Marvel to see if they'd adapt the film as a comic. In the past, Martin Goodman told editors he didn't want rockets, ray guns, or robots in his books; though Goodman was gone, Marvel rejected the idea of a *Star Wars* comic. Ed Summer and George's right-hand man, Charles Lippincott, were undeterred. During a subsequent visit with Roy Thomas, they asked him to persuade Marvel to reconsider. Thomas figured Marvel would reject it again but told the company they'd receive the license to a big movie for next to nothing. The circulation director asked Thomas to get the adaptation done in one or two issues and kept trying to cancel the book even as Thomas followed his six-issue adaptation with new *Star Wars* stories. "*Star Wars* single-handedly saved Marvel," Jim Shooter said later. "And that kept us alive."

Jack himself felt the name Luke Skywalker sounded suspiciously like Mark Moonrider from *The Forever People*, and that Lucas's the Force was similar to the New Gods' vague cosmic essence the Source. In *Star Wars*, a kind, gray-haired mentor urged Luke to join a galactic battle and returned from the dead, just the way Himon recruited Scott Free in *Mister Miracle* and also overcame death. Like Darkseid, Darth Vader ruled Stormtroopers and lived on a planet that had a huge circle carved into its side (like the flaming fire pit he'd always drawn on Apokolips). And Darth Vader served the Dark Side. Later, actor Mark Hamill, who played Luke Skywalker in the film and had read and enjoyed his Fourth World books, told Jack that upon arriving on the set and first seeing Darth Vader, he'd thought, Oh, it's Dr. Doom.

The film's light sabers resembled the Mega-Rod carried by Mister Miracle's girlfriend, Big Barda, and opponent Granny Goodness (who strapped hers to her right hip). Halfway through *Star Wars*, the heroes landed in a pit in the Death Star and tried to prevent walls from crushing them. Pages sixteen to eighteen in *Mister Miracle* No. 2 showed Miracle and his tiny sidekick, Oberon, falling into their own pit, Miracle touching the walls, mud rising, and Oberon yelling, "Scott! Do something! Before this mud covers us!" Like the Fourth World, *Star Wars* hinged on past events that included infants being taken from their planets and their real fathers. Lucas showed flying cars similar to those in *Mister Miracle*.

The more he considered *Star Wars*, friend Mike Thibodeaux explained, the more he noticed other connections. "Oh, constantly," Thibodeaux said. "I don't know if we should get into this. Jack didn't want any money or anything from Lucas, but he wished that Lucas had at least admitted where he got most of those ideas. I remember him saying one time, 'Just admit.' He even signed something to say he wouldn't go for any financial gain."

Where Lucas might have seen the future of film in Jack's work, Marvel kept calling him a tired old hack. But he figured he could stick it out until his contract expired. In early 1978, however, months before it expired, he learned Stan was preparing to leave for Hollywood. Jim Galton agreed with Lee Gunther that Marvel and DePatie-Freleng should form a partnership, and Galton wanted Stan to work closely with Gunther for a year, to sell more characters to other studios.

As a result, Stan was trying to persuade Jim Shooter to accept an editor in chief position no one seemed to want for very long.

Roy Thomas told Stan he should reconsider hiring Shooter for the top spot. "In fact, I advised Stan in writing not to give the job to Shooter – not to fire Shooter, but not to give him that job – because the people I knew really would not want to work under him." But Archie Goodwin had just announced that he was leaving. And, Thomas claimed, "Stan showed Shooter my letter, and I'm sure that helped our relationship enormously. I was willing to start, as Jim said he was, from square one, but it never really worked out."

Shooter felt that some writers had lost their way. One of the first things he wanted to do, he told Stan, was abolish the writer-editor position. Stan replied, "Okay, draw up a plan." Many writer-editors, accustomed to a high level of freedom and independence, protested and left for DC. Then, since U.S. copyright law had changed in 1976 – so that freelancers could now claim copyrights on anything created before this year (unless they signed a paper acknowledging that it was done under a work-for-hire arrangement) – Marvel's business department and legal counsel told Shooter he'd have to ask creators to sign a separate document giving Marvel the rights to characters and concepts they'd included in their stories. With Galton, Gunther, and Stan pitching characters to network television, and television networks interested in cashing in on the trend for superheroes – now that a live-action *Superman* movie had begun – copyrights were more important than ever.

But some creators refused to sign. "As long as they didn't sign,

Marvel was buying first North American rights to their work," Shooter explained. "And of course, the pile of work we didn't own was getting bigger and bigger." In response, Marvel began to include tersely worded work-for-hire contracts on the backs of paychecks issued to freelancers. Signing the check was akin to agreeing to a non-negotiable contract. "If you didn't sign that check," Jack said, "you didn't get paid." Jack's refusal to sign this or any other work-for-hire agreement worried Marvel.

It was a delicate time. By now Siegel and Schuster were making as many headlines as Warner Brothers' big-budget *Superman* movie. The creative duo – who, as two high school kids, had sold for $130 the rights to a hero who birthed an industry – hoped to receive credit and royalties, a precedent that could affect how every major publisher conducted business and treated the creators of their celebrated, money-spinning properties. "Jerry Siegel and Joe Schuster had disappeared from the world for about fifteen years because they were preparing a lawsuit to take to the Supreme Court to recapture the rights to Superman," artist Neal Adams explained. "Their lawyers had told them they should not talk publicly about this subject and had advised them, considering the circumstances that they had been in previously, to wait the amount of time it would take to recapture the rights to Superman. They must have been about forty-five years old when this advice was given to them. They waited until they were nearly sixty. They would have been much better off had they gone directly to DC Comics and tried to get some rights along the way or payment or something. But they were taking the big gamble. Now Jerry Siegel had a heart condition and Joe Schuster continued to have an eye condition that made him essentially legally blind. In those fifteen years, Jerry for the most part was working as a clerk making $7,500 a year. Joe, the artist, who was legally blind but could draw, was essentially blackballed from the industry and had to become a messenger. So the creator of Superman was a messenger in New York City, often through a winter where he couldn't afford an overcoat. I had asked about these guys for several years, and every time I was told, Don't ask: You don't want to know."

When he was fifty-nine years old, Siegel wrote a nine-page letter to the Academy of Comic Book Arts, where Adams was the president. The letter, also sent to newspapers and television stations and written up in *The Washington Post*, described what had happened to them and detailed how they had depended on lawyers to get them to the Supreme Court but, as the time approached, their lawyers did not remain in contact with them. They tried to call them and couldn't get hold of them, and they missed their window of opportunity to make the appeal. After waiting fifteen years and not saying anything to anybody, they lost their chance. What were they to do? "I watched the trail of articles dwindle and disappear," Adams recalled, "and realized that no matter what efforts they were going to make, essentially it would lead to nothing, because it would just dwindle away." Adams called Siegel and said, "Look, I know your lawyers aren't going to do anything for you and any opportunity they have to do anything is gone, so I would like to represent you. I'm not going to represent you as a lawyer. I'm just gonna represent you as a person and then make some effort to get some money for you, to take care of you for the rest of your life.

"I can't guarantee any success," he added during their telephone conversation, "but I will spend whatever time it takes for me to undo this."

Siegel agreed, as did Joe – "Joe would do anything that Jerry said it was okay to do, and from that point on," Neal recalled, "I essentially represented their cause in the press and on television and however I could to let people know the creators of Superman were basically hung out to dry and that somebody ought to do something and the people that *should* do something are the people who run DC comics and have all this money."

Adams flew Siegel and his wife to New York. A news show picked up the hotel tab in exchange for an interview. "And after three and a half months of hard work and effort – on the part of myself, people who helped me out, and the National Cartoonists Society, who jumped in at the end – we got a living wage for these guys for the rest of their lives." DC also included a credit in each *Superman* comic that announced, "Created by Jerry Siegel and Joe Schuster."

At Marvel, editors kept a new generation busy imitating Jack's style. And if another company used his style – angular, muscular heroes with decorative squiggles and bold lines – to market non-Marvel toys or products, company lawyers promptly threatened to take legal action and claim infringement (it was the "Marvel style," they claimed, and they owned it). Jack didn't respect many of the people who spent their lives imitating what he'd done, but he did admire July 1977's *The Defenders* No. 50, by Keith Giffen and inked by Royer – a work that included a stunning two-page spread presenting a big bulky Hulk that looked as if it had been torn from an old Kirby comic and pasted into this modern team. "He did a pretty darn good job," he told his friend Mike Thibodeaux.

Meanwhile, Roy Thomas kept asking Jack to draw *The Fantastic Four*. Thomas tried to make things as beneficial and fair for Jack as possible. A top name in comics, Thomas said he'd do the writing but speak to Stan and others to ensure that Jack received credit for the plots he created with his artwork. He wouldn't receive much more money, he told Jack, but he'd be able to do as he pleased and see his name appear first in the credits. It was a decent offer, but Jack rejected it nonetheless. He'd only do it, Jack said, if Thomas gave him a panel-by-panel breakdown of each story. Thomas rightly felt this was ridiculous. "We'd have had such a closed-off relationship," he said later, "it wasn't worth doing. So I dropped the idea."

But he did ask if Jack would be willing to draw the Fantastic Four in an issue of *What If* titled "What If the Fantastic Four Were the Original Marvel Bullpen?" In this tale, instead of Reed Richards, Ben Grimm, Sue Storm, and Johnny Storm, Stan would appear in costume as Mister Fantastic, Jack would be the cigar-chomping, rock-covered Thing, former production manager Sol Brodsky would be the Human Torch, and Flo Steinberg – who quit the company when Goodman wouldn't give her a raise – would be the Invisible

Girl. Roy Thomas wanted to write the issue, but Jack said he wouldn't work with another writer. And if another artist handled it, he added, he wouldn't let them use his likeness. Roy let him create the story, but after reading the final work, Stan said that he disliked how Jack's character kept calling him "Stanley." Roy dutifully changed each reference to "Stan." And Jack never drew the Fantastic Four again in a Marvel comic.

With the Hulk on television each week, the character was more famous than ever. Jack had mixed feelings about the program. When he learned that its producers had asked Mark Evanier to write an episode, and Evanier had turned them down, he thanked him. Next, one of the show's writers – who lived nearby and admitted that prior to working on the show, he'd never read a comic – kept asking for free ideas, but Jack refused to provide any. Yet he watched the show each week and, strangely enough, accepted an invitation to appear in one episode. "They hired him to be a police artist sketching the Hulk in a precinct," recalled Thibodeaux. "He liked it. He liked Bill Bixby. He thought they did a good job on it."

By now, Stan's work in Hollywood kept him almost completely disconnected from the comics. At Marvel, Jim Shooter called the shots. "Stan was the publisher, but he never really had any authority and really didn't do anything," Shooter later said in an interview. His real job was to sell things to Hollywood. Shooter looked back fondly on his work with Jack during the 1960s – and sat with an old Kirby comic starring Captain America and the Human Torch, telling new artists Frank Miller and Steve Rude, "This is what comics ought to be." (To which Miller added, "He was not wrong.")

Times continued to change at the company. More young people were entering the industry. John Romita watched in horror as his son John junior expressed interest in a career as a comic book artist. "My son wanted to work at Marvel as soon as he got out of high school," the comic legend recalled. At age thirteen, John junior had created the well-regarded Spider-Man villain the Prowler. "Stan used one of my costumes and John junior's name," Romita continued, and from that moment on "there was no way I could have kept him out of comics."

Still, he tried. He was nervous about having his son enter a business he felt "was always a year away from extinction." Why would he want to be in it? "And also, why would you want to work seven days a week when you can work five days a week like your friends and make more money? Because frankly, I never made a lot of money in comics until the last five years I was in the business. Up until then, I worked much too hard and for too many hours and made much too little money." He told his son he'd be better off in advertising and begged him to attend college for two years before starting at Marvel. "He used to see me work through the night many times," Romita remembered. "He would come up before he went to school and see me still looking haggard and exhausted, and he'd rub my back because I used to get a pain right in the middle of my trapezius muscle. And he would rub it for me and he was practically in tears, saying, 'Gee, you didn't sleep at all, Dad. You must be dead tired.'

"I'd tell him, 'Nah, I'm okay.' But he could feel it. He was sensitive to it.

"That's why I used to throw that up to him and say, 'Don't you remember when you used to see me looking like a dead man in the morning?'" But John Romita Jr. was soon working on *Iron Man*, on a memorable run that ended with an award-winning story in which Tony Stark – the carefree, dashing, but ailing millionaire arms manufacturer of the bright pop art 1960s – succumbed to alcoholism, hit bottom after a few heart-wrenching issues, and entered Alcoholics Anonymous.

In Hollywood, Marvel started pushing *The Silver Surfer* as the next big film property, and one executive – singer Olivia Newton John's boyfriend at the time – optioned the rights. Stan was asked to create a new Surfer story and soon called Jack for help. Jack loved movies and felt this story might actually make it to the big screen. And the terms were generous: Jack would receive money, see the new story copyrighted to him and Stan alone, and have power to prevent Stan or anyone else from leaving his name out of the entire book. The pages he drew would also count toward the quota called for in his contract.

Marvel's production manager, John Verpoorten, then called Joe Sinnott to say, "We're doing a graphic novel on the Silver Surfer, and Stan and Jack would like you to be a part of it. Would you like to ink Jack's work?"

Sinnott answered, "I'd like to do it. But John, my only request is that I get credit on the splash page with Jack and Stan."

Verpoorten said, "No problem, Joe, no problem."

To convince movie producers that the new story, *The Ultimate Experience*, would make a great screenplay – and could easily be filmed without having to untangle rights from other studios – Stan and Jack retold the classic Galactus trilogy without the Fantastic Four. "The main idea was mine, and as usual I told Jack what I wanted the story to be and he went home and drew it in his own way, which was magnificent," Stan claimed. "I mean, it was so much fun for me to put in the dialogue, just looking at those drawings."

Mark Evanier, however, remembers Jack sitting at his typewriter, in his office, writing the plot and including a new love interest – then sending this outline to Stan with his penciled pages. He remembers Stan requesting changes that meant having to redraw over ten pages and changing the thrust of the story. He recalls Jack's vehement protests, heated arguments, then Jack finally capitulating and redrawing pages that accommodated Stan's revisions and dialogue.

When he saw the pages, Sinnott was stunned. Despite what John Verpoorten had promised, the book's first page read "Stan Lee and Jack Kirby present *The Silver Surfer*." "Of course there was no mention of me contributing. So when I inked this page, I penciled under Kirby and Stan Lee, 'Inking by Joe Sinnott,' and sent it back. But when the book came out, naturally, there was no credit given to me on the splash page." His name appeared in the rear of the book, near the colorist and letterer.

Jack was equally frustrated. As with 1974's *Origins of Marvel Comics*, 1975's *Bring on the Bad Guys*, and 1976's *The Superhero Women*, Fireside planned to credit the book *Ultimate Experience* to Stan alone. This time, however, Jack and Roz threatened to speak to a lawyer and take action. Jack's name was swiftly added to the cover. Though they shared credit and the copyright, Jack privately decided never to work with Stan again. He reached this decision just when Stan was viewing their collaboration as another masterpiece, proof that they still had it as a team. "My problem is I don't control the Marvel movies," Stan said decades later. "I have nothing to say about them. But if I did, I would just find a producer and give him that book and say, 'Here's your story, start filming.'"

When it came time to renew his contract with Marvel, Jack admitted to himself that he was tired of worn-out characters and clichéd stories and churning out fifteen meaningless pages a week for a company he couldn't trust. In the animation industry, the pay was better, the work was more challenging – he was able to fill board after board with new heroes, villains, gadgets, and settings, finally letting his imagination run riot and operate unfettered – and the people were more respectful: Veterans told him they'd grown up on his work, and Joe Barbera, himself a brilliant idea man, valued his contributions, his unassuming nature, his eagerness and sincere interest, and his hard-charging work ethic. "So when he got the opportunity to go into animation and make more money doing presentations than he could for doing a book, he dropped comics in a flash," said Steve Sherman. "'Fine! I'm done! I get a pension, I get health benefits, I get treated like a human being.'" He told people, "That's it! That's it with comics." After refusing to renew his contract with Marvel, telling the *Comics Journal* now was the right time to try other things in life, completing the final stories he owed the company, and shipping them off in the mail, he said with relief, "Okay, that's it."

Chapter 16

While freelancing for Hanna-Barbera, Jack sought for ways to maintain his involvement with comics. He considered opening a comic book shop and actually looked at spaces to rent but finally decided it was too risky. Then a businessman wanted to publish a line called Kirby Comics and suggested that a graphic novel that read like *Star Wars* would sell. At his board, Jack turned an old screenplay into the adventures of a hero named *Captain Victory*. Victory, the blond-haired, muscle-bound commander of the gargantuan spaceship *Dreadnaught Tiger*, led his Galactic Rangers – talking lions, reptiles, and aliens who walked like humans – into battle against the insect Lightning Lady, a villainous alien hiding on planet Earth with her armored troops and planning to turn citizens of a nearby small town into slaves in her Hive. *Captain Victory* countered Spielberg's feel-good ending in *Close Encounters of the Third Kind* by showing that aliens that went through the trouble of developing spacecraft capable of crossing the universe would visit planet Earth for one reason and one reason only: to take over – not hang out in the woods and shake hands with friendly earthlings. He hoped to further explore this theme in the sequel "Encounters of a Savage Kind," but the investor couldn't even cough up the cash to publish the first book.

Just as Jack set aside these pages, he heard that the new animation studio Ruby-Spears needed someone to create presentation art for ABC. The company had commissioned legendary artist Alex Toth to design the main characters for its *Kamandi*-like series *Thundarr the Barbarian*, and Toth had wowed ABC executives with his fair-haired barbarian Thundarr, who carried a laser sword; Thundarr's giant, shaggy assistant, Ookla the Mok (whose form and growls evoked the Wookiee Chewbacca of *Star Wars*); and curvy brunette sorceress Ariel, who flung destructive orbs of light from her delicate little hands and wore what resembled a blue, form-fitting, one-piece swimsuit with go-go boots. When the network asked to see more – the mutants, wizards, and monsters Thundarr would combat in his postapocalyptic world – and with Toth unavailable, Jack's former assistant Mark Evanier, by then writing for television (among his credits he was story editor for the crowd-pleasing hit sitcom *Welcome Back, Kotter*), and writer Steve Gerber, creator of the new series and also of Marvel's popular *Howard the Duck*, both recommended Jack to Ruby-Spears executive Joe Ruby.

ABC executives looked at Jack's designs and quickly bought the show. "Those characters were really outstanding," said Joe Ruby. "And I liked him so much, I asked him if he wanted to be on our staff, and he accepted."

Jack enjoyed creating each episode's ancillary characters and working with Ruby on proposals for other shows. Once a week, Roz drove him into Hollywood, where he dropped off pages and then took her to lunch. After decades of struggle, things were looking up. He was paid well, had health insurance for himself and Roz, and received vacation pay for the first time in his life. He could breathe and say proudly, "I'm out of comics."

At home, he'd fill twenty-by-thirty-inch presentation boards with detailed black-and-white drawings of characters, settings, villains, and more. Ruby-Spears would receive six of these a week. But Gil Kane (also working for the company) felt some weren't up to his usual standard. Wheels on vehicles weren't as round. Figures were short. Even so, many were excellent. "In fact, I wanted to steal one of the boards," Kane admitted. "They had all this stuff standing around there that they weren't able to use, and I figured that no one was going to miss one of 'em!"

After two years, ABC decided to cancel *Thundarr*. "They thought it was too violent for television," said Joe Ruby. NBC aired reruns for a year, to good ratings. "We were going to go do a spin-off with *Thundarr*, another season where they would meet kids along the way, some orphans who would tag along, and expand the episodes in that direction a little bit, but they didn't pick it up. Again, I think, they were afraid of the show. In those days, there was an awful lot of stuff about violence. By today's standards, it's very tame."

Jack continued to help develop ideas for new series. He'd submit them in pencil drawings or draw characters Joe Ruby described. But his ideas failed to sell. Ruby felt he was "a little too ahead of its time." His concepts struck television executives as being more like comic books than the simple fare networks preferred. "They were buying softer stuff," Ruby said. "They had *The Smurfs* on. We had *Punky Brewster* and *Alvin and the Chipmunks*."

After Taft Broadcasting bought Ruby-Spears and moved the studio across the street from Hanna-Barbera (which it owned), Jack was loaned out to Hanna-Barbera and drew concepts for *Super-Friends*, *Scooby-Doo*, and *Space Ghost*. In addition, Mike Thibodeaux recalled, "There were times on the weekend when you think he'd be relaxing. But he'd be in there drawing something else for a comic idea."

Though he was "out of comics," his name could still lure readers, so Bill and Steve Schanes – owners of the successful mail-order business Pacific Comics – asked Jack if he'd like to draw the first comic they'd publish themselves. He considered the two screenplays he'd written (*Captain Victory* and his collaboration with Steve Sherman, *Silver Star*) and agreed.

The Schanes brothers turned the *Captain Victory* graphic novel into two issues of *Captain Victory and the Galactic Rangers* and added *Silver Star* to their schedule. When Marvel learned even more artists were working with Pacific for royalties, ownership, and a higher page rate, "that's when Marvel started paying artist royalties and tried to be more competitive about keeping artists," Bob McLeod explained.

Every night, Jack worked on the series until three or four in the morning. His grandson, Jeremy, remembered waking up in the middle of the night: "You could see him with his back facing the window, just drawing at the board." He filled *Captain Victory* with insect villains that resembled armored warriors in *New Gods*, animal sidekicks Orca and Tarin that evoked the Inhumans and Kamandi, and a hero with direct ties to the Fourth World. "Captain Victory was supposed to be the grandson of Darkseid," explained Mike Thibodeaux, who inked the books. "That was his plan." And about Victory's biggest opponent, Blackmass, Jack told the inker, 'That's really Darkseid.'"

Since he was also a night owl, Thibodeaux would drive over in the middle of the night to pick up Jack's latest pages. After handing them over, Jack would return to his chair and favorite videos. "He really loved Charles Bronson. I'd always give him those tapes for his birthday. You know *Death Wish*? And Clint Eastwood: He loved the spaghetti westerns. I remember buying him all of those. He would watch those tapes over and over."

Jack also spent a lot of time reminiscing. He once told Thibodeaux about how, one rainy day in the 1940s, people at Timely laid pages from *Captain America* facedown on the floor so visitors wouldn't get the rug wet. He said he was proud of what he and Joe had done at Mainline and felt wounded when it fell apart. He didn't speak ill of Joe, "but I could tell at times by the tone of his voice that he wasn't happy with the way some things went down." Jack tried to avoid discussing Stan Lee but did become livid sometimes. Then again, he also told Thibodeaux that he loved the work he did during the early days of Marvel.

His experiences in World War II, however, were what he enjoyed describing most. When he interrupted conversations to tell an anecdote, Roz might say they had heard this already, while daughter Lisa rolled her eyes. "But the war definitely had a traumatic effect on him," she said later. "He made some of his stories humorous, and that somewhat took the edge off them, and then he had some that were actually very tragic."

He'd describe the day Germans left the woods disguised as American soldiers, stood in the mess line, and were beaten and then thrown in prison. Or times he had been shot at or captured while on patrol. Or how he suffered severe frostbite – seeing his legs turn black – after walking through snow. "He would tell that story a lot," said Thibodeaux. "He really thought he was going to lose his legs."

Jack's days were mostly quiet, domestic. After a late night, he'd wake to the sound of his grandson running across the house, coming toward his room. Five-year-old Jeremy would leap happily onto his back, imploring him to wake up. Jack would spend the next thirty minutes telling him stories about Goozlebobbers, fictional aliens out to conquer the world. Then he'd point and yell, "There goes one now, running past the window!" Jeremy would hide under the covers. (Soon these creations appeared in *Captain Victory*.)

When it was time to return to work, he'd put on his favorite New York Yankees cap, walk by the hanging drawing of the Thing in a yarmulke and the shelves teeming with his complete collection of *National Geographic* magazines, dog-eared, yellowing sci-fi novels, and photos of him with fans in homemade costumes. Breaking for a meal, leaving the beat-up drawing board, he'd stroll past the original *Boy Commandos* page on the kitchen wall, fix a sandwich, and maybe read the paper. Or he'd get into his trunks and swim in the pool, maybe watch some TV, or spend time with his son, Neal, his daughters, and his grandchildren. He'd attend their birthday parties, school plays, softball games, and Girl Scout meetings. And during sleepovers, he'd sit and watch movies with them or watch his granddaughter Tracy play with the toys in his office and Jeremy scribble drawings at his table. If they both wanted to draw, he'd pull up another chair and gently offer a few tips.

One day, Steve Gerber (creator of *Thundarr* and a wonderfully gifted comedian to boot) asked for his help. Gerber had sued Marvel for Howard the Duck. "I felt the ownership of the character was controversial," he explained. "At the time, Marvel secured the ownership of all of its characters with a statement stamped on the back of the checks, and I had frankly X'd out about half of those statements just to see if they'd still cash the check, and they did." *Howard the Duck* No. 1 had been an enormous hit – receiving glowing reviews from the mainstream media – and the subject of a newspaper comic strip. When Marvel refused to advance the strip's artist any money, and two artists couldn't afford to wait months for the syndicate to pay them, "I begged them to just pay comic book rates so that an artist wouldn't lose his shirt while working on the strip," he recalled. Marvel's refusal led to "a huge blowup," and Gerber left Marvel in 1978, feeling "they were dooming the strip to failure, and they could not see that."

Since then, Gerber had sued for ownership. After mortgaging everything he owned, hoping to create a fund-raising comic, Gerber dropped by Jack's home to ask if he'd draw it. "Sure, I'll pitch in," Jack replied evenly. "You want me to help you? I'll help you."

"He was pretty vehement in his resentment of Marvel," Gerber recalled. "And he had every right to be. Along with Stan, he created almost all of the characters. There are a few exceptions – Spider-Man is controversial, Daredevil, as far as I know, Jack had nothing to do with – but virtually everything else was essentially a Stan Lee and Jack Kirby co-creation, and Jack never received any compensation for that."

Gerber's *Destroyer Duck* quickly sold eighty thousand copies. And by filling its first four-color comic with sound-effect captions and lettering that resembled those in Marvel books, publisher Eclipse Comics showed the entire industry that another company could easily deliver this style.

While he was working on this comic, however, Jack learned of Marvel's latest shenanigan. Since he had left, Marvel attorneys had said he shouldn't draw squiggly lines, muscles, and machines since the company owned the copyright to his characteristic style. As if this weren't enough, various artists and writers then tried to include him in their stories – even though he didn't want his name or likeness in anything DC or Marvel held the copyright to. Claiming they could use his name whenever they pleased, Marvel planned to include his name and face in a *History of Marvel* comic series that would have him, Stan, and Steve Ditko acting out the company's official version of events (Stan as sole creator telling them what to draw). Taking umbrage to this, Jack had his lawyer put a stop to it, then just as quickly learned that another artist wanted his image near Stan's on a cover of *The Fantastic Four*. After his lawyer prevented this use as well, the matter seemed resolved: Marvel attorneys claimed his face wouldn't be featured without his permission.

Then someone at Marvel asked him to collaborate with Stan on a special story for the Fantastic Four's anniversary issue. In recent years, Stan's writing had consisted mainly of retreads of their old collaborations. With Roy Thomas, he'd filled *The New Fantastic Four* cartoon with rewrites of *The Fantastic Four* Nos. 5, 11, 35, and 36 and *Annual* Nos. 2 and 63. Three weeks after NBC axed the show, the network started airing Hanna-Barbera's *Fred and Barney Meet the Thing*, a child-friendly work created after network president Fred Silverman told the animation studio their boy-with-a-magic-ring proposal needed a celebrated attraction. When Jack saw his co-creation dancing with the Flintstones during a misleading opening sequence, he laughed. Since then, Stan had worked on dismal cartoons like *Spider-Woman* (canceled after half of a season), and the program that began as *Spider-Man* turned into *Spider-Man and His Amazing Friends* and was now called *The Incredible Hulk and the Amazing Spider-Man*. Jack told Marvel he had no interest in working with Stan again.

A few months later, someone handed him November 1981's *Fantastic Four* No. 236. On the cover, artist John Byrne had drawn the Thing holding Reed Richards in one arm and Sue Storm in the other. The Human Torch flew past them. Surrounding them were Luke Cage, the Avengers, the Defenders, Daredevil, Black Panther, the New X-Men, Dr. Strange, Hulk, Spider-Man, and Stan in a green pinstripe suit. Where it usually read "Marvel Comics Group," the cover announced, "The Marvel Comics Group Proudly Presents . . . the 20th Anniversary of the Fabulous Fantastic Four." Another blurb added, "Special Triple Sized issue of the world's greatest comic magazine!" A third read: "Plus: An All New Blockbuster by Stan (the Man) Lee and Jack (King) Kirby!"

In shock, Jack opened the sixty-four-page, dollar-priced edition and read an unsigned column ("A Note on Our Special Feature") that described the story as "the first collaboration by that titanically talented duo since King Kirby left Marvel some years ago for the wooly wilds of animation studios. . . ." It mentioned how he produced storyboards for *The New Fantastic Four* series, then added, "When we were looking for a special feature, someone suggested we modify Jack's storyboard into a comics format and voilà!" After the column thanked Jack and David DePatie "for their consent and cooperation in this somewhat unusual undertaking," he was stunned to see that this "All New Blockbuster" ("The Challenge of Dr. Doom") was nothing but the storyboards he'd drawn for *The New Fantastic Four*'s eighth episode, a retelling of *The Fantastic Four* No. 5 – boards that were not intended for publication. "He felt it was a cheap thing to do," said Steve Sherman. "He felt it was sort of a rip-off to the readers, but there wasn't a heck of a lot he could do about it."

Stan blamed an unspecified employee at Marvel. "He must have just thought it was a good idea. That's how everything came about. Like 'Hey, here's a good idea! Why don't we do this?' And we'd do it."

Jack, however, was fuming. "I had nothing to do with it," he said publicly. "Some friend of John Byrne's called and asked if I would do something for the twentieth anniversary issue. I said no. So they took the roughs I did for DePatie and put six inkers on it. I didn't know anything about it until the goddamn thing was published."

Chapter 17

In 1984, DC Comics wanted to create a toy line, and companies lined up to obtain the lucrative license. Kenner Toys, which had enjoyed immense success with its *Star Wars* line, put together a presentation for DC that included concept art, packaging, test shots, and production samples: an old Robin doll, by Mego Toys, painted to resemble Batman, and a "Glamor Gal" doll and *Star Wars* figure sloppily painted to resemble Supergirl and Captain Marvel. Kenner talked up the punching feature – or "superpower" – they'd give each doll (activated by buttons that moved its arms or legs), and sample packaging prominently displayed drawings of Batman, Superman, Wonder Woman, Robin, the Flash, Green Lantern, and Green Arrow. Each sample included the phrase "DC Presents Super Heroes . . . with 'Super Power Feature.'" Since Kenner emphasized artwork, and would not blight the characters' likenesses with switches, DC turned Mattel down and awarded them the license. After selecting which heroes would constitute the first wave of dolls, and the lineup in the new cartoon *Superfriends: The Legendary Super Powers Show*, DC and Kenner felt the concept needed better villains than the Penguin and the Joker. "They discovered that they had lots of superheroes but not enough good villains for toys," Mark Evanier explained, "and someone suggested Darkseid and they went, 'Oh, that's a perfect villain.'" Since Desaad, Kalibak, and Jack's other Fourth World villains accompanying Darkseid were also impressive, DC was enthusiastic about including the characters as a theme in the new toy line. "So they said, 'Well, we need someone who can do some artwork and redevelop these things,'" Evanier continued. By now, executives Paul Levitz and Jenette Kahn were the heads of DC, making it a more creator-friendly environment; people who created new properties could share in the revenues – including Jack Kirby, who back in the 1970s had signed away his rights to the New Gods.

At the time, Jack was stinging over the cancellation of *Captain Victory* and *Silver Star*. "Jack never got to finish them, really," said Mike Thibodeaux. "He was disappointed. He wanted to continue *Captain Victory* for another ten or twelve issues because he had somewhere he wanted to take it." Pacific Comics issued a *Captain Victory* special issue and announced he'd be creating a series called *The Midnight Men*; but after providing his outline for the series to another writer and experiencing creative difficulties, Jack moved on. Since then, Jack had been developing another trilogy of comic books, *The Secret City*, about the ancient city Gazra – buried during the "Great Flood of Noah's day" under "modern-day Chicago" – rising again after an unexpected earth tremor and causing the "Triad-Cell" machine to awaken three costumed heroes. In the first series, Bombast, who had superhuman vision and mastery of temperature, would cope with 1983 technology, having trouble using telephones or driving a car. In the second series, Glida, a woman with wings attached to her costume, would welcome technology, and frustrate a "'Red Baron' type by outwitting him in aerial combat." The third series would show a hero assuming the identity of deceased detective Keltan McCord. Upon defeating a crime ring that framed "a poor schnook of a Vietnam war veteran" in a "flag-waving conclusion," citizens would hail him as "Captain Glory," and the new superpatriot would have to cope "with the problems we live with in the shadow of the H-bomb."

But then DC called.

After checking into a Beverly Hills hotel, Jenette Kahn arranged to meet with Jack and Roz. She told them DC wanted to create New Gods figures, Roz recalled, and the dynamic young brunette executive added, "Look, we know what Marvel always did to you. You were always getting screwed all your life, and we want to be fair. We feel that you created this, and that you should get something out of it."

Jack was utterly delighted and relieved. If anything happened to him, especially now that his health was failing, he'd leave Roz some royalties, something he couldn't say about his work for Marvel. "So DC went to Jack and said, 'We'd like you to come in and do this drawing, and we'll give you the same type of deal as if *The New Gods* were created today,'" Evanier said. "Because the deal would not ordinarily apply to preexisting characters."

In New York, DC executives led Jack to a desk where Keith Giffen, the young talent responsible for the fiftieth issue of *The Defenders*, with its old-style Hulk, was working on drawings of Darkseid, the Parademon, Mantis, and Kalibak to send Kenner. Recently, Giffen and DC executive Paul Levitz had included Darkseid in the series *The Legion of Super-Heroes*. Jack appraised the young talent's faithful versions of his ultimate villain and said, "These are going to do just fine." Then he wowed Giffen by showing a mammoth board covered with his own designs.

DC wanted to introduce the New Gods to a new generation by reprinting the series in six comics with superior paper, brighter color, and a higher price. "And someone at DC said, 'Let's get Jack back to do an ending for the *New Gods* series he was never able to finish in the seventies,' which was probably a bad idea, because he had never developed the series to the point where he could finish it in fifty or one hundred pages," said Evanier. In the past, Jack had told people the saga would conclude with Darkseid and his warlike son, Orion, meeting, but not fighting. "A son in the end will never hurt his father – that's my personal belief – and a father will never hurt his son. I know that I never will. My son can do anything to me that he damn pleases. It's just the way I feel. I can't hurt my own flesh and blood."

At his typewriter, in the office in his home in California, he wrote an overview of the New Gods saga for Kenner Toys and for use as a treatment for a movie people now felt might happen. During the last few years, he'd said, "When I do write the finale for the *New Gods*, it'll be something spectacular." He hoped to include a big surprise but changed direction after the third *Star Wars* film – George Lucas's effects-filled spectacular *Return of the Jedi* – ended with Darth Vader switching sides and helping his son, Luke, destroy the wicked, wrinkled, red-eyed emperor.

When Jack submitted his twenty-two-page story, editor Joe Orlando rejected it.

"What do you mean you don't like it?" he asked.

Orlando then called Evanier for advice on how to tell Jack he wanted someone, like Evanier, to help write the dialogue. "I told him to just confront Jack directly," Evanier recalled. "I told Joe that I doubted Jack would or could work with another writer and that if Jack asked me, I'd help out, but I didn't expect that to happen. For some reason, an article then appeared in the *Comic Buyers Guide* saying that I was rewriting *The Hunger Dogs*, which was never true." The article angered Jack, so Orlando had to fly out to California, Carmine Infantino recalled, to say they wouldn't let anyone else write the book but him.

With DC insisting the ending wasn't strong enough, Jack had to redraw the story and create a concept better than the one he originally felt was first-rate. In the end, DC decided that rather than scrap what he'd done, Jack could draw another story, a sort of framing device, around the pages, and they'd publish it as a graphic novel called *The Hunger Dogs*. And for the reprint series, he could create a second new story. Once they agreed on what needed to be done, Evanier explained, "Jack did all the revisions himself." Instead of his epic finale, he wrote and drew the pedestrian "Even Gods Must Die," which presented Big Barda and her armored Female Furies bemoaning the fact that they were now desk jockeys who relied on computers. Artistically, Jack told his story in rectangular panels that evoked artist Frank Miller and his incalculable imitators.

That *The New Gods* reprints – published from June to November

1984 – didn't sell, despite arriving with new covers, better paper, and a new tale, depressed him. But he finished adding pages to his first story, for *The Hunger Dogs*, and turned it in. DC then passed photostats to Greg Theakston, who was only supposed to paint the graphic novel's cover. When Theakston – a comic fan who had met the Kirbys and sometimes drove them to the San Diego Comic Convention – saw Jack's *Hunger Dogs* pages, he immediately thought, What the hell's going on here? There was a giant contrast between D. Bruce Berry's and Mike Royer's inking styles. And since Jack insisted they not change one line, both Berry and Royer had inked weird-looking bodies, eyes that were askew, and fingers that were clearly too square, and both had misinterpreted lighting effects, which were "very abstract, and you had to decipher what he was saying." Theakston told amiable, easygoing DC editor Andy Helfer, "Andy, goddamn! Andy, geez, these two styles, they simply don't gel."

Helfer replied, "Do whatever you want with it."

"So I took it home and worked on it for a week, for nothing, for free, and reinked numerous faces and figures and readjusted some stuff and then colored it."

While Theakston finished *The Hunger Dogs*, Jack coped with the fact that Marvel continued to turn a profit off of ideas he created. One afternoon, while Roz was shopping and he and Evanier sat in her car in a parking lot, Evanier suggested they kill some time in a nearby Toys "R" Us store. Jack shook his head. "I can't go in there," he said. Evanier tried to persuade him, but he repeated, "No, really, I can't go in there." Seeing scores of Hulk and Captain America dolls on sale, when he wouldn't receive a penny, made him physically ill.

He now felt the same about his original artwork. When he went to big conventions, he saw dealers selling pages his lawyer had tried for years to get back. By this point, his attorney had told him he'd never seen a company like Marvel, which wouldn't speak to another lawyer or answer his letters. During Jack's second stay at Marvel

– from 1975 to 1978 – when tall, stocky production manager John Verpoorten returned his work for *Captain America*, *Black Panther*, and *The Eternals* books, all Jack had had to sign was the same four-sentence release every other artist received. Now, Marvel was stonewalling him about pages from the 1960s – his most classic work, collectors and fans felt – pages he wanted to leave for his grandchildren. "Then, the reasons for their refusals became clearer," said Roz. "The originals began appearing for sale among the dealers at every convention across the country."

At conventions, when he and Roz strolled across enormous spaces, fans nervously approached to ask Jack to sign pages, but he wouldn't do it. One day, someone actually sent his two children over with a page to ask for an autograph. With a sigh, he signed it. Then, at a convention in Chicago, he and Roz ran into Marvel's editor in chief, Jim Shooter, who cried, "Jack, when are you going to come back and work for Marvel?" Saying he was working on a way to get Jack his artwork back, Shooter added, "Don't worry, everything's going to work out fine."

After this, they didn't hear from Shooter for months. Roz called his office repeatedly and remembered him saying it would take time for them to arrange for someone to go down to the vault. Roz said they could send Greg Theakston, who was willing to take inventory, but Shooter said Marvel wouldn't let him in.

"All right," she told him. "We'll come down there personally."

"No, you guys can't do that. We can't work it that way – there are already too many guys involved."

Soon, Jack and Roz heard that Marvel was returning pages to other artists. "Oh, great," she told him, "it's happening." But instead of the usual one-page form, in August 1984, Marvel sent Jack a four-page agreement.

The agreement said the company would return eighty-eight pages as a gift for having created artwork or written material on Marvel's behalf. In return, Jack had to acknowledge that Marvel was giving him only physical custody of the pages. Marvel would retain all rights, including the worldwide copyright. The gift didn't mean that

Marvel was transferring any rights. Jack also had to acknowledge that the pages had been commissioned and ordered by Marvel and prepared subject to the company's supervision, direction, and control. He had to agree that he'd been fully paid and that Marvel didn't owe him royalties; Marvel was the sole and exclusive owner of all copyrights and could do what it pleased with them; if Marvel didn't own any copyrights, this agreement would hand those over, too.

His signature, it continued, would also prohibit him from disputing Marvel's complete ownership of copyright and the art or helping anyone who tried to do the same for their own work. He couldn't object to revisions or new material created from the artwork or Marvel using his name and biography in advertising. And if Marvel didn't want to mention his name in connection with the art or characters, it didn't have to. Furthermore, he couldn't copy the work, exhibit it without permission, give the pages to someone else (without this person signing a similar agreement), use the name Marvel or any of the characters, or refuse to allow Marvel to make copies if it gave reasonable advance notice and needed the pages for its business or licensing. The agreement also prohibited him from saying he had a right or claim to any of the art in Marvel's possession, to allow Marvel to hand this art over to anyone it wanted, to sign and return any additional documents Marvel might send, and to accept that Marvel could sign these documents for him if he didn't return them in a timely fashion.

Though he'd drawn from three thousand to eight thousand pages during the 1960s alone – and this agreement said Marvel would return a mere eighty-eight – he took the agreement to a table to sign. Looking over his shoulder, concerned, Roz asked, "Have you read all of these paragraphs? Let's think about it."

By the time his former assistant Steve Sherman dropped by, Jack had considered what Marvel actually wanted him to agree to. He was livid. "Look at this!" he shouted. "Read this!" After a few paragraphs, Sherman said, "Whoa! What nerve!"

When Sherman reached the paragraph that asked Jack to relinquish all rights to the characters he created, to never be allowed to say he created them or describe himself as a co-creator, he said, "Well, this is a perfect time to sue them, Jack." Though Sherman felt a nuisance suit would lead to a settlement with Marvel, Jack really didn't want to go to court.

"Look, you're getting all your DC art back," Sherman told him. "The Marvel art, I can assure you, Jack, has all been splintered from the warehouse." Back when he'd worked at Marvelmania, Sherman and Chip Goodman had visited the warehouse; Goodman had given him original pages to take back to Marvelmania. Since then, he knew many of Jack's pages were gone. "Why fight for it, Jack?" he asked. "Even if you get it back, what's it gonna do for you? You'd be better off suing them and collecting that way."

Jack wouldn't do it, but Roz sent a copy of the agreement to their lawyer, who looked it over and said, "Look, you're going to have to make the decision."

For three days, Jack couldn't sleep. He was nervous, edgy, and pensive. Finally he told his wife, "Roz, I can't sign it."

She called Jim Shooter. "Jack can't sign this," she revealed. "All the other guys have the simpler form. Enough's enough. Let's get started."

Shooter, she recalled, told her to sign or forget everything.

"We have this list for eighty-eight pages from seven books," she replied. "How do I know we'll get anything else?"

"You have my word on it."

This wasn't good enough. She asked him to send someone into the vault and to mail her an inventory describing the art pages Marvel possessed. Shooter refused. "It seemed very innocent on the surface," he said later. "It was a trap. It was phrased in a way that if we responded with a list of artwork, it was an admission that it was Jack's." Since Jack had never signed the work-for-hire contract, Marvel's attorneys worried that he might sue for copyrights; they analyzed each word in letters from his attorney.

"Now you'll notice, right about the time that all of these characters are coming up for renewal, Marvel takes steps to change their major characters," said Greg Theakston. "Spider-Man was now in a black costume. I believe that the Hulk was back to his original gray form. The FF, I think Byrne redesigned their costumes. They went out of their way to significantly change the characters so the claim on them would not be as strong. They were thinking ahead on this in their attempt to retain the ownership of characters."

Be that as it may, Jack had no intention of taking legal action. "We've never sued anybody." He and Roz were also both over sixty years old. Battling Marvel could easily last a decade in court. "And what were they going to give us?" Roz asked incredulously. "Eighty-eight pages?"

Once Roz developed high blood pressure for the first time in her life, and Jack started experiencing stress-related chest pains himself, he realized he might finally have to stand up to the Marvel Comics Group. "If I can afford it," he told a reporter, "I will try to get a court of law to decide the important questions of copyright law for the sake of myself, other artists, and the comics industry itself."

"He had the best contract he ever saw, so he got a little spoiled and started demanding his artwork back from the sixties," said John Romita. "And the problem was, a lot of it had been misplaced."

Behind closed doors, Marvel worried about the thirteen thousand original pages. During the 1960s, the company claimed it had routinely destroyed this work. And to this day, Flo Steinberg says the same. "It was like an old script," she said. "I mean, I used to throw the artwork out when the shelves got too full. Imagine that. I mean, you threw out the old scripts; you threw out the old artwork."

By the late 1960s, however, two young editors arrived at a convention and sold dozens of original pages to eager art collectors for $10 to $15 each. And during the early 1970s, artist Gil Kane – who once worked for Jack and Joe Simon during the 1940s – visited the Marvel office with an empty portfolio and left with it full of pages. Another time, Kane watched everyone ogling a page by John Buscema and then quickly left the office. Production manager

John Verpoorten chased the divorced, financially distressed artist down a crowded Manhattan street, shouting that they had to print it first before Kane could bring it home with him. Verpoorten himself was said to have carried pages home with him every night when he left the office.

In an effort to reduce theft during this period, Marvel put the pages in an art return room and asked visitors to sign in. After the art was moved to a warehouse in 1975, employee Irene Vartanoff (a colorist also in charge of returning original pages to their creators) began to catalog and organize the pages. By the end of the year, Vartanoff had cleaned things up and meticulously cataloged the pages – even while Marvel staff kept handing original art pages to people they wanted to be in business with. Three years later, when Jim Shooter rose to editor in chief, the warehouse was supposedly burglarized and ransacked. Nothing appeared to be missing, but Shooter nevertheless ordered all of the original artwork moved into his office, the safest place in the building. Marvel moved to another office in 1979, and the original art – save for one box – was moved to a new warehouse. For whatever reason, someone placed this box of valuable original pages in the middle of the Marvel lunchroom. "When I was made aware of that," Shooter claimed, "I went to Bernie, the office manager, and said, 'That box goes to the warehouse right now!'" Bernie told Shooter the box wasn't there. "Somebody had obviously grabbed the box, straight out to the freight elevator – which was near there – and left," Shooter explained.

These pages – and many more drawn after this supposed robbery – appeared on dealers' tables at comic conventions nationwide, and rumors in comic circles continued to accuse some Marvel employees of stealing artwork.

When he wasn't struggling to convince Marvel to return his pages – without his signing the four-page agreement – Jack saw comic fans largely ignore February 1985's *The Hunger Dogs*. "So many years had passed that he was no longer immersed in the themes that had informed his earlier work," Evanier explained, "so he produced this *Hunger Dogs* book, which I don't think pleased anyone too much, and a lot of people have since kind of pretended it didn't exist." Then he learned about an ad Cannon Films had placed in the March 6, 1985, edition of *Variety* for their proposed *Captain America* movie. Next to a Romita drawing of a smiling Cap, a caption screamed, "America's Star-Spangled Super-Hero Battles the Forces of Evil!" Underneath it was the credit "Based on Stan Lee's Marvel Comic Strip Character."

Jack was enraged. He called his lawyer and told him about the ad. Joe Simon was just as annoyed. "He was upset when Stan was taking credit for creating Captain America," said Joe's son Jim (who coauthored his father's landmark biography *The Comic Book Makers*). "They'd spoken several times, and Stan would say, 'You know, Joe, I'm not taking credit, it's Marvel press machine,' and blah blah blah."

Jack's lawyer asked Cannon to change the credit. The film studio said it was up to Marvel. The lawyer wrote to Marvel, and the company said it would make sure Stan was no longer credited with creating Captain America.

At this point, everyone around Jack told reporters he'd been injured in a car accident, "but that actually wasn't the case," Steve Sherman revealed. "They just didn't want anyone to know that he'd had bypass surgery. They felt if publishers knew Jack was sick, he wouldn't get work. So they told everyone it was a car accident."

Once he recuperated, he resumed work on a second miniseries based on the latest Super Powers dolls and the new season of cartoons (*The Super Powers Team: Galactic Guardians*). But by now, his hands wouldn't do what his mind wanted them to. He had already stopped signing autographs at conventions – now his vision was failing. He started getting the costume details wrong, drawing Metron's Moebius Chair (which he created) differently each time, making his figures short and stunted, their arms too long; his straight lines wobbled, and his overall style became less detailed, more exaggerated and cartoonlike. Since 1962, he'd worked every day, but now, at sixty-eight, he was exhausted. He had had throat cancer, had undergone chemotherapy, and had endured bypass surgery; his eyesight was failing, and his hand trembled a little when he held a pencil. "And psychologically, he didn't want to do it anymore," Greg Theakston said.

Though the drudgery of a panel-to-panel twenty-two-page book wore on him, he worked to finish the series as reciprocation for the money DC had given him for the Fourth World toys. He tried to continue drawing a mind-boggling four pages a day – unheard of for most other artists – but health problems took their toll. "The first page would always be very strong," Theakston explained. "It was his morning page. He was pretty good. He had his strength; he was awake and ready for a day's work. The second page was not bad. The third page was weak. And the fourth page was barely done. By eleven at night, Jack was just burned out, absolutely tired; the work was thin, and the proportions were somewhat off. He wasn't taking the kind of care that he did on the first page." Theakston would ink the pages in reverse order so that Jack's weakest page would be his first and strongest.

At the same time, Jack was bored with the scripts. Theakston claims he developed the general idea – Darkseid sending five menaces to planet Earth to prepare for an onslaught – in an effort to provide something fun to draw. Instead of an update of the old *Justice League of America* – those halcyon three-act stories in which a villain nearly defeated the superteam, the team was forced to go out in pairs to perform some mission, and then the team, together and trapped, all used their powers to help the next member escape their bounds – another writer was handing Jack scripts so poor, he actually called editor Andy Helfer after the second issue to say, "Look, these have to be better, you've got to do a better job." Upon seeing the script for the third issue, he told Theakston, "Oh boy, Easter Island, how many times have I done that? Dinosaurs? I'm just off *Devil Dinosaur*. I don't want to draw another one.'" Not only was he tired and unenthusiastic, Theakston said, but "the stories stank."

He tried to suppress his boredom, to draw twelve characters he didn't create, whose costumes went against his entire design sense, but soon he stopped drawing the Superman logo on the hero's chest, telling his inker, "Greg, you just do that. You know what it looks like. You draw the Superman logo in." Next he called to say, "If Green Lantern's gloves are the wrong length, correct them, will you?" Then Roz called Theakston with Jack on the line to ask if he'd do more of the actual drawing. "No, absolutely not," the inker replied. "I mean, I'll do the logos 'cause there's nothing creative about that. But it's really not my spot to be drawing or redrawing anything in this book." After the second *Super Powers* miniseries was finished, Jack told Theakston he'd never again do a regular book. DC asked him to do the third sequence and other work, but he turned them down.

On April 15, 1985, Jack's lawyer tried to get a response from Marvel's tight-lipped attorneys by writing a letter that mentioned Jack had created characters like Spider-Man, the Hulk, and the Fantastic Four. Marvel's lawyers showed people excerpts and claimed Jack was going after the copyrights. By now, Cadence was selling Marvel to New World Pictures, and Steve Sherman told Jack, "This is the perfect time to sue. If you hit them with a lawsuit, they're just going to freak out because they won't be able to sell the company and they'll have to settle with you." Though Sherman went out and researched lawyers, Jack still wouldn't do it. It was too expensive. It'd be too much of a fight. He just wasn't up for it. "I think that was when he'd just come out of heart surgery." A lawsuit at this point would put too much stress and strain on him, Sherman added.

But more people began speaking about Marvel's alleged mistreatment of Jack, and the company saw deals threatened or called off. Evanier told a reporter that in Marvel's letters, asking him to sign away rights, "the offers were like 'Mr. Kirby, you have absolutely no rights to this material, but if you sign this paper, affirming you have no rights to this material, we will pay you one thousand dollars.' Jack has a whole file folder of those goodies."

Soon, Gary Groth, the dynamic, outspoken publisher of the *Comics Journal*, requested an interview. Jack had met Groth once or twice in the past, but now, on the record, he told him about the agreement, the original artwork pages, and how he didn't want to take this to court. Marvel owned the characters, and a lawsuit would get him nowhere. When Groth called Stan's office in California for a quote, someone claimed Stan didn't grant interviews. Then Neal Adams called to say Stan should persuade Marvel to return the artwork: Adams recalled that Stan felt Jack should have it back, but – despite the fact that every Marvel comic included the phrase "Stan Lee Presents" and Stan was being credited as publisher (when Mike Hobson was seemingly doing the job) – it was out of his hands.

Either way, July's hundredth issue of the *Comics Journal* broke the story in the article "Marvel Withholds Kirby's Art," revealing that inkers like Joe Sinnott were receiving pages Jack had drawn (while Jack himself was locked in a stalemate with the company over his refusal to sign the four-page document). The article quoted Roz saying she had asked Shooter for the shorter release form and been told, "With Jack, it's more complicated." Then Jack said, "They'll return my art if I'll sign that release, and I can't sign it."

After the *Journal* story and a subsequent editorial describing Marvel's four-page agreement as a way to "nail down their copyright to characters that they're not entirely sure they would own if challenged in a court of law," Jack's battle became an industry cause. At the San Diego Comic Convention on August 3, 1985, he sat on a panel with *Comics Journal* publisher Groth and some of the industry's most popular and influential talents, including artist Frank Miller and writers Alan Moore and Marv Wolfman.

"He was really little . . . little guy . . . but really good," Miller recalled. "There was a goodness to the guy." He added: "But he was a very angry man." Jack was also unusually perceptive. "He had an uncanny manner where he would simply turn and say, 'You're lonely,' and he'd be right." At the same time, "He was just a guy like the rest of us. Like Eisner, he knew that what he did for a living was a job. And there's a virtue to that."

Moore, a fan since the early *Fantastic Four* issues, and Miller, who made *Daredevil* the most powerful book in comics, were about to forever change the direction of comics with their projects *Watchmen* and *The Dark Knight Returns*. Wolfman, meanwhile, had followed his classic *Tomb of Dracula* run for Marvel by handing DC a solid hit with *The New Teen Titans*. Addressing Moore and Miller, Jack said, "You kids: I think you're great. You kids: What you've done is terrific. I really want to thank you." Embarrassed, Moore said he should be thanking *him*. "He had a glow around him," Moore recalled. "He was somebody very, very special."

During the panel, they noticed tall Jim Shooter sitting in the audience. Since assuming the top spot at Marvel, Jim Shooter had made a number of decisions that rubbed his critics the wrong way. When Mattel offered to create dolls based on Marvel heroes, Marvel agreed to create a new comic, and Mattel suggested they call it *Marvel Super Heroes Secret Wars*. Shooter had alienated writers by deciding to write this twelve-issue limited series himself. He told writers they had to end their current stories with their characters being kidnapped from earth and then to begin the next month's installment with different versions of the heroes returning to earth and taking up where the old models left off. While readers encountered new versions of some heroes in their individual titles, they'd also see the original versions going through changes in the yearlong *Secret Wars* book. In response to the instant and major alterations Shooter wanted to make, and resenting that he chose himself to write a high-profile series that could potentially earn its creator lucrative royalties ("I'll grant you, I made a couple of bucks on that," he said later), some writers were upset. When freelance artists were no longer allowed in editors' offices or to loiter in the halls, they also took umbrage and felt, as artist Bob McLeod expressed, "It wasn't the same relaxed 'anything goes' atmosphere after 1976. It started becoming like any other business office."

Shooter's ensuing edict caused yet more bad blood. He told artists he wanted to see more establishing shots, ceilings, floors, crowd scenes, and thin lines on backgrounds – and no heavy shadows in foregrounds of panels – in their comics. "He wanted everything done the same way he had seen work on a particular Jack Kirby comic," McLeod recalled. After Shooter got into it with Gene Colan – over what Shooter felt was Colan's habit of earning money by filling pages with easy-to-draw explosions – Colan defected to DC. Writer Doug Moench later claimed in a published interview that Shooter had told him, regarding Thor, "No more Asgard. Thor is Superman and Donald Blake is Clark Kent, and it all takes place on earth." Moench also claimed that Shooter wanted to end the Stan Lee era of Marvel by killing off every character's alter ego. According to Moench, Shooter wanted Tony Stark to die and someone else to wear the Iron Man armor; lame physician Donald Blake's death to lead to someone else wielding the Mighty Thor's hammer; and Steve Rogers's demise to allow an investment banker to wear the famous Captain America uniform. "Shooter was going to do this across the board!" Moench claimed. "Peter Parker and the Fantastic Four were all going to die!"

At a press conference, Shooter denied Moench's allegations, which were published in the *Comics Journal* after Moench left for DC. "This is an allegation by a disgruntled former employee," Shooter insisted. But more and more Marvel talents privately claimed that he did in fact want to do this. Jim Starlin, creator of the graphic novel *The Death of Captain Marvel*, remembered Shooter saying, "We don't know what to do with this character; we haven't for a long time. Kill him off so we can bring somebody else back as it." And today, Moench's frequent collaborator Paul Gulacy mentions, "He wanted to kill off a lot of major characters and start all over again with new guys." Despite his denial, May 1984's *Marvel Super Heroes Secret Wars* actually included many of the changes Shooter denied wanting to make: By the end of the series, African American Jim Rhodes was the new Iron Man; Bruce Banner's personality controlled the Hulk; Professor X could walk and fight with the X-Men; *The Fantastic Four*'s Susan Richards was pregnant with a second child; and She-Hulk replaced the Thing. A new Spider-Woman debuted. Shooter's most controversial move, however, was replacing the famous Ditko-designed Spider-Man costume with a form-fitting black outfit that had a white spider emblem on its chest (with the spider's legs stretching across his ribs and back). When fans saw the new suit, editor Tom DeFalco recalled, they wrote to say, "You guys crazy? Are you idiots? The most classic costume in comics! How could you do this?"

Shooter was sensitive to their grievances and soon told DeFalco, "Listen, this new costume. Issue 252 is the first where we introduce it? Get rid of it in 253." DeFalco, however, convinced him to keep it around "at least until it was introduced in *Secret Wars*." The irony was that once they got rid of it, more readers wrote to say they missed the new suit, "which is why it came back for a few months. And when Peter Parker had both costumes and couldn't make up his mind? The readers couldn't. Whichever costume we had, readers kept saying we should have had the other." Shooter's hard-charging style offended some creators, but his success – *Marvel Super Heroes Secret Wars* sold between eight hundred thousand and a million copies a month – and his high standards helped make Marvel the undeniable industry leader. As the company still refused to return Jack's artwork, however, and magazines like the *Comics Journal* kept reporting on the situation, Shooter was unfortunately described as the villain of the piece. "He was supporting the corporate point of view," Groth said. "I think Shooter claimed that he was trying to work from the inside and get Kirby a deal and so on, but I don't know to what extent that was true."

The August 1985 San Diego Comic Convention panel began with Groth discussing Marvel's position regarding Jack's original pages. Shooter recalled: "Jack gets up and in the gentlest, sweetest way he says, 'Well, yeah, there are some issues in dispute, but we're working to resolve them. It's really just between me and Marvel and it's really not to be discussed here and we really appreciate everybody's support and concern.'" Then Groth, Shooter added, told the audience, "If he's not going to tell you, the rest of us will." After panel members each commented, Frank Miller said, "Jim Shooter's in the audience; let's hear what he has to say."

Shooter rose to his full, imposing height. "Listen, I heard this thing start with Jack saying he was going to work it out, and I know from my side that I would like nothing better," he began. Marvel would like to return the artwork, he continued, but couldn't, for reasons he couldn't disclose. Once Shooter mentioned copyrights, however, Roz leaped to her feet, furiously, and said, "I hate to interrupt you, but during the entire thing, we've never tried to get the copyrights back from Marvel. It's you people who keep bringing it up."

She was clearly emotional, Shooter said later, and he couldn't blame her. "She's the one who really kind of gave me hell, and I didn't really want to debate Jack's wife! The whole thing deteriorated to the people on the podium saying nasty things about Marvel; it became sort of chaos."

Jack saw things differently. "It was unfair for Shooter to be present, because he was trying to scare the panelists." He added: "Shooter had the right to be there, of course, because they have their side, too. But still, I felt there were a few instances in Shooter's answers that carried threats. The panel was very forthright with their answers and views."

Chapter 18

During the artwork battle, Jack continued to meet some of the new generation of artists. The image of a comic book artist was that of a guy at his desk, looking up from his page only when his writer stopped by to see how everything was going — an image perhaps reinforced by all those Siegel and Schuster photos during the Golden Age of the 1940s: the artist in his white shirt and tie, facing the desk while the taller writer, in a conservative suit, stood behind him. It was a pose he and Joe and many other creative teams had mimicked in their own black-and-white photos. These new artists, however, were wild: They met girls, drank one another under the table, feuded in public, insulted their own editors and bosses in print (Jim Starlin named a clown villain "Len Teans," or Stan Lee with the letters transposed and an extra "n"), demanded higher pay, argued with their fans, charged high prices for their autographs, and (some of them) smoked good pot before drawing some pretty phantasmagoric pictures. When they met Jack, however, no matter how long their hair might be, how much of a scowl they flashed toward their fans, how difficult they were rumored to be to work with, or how contemptuous they were of what they called lowbrow superhero comics, almost invariably they were in awe.

The *Comics Journal*'s February 1986 issue was "dedicated to swaying Marvel's heart, if indeed the corporation has one." In the editorial

"House of No Shame," publisher Gary Groth wrote, "You don't need to have grown up reading Jack Kirby's work to recognize that Marvel's treatment of him is criminal." The same issue contained a letter by DC executives Jenette Kahn, Dick Giordano, and Paul Levitz. "The ownership of the page, the actual object, belongs unequivocally to the artist, and the artist alone," it read. Marvel was under no legal obligation to return Jack's pages, but the longer it didn't, the more some people felt the company was trying to bully the little old man who helped create their most celebrated characters. "I mean, that's when people realized that it wasn't this big happy family that it pretended to be," said Groth.

The battle became even more public. One day, Jack joined former assistant Mark Evanier (who had gone on to write television shows and critically acclaimed comics like the hilarious barbarian spoof *Groo the Wanderer*), writer Steve Gerber, artist Frank Miller, and writer Arthur Byron Cover for an interview on Los Angeles station KPFK 90.7 FM. Usually, Roz would join him during interviews to try to prevent him from making outrageous or erroneous statements – claiming he'd created Spider-Man's costume – or losing his temper and lashing out at Stan. But she couldn't make it this time and asked Evanier to keep an eye on him.

In the studio, Jack explained what the hoopla was all about. "My release was quite different from the others." He said he wondered why they sent a longer release; he'd have easily signed the shorter one; he was sorry it became a legal thing, but he couldn't sign this agreement. "So they kept my pages." When the host mentioned for listeners that Jack had drawn thousands of pages for Marvel, Jack added, "According to statistics, I've done one quarter of Marvel's entire output." Frank Miller called the four-page agreement the most offensive legal document he'd ever read. Evanier explained that Jack continued to inspire Marvel; editors routinely handed new artists old Jack Kirby books and said, "This is what we want."

"It was done with me," Miller added.

Evanier then told listeners that DC had paid Jack more money for redesigning Darkseid than Marvel had for the entire universe.

When the host asked if he had any last words, Jack said, "I'm from the old school. I'm from a generation you fellas know nothing about. I ask nobody to do anything for me." He was here only to let people know about the comic book industry. "But I ask them to do nothing," he stressed. "If they feel like writing a letter, fine. If they don't, it's still fine with me. I'll continue my own fight. It'll go on because I want it to go on. If it stops, it'll be because I stopped it. I ask nothing of anybody. It's because of my own love for the individual that I ask nothing from it. If there are any people on my side, I thank them."

The sight of young people arguing his case in public led some people to believe Jack was being provoked into pursuing the issue. "He had friends, and a lot of other people with axes to grind against Marvel, sort of pushing him and saying, 'Oh, you're not like everybody else,'" said John Romita. "In other words, if John Romita's artwork is being stolen or lost, that's one thing. 'But this is Jack Kirby's stuff. This is Michelangelo we're talking about.' They fed his ego, and he started to say, 'You know, you're right, I should have it back.'" The problem, he added, was that Marvel simply didn't know where half of the artwork was. "And the legal department was asking him to sign away any rights to the ownership or proprietary or creative rights of these things. They wondered if Kirby having the original art would allow him to go to court and say they should never do a story with the Silver Surfer in it. The legal department was whispering in Marvel's ear and his friends were whispering in Jack's ear, and they made it a mess that it should never have been."

The next salvo arrived on March 13, 1986, when a company attorney sent Jack's lawyer copies of documents he'd signed in 1969 and 1972. The first document supported Goodman's claim to copyrights for the first ten issues of *Captain America*. The second, three years later, was signed because he hadn't been paid the same amount Simon received in his settlement, something Goodman had promised. "Marvel had these documents sitting in a pile for years," Shooter explained, "but had been afraid to 'show their hand' because they,

Marvel's lawyers, believed absolutely that Kirby's lawyers must be aware of these documents and therefore must have some ace up their sleeve." Marvel's lawyer wrote that he hoped these would eliminate any lingering doubts about the company's ownership of copyrights and added that the company would accept the standard one-page artwork release form if Jack also sent a letter saying his copyright renewal claims in the April 1985 letter were groundless and wouldn't be repeated.

By now, the "Kirby Artwork Battle," as it was known in comic fandom, had become such a cause célèbre that the *Comics Journal* circulated a petition asking Marvel to return Jack's artwork. Marvel was under no legal obligation to return the pages, but comic creators felt it was the right thing to do. It was a star-studded petition: Neal Adams, the legendary Carl Barks, C. C. Beck, Robert Crumb, Harlan Ellison, Jules Feiffer, Steve Englehart, Steve Gerber, Burne Hogarth, Jerry Iger, Gil Kane, George Perez, DC's Julie Schwartz, Don Heck, Superman co-creator Jerry Siegel, *Maus*'s Art Spiegelman, *Doonesbury*'s Garry Trudeau, *The Simpsons* creator Matt Groening, and 132 other professionals had signed it.

Will Eisner issued an open letter to Marvel. "I wrote that I thought it would be in their best interest and the best interest of the industry to return the original art, because I felt no artist really intended to give it away," Eisner explained. "The intention was to give them the rights to publish his work, but that was certainly another subject." Marvel wrote back to say he should mind his own business. Artist Steve Rude, meanwhile, wrote Shooter to say, "Just give him his artwork back. He's not going to be alive forever. What's the point going to be if you give it to him when he's not here?" Said Rude, "I got a letter back from Shooter that claimed he was innocent of all the accusations."

While seeing the community behind him added to his determination – "He realized it was not simply a one-man war," said Theakston – the battle permeated every inch of his life and took its toll physically and psychologically. Meanwhile, his supporters expanded their attacks to include Stan, though the return of artwork fell under the jurisdiction of Marvel's business department. "I think because of the fact that I was the publisher or whatever the hell I was at the time, Jack must have felt mad at the company and at me because I represented the company," Stan said.

When Stan finally did speak to the *Comics Journal*, he repeated that artists helped create plots. But in *Variety*, he said, "In the case of the Hulk and the Fantastic Four and others, Jack Kirby created the characters visually – and it's important to keep the word 'visually' in there. He drew the characters that I described to him." And during a promotional appearance at the 1986 San Diego Comic Convention, in response to a fan asking about Jack's involvement, Stan said, "As far as I can remember these things happening, I was the editor and head writer at Marvel, and Jack was an artist who worked for us."

Jack's supporters were furious and asked reporters to look no further than Stan's career for proof that Kirby had created the characters. "At the point the so-called Marvel Age began with *The Fantastic Four* number one, Stan had been in charge at Marvel for twenty years," Evanier said publicly. And while he'd written countless stories, "Have you ever heard anyone single any of them out as 'well-written'?"

Marvel, however, continued to promote Stan as sole creator. During the same month the *Comics Journal* printed their petition, a special episode of ABC's *20/20* celebrated the company's twenty-fifth anniversary and credited Stan as sole creator of the Fantastic Four, Spider-Man, Hulk, the Silver Surfer, Thor, and Dr. Strange. On the heels of the episode, Marvel vice president Michael Hobson issued a press release. Marvel was willing to return the art, it read. Jack had received all his pages from 1976 to 1978. Jack had refused to acknowledge Marvel's ownership of the copyrights and made ownership claims for some characters after signing several documents acknowledging Marvel's ownership of the same. Since Jack's attorneys asserted claims of copyright ownership during the past four years, the press release continued, Marvel had sent a longer release form only to have Jack refuse to sign it. Despite the press release, Marvel's image continued to suffer. "It's almost as if they didn't read their own comic books," said editor Jim Salicrup. "It's like the Stan Lee cliché: When the villain becomes too overconfident, that's when he's most vulnerable."

August 2, 1986, a month after the *20/20* special and Hobson's press release, Jack attended the San Diego Comic Convention. At a table, greeting fans and supporters, artist Jim Starlin – who had signed the petition – called Jim Shooter over. At this point, Marvel wanted to return the pages, but Jack had requested a creator credit similar to the one DC had given Siegel and Schuster in *Superman*.

Shooter claimed that he asked Jack, "Doesn't Stan deserve some credit?"

"Yeah, he does."

"So you'd be okay if we put 'Stan and Jack'?"

"Yes."

"In your letter you insist you created Spider-Man, and I know you developed a version of Spider-Man, but it wasn't the one that was actually used. The one that was actually used was the one Steve did."

"Yeah, you're right, that's his."

Roz remembered the meeting differently. "I just told him what we wanted and we were going to stand firm."

By October 16, 1986, Marvel sent Jack the inventory list of the artwork in their possession, close to 1,900 pages – as opposed to the 88 mentioned in the four-page agreement. They also sent the original one-page release he'd always been willing to sign and an additional two-page contract. Jack signed the papers, handing Marvel the copyrights, promising never to repeat certain claims, and reaffirming his signatures on the 1972 agreement and his 1975 contract.

Six months later, on April 15, 1987, Marvel fired Jim Shooter. The tall editor in chief's final days were an emotional roller coaster, former assistant and editor Tom DeFalco recalled: "Jim was, toward the end there, fighting with everybody. He was fighting with the creative people; he was fighting with his bosses and the owners of the company; he was fighting with me. He had helped build Marvel into a powerful juggernaut and then decided that he didn't like the way it worked anymore. And that it needed to be completely rebuilt instantly. And you know, juggernauts don't get rebuilt instantly."

Sensing that he and Jim would be fired, DeFalco had tried to convince him that they should find a safety net on the West Coast. "I maintain that Jim looked at that as a kind of disloyalty because he never thought he'd be fired." Shooter, he continued, suspected DeFalco of angling for his job. Either way, Marvel president Jim Galton and Mike Hobson asked DeFalco to lunch and told him, "The time has come to make a change. Jim is going to be let go, and we're going to put you in charge." After Shooter's dismissal, a few employees held a party in the conference room and hung him in effigy.

During an interview at the time, Jack told a reporter, "Shooter used to walk around like he was the king of England."

Roz cut in. "Jack, you don't want to get into any of that right now."

"Okay," he answered.

On May 16, 1987, Jack received 2,100 pages of original art, less than what he'd drawn for *The Fantastic Four* alone during the 1960s. Marvel also refused to pay the $800 insurance freight. "He just said they were pricks," Sherman says, laughing. "You figure that's par for the course. You have to remember he'd dealt with Nazis, so Marvel and DC didn't faze him that much."

Once the pages arrived, Jack called Mike Thibodeaux and Mark Evanier. "And we raced over there and just went through them page by page," Thibodeaux recalled. "He was thrilled. He was really thrilled about getting it back. He was standing there, holding the splash to *The Avengers* number seven, and just staring at it for the longest time. You could just see he was into it. He was into what he had done, which I'd never saw him do before."

Marvel reprinted the old Lee-Kirby stories in their more expensive hardcover *Marvel Masterworks*, and included Jack's name on each cover.

Chapter 19

Stan Lee emerged from the Kirby Artwork Battle with his professional reputation intact. Jack's supporters had ridiculed his many achievements, but to a new generation it didn't matter; when he stopped by the office during his rare visits, new employees gathered around to praise the many wonderful stories he had written with and without Jack. They had heard tales about him depriving people of credit but chalked it up to rumors by industry gossips or bitter old-timers. "Unlike them," young new Marvel editor Matt Morra opined, "Stan Lee was never a freelancer for Marvel Comics. Stan Lee was an editor from day one, an employee of the company. He was never in the same boat that they were."

After investor Ronald Perelman added Marvel to a portfolio that included Technicolor, MacAndrews & Forbes, Pantry Pride, and Revlon in early 1989, Stan met with Perelman's employee Bill Bevins. By this point, he'd worked for Marvel for forty-nine years: He'd kept the company going after Simon & Kirby left; when heroes no longer sold after World War II; when monsters suddenly came into vogue; and when his superheroes with Jack struck a nerve during the carefree pop art years. After some small talk, Bevins asked his annual salary. Stan told him, and Bevins's face briefly registered shock. Then he said they'd triple it. Stan couldn't believe his ears. At home; he told his wife of Bevins's offer, and both felt that he must have misheard. Then payday arrived and his check was three times larger.

His salary wasn't the only thing that had changed.

Shortly after his raise, the new owners issued a memo announcing that Stan would now be chairman of Marvel. The new employees running the company, taking it in another direction, were largely indifferent. "Stan was hands-off at that point in time," Morra recalled. "It wasn't as though it made a difference in our daily lives. It wasn't a big deal."

The owners would also close Marvel Productions, the animation arm, but continue to have Stan pitch characters for film and television projects.

In recent years, the film deals had resulted in a few embarrassments. After five years, *Captain America* arrived and tanked. "It was filmed in what was Yugoslavia at the time, and it had to do with the Red Skull," Stan explained. "They made him an Italian in that movie. They did the best they could, but it was low budget and really not very good."

At Marvel, during lunchtime, an editor once wheeled a cart out into the bullpen. The cart held a TV and a VCR that would play a videotape of *The Punisher*, another low-budget straight-to-video disaster. "And it was just a solid hour of howling laughter," Morra recalled. "That and the *Captain America* movie."

The Fantastic Four movie, however, was easily the worst of all. Stan's friend, director Oley Sassone, tried his best, but Bernd Eichinger of Constantin Films – who later brought the superior, effects-laden horror *Resident Evil* to theaters – had supposedly rushed the movie. Eichinger, who held the rights for years, was waiting for a stronger script. But Marvel hinted that they wanted the rights back, to sell to another outfit. If he didn't start principal photography by December, Eichinger would lose the rights. He contacted film producer Roger Corman, known for churning out exploitation films at microscopic budgets. Cameras rolled in September. "We actually got ahold of the tape of *The Fantastic Four* movie," Morra recalled. "More howling laughter. Internally, we knew this thing was never going to be released to the public. It was a low-budget thing that stepped into that realm of 'so bad, it's good.'"

In Hollywood, Stan kept visiting studios to pitch *The X-Men* as a cartoon. Amid cordial greetings and compliments, executives told him comics wouldn't do well as a series for children. Comics, they felt, were for eighteen- to twenty-four-year-old males who didn't watch cartoons. Stan emphasized the phenomenal success of the comic series, but networks kept rejecting *The X-Men.* At the same time, he knew a *Spider-Man* movie could reverse the trend of cinematic embarrassments. But producer Menachem Golan of Cannon Films – another studio known for low-budget movies – bought the rights for a mere $225,000 and a percentage of the gross and had screenwriters turn in ten drafts. Then Golan left his company with the rights for Spidey and Cap, asked Marvel to extend the option to his new company, and started trying to raise money to attract a big-name director by selling worldwide television rights to Viacom, home video rights to Columbia TriStar, and signing a $5 million deal with executives at film studio Carolco during the 1990 Cannes Film Festival (a deal that would raise the film's budget to $50 million). With all of these deals being made, and director James Cameron (*The Terminator*) writing a treatment, a *Spider-Man* movie, in Stan's mind a surefire hit, would take a while.

Soon, Stan's thoughts turned to writing comics again. At the time, the industry was undergoing another major change. The positive morals that he and Jack – and Colan, Buscema, Trimpe, Heck, and Romita – included in their stories were now considered old-fashioned and irrelevant in the age of the "grim 'n' gritty" comic book. "Grim 'n' gritty comics were pretty much an editorial response to things like *Dark Knight* and *Watchmen*," explained comic writer Steven Grant. "It was editors looking at those books and going, 'Oh, well, this must be what people are responding to,' and picking out specific elements from them and applying them to other books." As a result, instead of superheroes that were, as Evanier once joked to an acquaintance, super and heroic, Marvel now specialized in clenched-jaw vigilantes like Wolverine, Punisher, and Deathlok, a killer robot created during the 1970s and later revived. Marvel had scored a hit with an update of Ghost Rider, a high-testosterone version with a ponytail and a big shotgun, and the company was selling huge numbers of *The X-Men* – and up to eight monthly spin-off titles that included even more muscle-bound, gun-packing heroes like Cable.

In addition to bleak stories, the look of Marvel Comics had changed. Where Stan once urged artists to think like Kirby, detailing specifics in the popular book *How to Draw Comics the Marvel Way* with John Buscema, young newcomers like Jim Lee and Todd McFarlane moved away from clear, melodramatic storytelling. Instead, they filled pages with scratchy lines, lantern-jawed men with bulging biceps, enormous rifles, graphic violence, and scantily clad, anatomically exaggerated heroines.

Once magazines like *Wizard* promoted these newcomers as fan favorites and their works as collectors' items, other artists rushed to imitate them. Marvel's entire line began to look the same. Older artists, who had worked for the company during previous decades, reacted to receiving fewer assignments by trying to imitate the new pencilers. When editors rejected their attempts to pad their own stories with as many meaningless full-page splashes and half-nude heroines as younger artists did, they grumbled to reporters about Marvel not wanting to hire older people. "Here's the bottom line with all creative efforts," said Tom DeFalco, editor in chief at the time. "Either you're getting better or you're getting worse. There's no such thing as staying static."

The fact was that the new artists and the long-drawn-out epics that crossed over into virtually every title were helping Marvel's sales rise to unimaginable new heights. At one point, a summer annual introduced the story "Atlantis Attacks." By the time it ended, culminating in the Sub-Mariner's fiftieth anniversary, readers had purchased fifteen other double-priced issues. "This is when the industry went from this tiny little thing to this gigantic monster, to when Mr. Perelman started making more money off of comic books than eye shadow," said Matt Morra. Higher sales led to more titles and over twenty editors working on staff. And things got even better when, thanks to *Wizard* and other magazines geared for collectors, comic fans and nonreaders in search of what they believed would become good investments began to gravitate in record numbers toward certain issues. When *Spider-Man* No. 1 – a revamp of the long-running series written and drawn by "hot artist" Todd McFarlane (who later created *Spawn*) – arrived in stores in a plastic bag (which comic fans believe will preserve the quality of an issue and allow for a higher resale price) and printed with multiple covers, collectors snatched up a record 2,350,000 copies of the first printing and three hundred thousand of the second, making it the best-selling comic of all time. Marvel's marketing department tried to repeat this success by including more of these "enhancements" with other comics: covers with different colors, plastic 3-D holograms, glow-in-the-dark images, plastic bags, trading cards, and more. Soon, retailers wanted nothing to do with a comic that didn't include enhancements, and comic creators demanded them in their comics since they spurred sales. With "hot artists," enhancements, and editorial gimmicks like epic crossovers and beloved characters being killed off (and inevitably revived), Marvel saw every title skyrocket in sales. Even books with double the print run sold out in a week. Stan was absolutely stunned. "Suddenly a book that sold two hundred thousand was selling a million or half a million," he said later. "It was the greatest thing." He wanted to create a hit of his own.

Jack Kirby, meanwhile, was trying to get used to not working in comics. Two years earlier, he'd worked with Ruby-Spears on a September 1988 *Superman* cartoon for CBS, which commemorated the hero's fiftieth anniversary. Shortly after it was completed, he lost his job in animation. Ruby-Spears's parent company, Taft, merged with new owner Great American, Joe Ruby explained. Then Great American turned around and sold Ruby-Spears to Turner Broadcasting System. "When Turner owned it, they had Hanna-Barbera, which was their main company, and they had us and

Southern Star, a company from Australia. And they were just getting rid of what they called the excess weight." With studios pitching shows to the same networks, things were competitive enough. But once networks became more interested in licensed properties, with preexisting audiences, animation studios had to compete with one another for properties and pay higher prices for licenses. Studios also had to accept that despite paying huge sums, they might not own the lucrative syndication rights to whatever series they created. "So everybody was vying over the same projects, and it got into bidding wars," Ruby said good-naturedly. "It changed the business." Once costs started to rise, Ruby-Spears's new owner focused on Hanna-Barbera and got rid of Southern Star, Ruby-Spears, and many live-action properties in development. "So literally we went out of business," Ruby explained. "That's how Kirby stopped working for us."

Now, in 1990, Jack agreed to grant a three-part interview to the *Comics Journal*'s Gary Groth and uttered his most acerbic comments yet about Stan Lee and Marvel Comics. Describing Stan as a teenager at Timely, Jack added bitterly, "In fact, once I told Joe to throw him out of the room."

"Because he was a pest?" Groth asked.

"Yes, he was a pest. Stan Lee was a pest. He liked to irk people, and it was one thing I couldn't take."

"Hasn't changed a bit huh?"

He couldn't do anything because Stan was the publisher's cousin, Jack said, before adding that they never collaborated on monster stories. "Stan Lee and I never collaborated on anything! I've never seen Stan Lee write anything. I used to write all the stories just like I always did."

When Groth mentioned that credits read "Stan Lee and Jack Kirby," Jack, in a very angry and bitter mood, repeated that Stan did "nothing! Okay?" Stan didn't dialogue anything, he insisted. "If Stan Lee ever got a thing dialogued, he would get it from someone working in the office." He claimed Stan handed Jack's margin notes to another person, who did the writing. "In this way,

Stan Lee made more pay than he did as an editor. This is the way Stan Lee became the writer. Besides collecting the editor's pay, he collected writer's pay. I'm not saying Stan Lee had a bad business head on," he added. "I think he took advantage of whoever was working for him."

As the interview continued, Jack attempted uncharacteristically to take full credit at Stan's expense. He said he had created the Fantastic Four, Thor, Hulk, the X-Men, and the Avengers because monster books weren't selling. He denied drawing stories from Stan's plots and said that Stan's function at Marvel back then was to lead visitors in to see Martin Goodman. He also said that, upon arriving at Marvel during the late 1950s, he saw moving men carrying out the furniture and desks. "Stan Lee is sitting on a chair crying," he claimed. "He didn't know what to do, he's sitting in a chair crying – he was just still out of his adolescence. I told him to stop crying. I said, 'Go in to Martin and tell him to stop moving the furniture out and I'll see that the books make money.'"

This interview was not the first time he'd told this anecdote. But when Steve Sherman first heard it, Jack said he consoled a crying Stan by saying, "Well, you know, let's not be in a rush here, let's see what we can do. What's selling? What looks like it's gonna work?" Stan Lee meanwhile denies this ever occurred. "I am not a crier. I would certainly not cry in public in an office. It's the most ridiculous story I have ever . . ." Pause. "And I didn't say, 'I want you to come back and save the company,' either," he added with annoyance. "I mean, I don't understand it. I can't believe Jack said it 'cause I must tell you: He was the nicest, straightest, most decent guy you could ever find. It wasn't like Jack to make up things or to lie. I just do not understand that whole story."

During the interview, he told Groth that after agreeing to save the company, "somehow they had faith in me. I knew I could do it, but I had to come up with fresh characters that nobody had ever seen before." He then said, "It wasn't possible for a man like Stan Lee to come up with new things – or old things, for that matter. Stan Lee wasn't a guy that read or told stories. Stan Lee was a guy that knew where the papers were or who was coming to visit that day. Stan Lee is essentially an office worker, okay?"

Jack's embittered, derisive tone shocked friends and fans alike, especially those who had heard him say, in the past, that Stan had been an excellent editor and a great PR guy. "He always credited Stan with making Marvel Comics what it was because of his promotional ways and taking the raw material that Jack and other artists gave him and really punching it up," said Sherman. Now, fury and frustration took him to the other extreme "to say, 'Stan didn't do anything, I did it all,' just to counteract the whole business of 'Jack didn't do anything, Jack was just the artist.' When I first met Jack," Sherman continued, "he was more apt to say it was a co-creation, that they worked together in building this stuff."

After Jack told Groth he had also created the name Fantastic Four, he and Roz both weighed in on Stan's typed synopsis for the first issue, which had recently been printed in a fanzine. Roz said she'd never seen it. Jack called it an outright lie. Steve Sherman felt Jack was going to the other extreme again. "If Jack Kirby does a superhero, it's going to have a form-fitting costume." His most recent heroes at the time – the Challengers of the Unknown, Green Arrow, the Shield, and the Fly – had basically followed this aesthetic. Yet, the Fantastic Four first appeared in regular clothing. "Plus, you have Mister Fantastic, a rip-off of Plastic Man, the Thing, which they had done – it's a monster – Sue Storm, invisibility, and the Human Torch, an old Marvel character," said Sherman. "If you look at all that, it seems, yeah, Stan probably had a hand in coming up with that and talked to Jack, and by issue ten or twelve, Jack said, 'Wait a minute! This is the direction we should go in, this is how the book's going to be,' and Stan said, 'Oh, okay, go with it.'"

During the interview, Jack told Groth he had created the Hulk after seeing a newspaper article, and Roz added, "You also said the Hulk reminded you of Frankenstein." Groth mentioned Stan's claims for having created the Hulk's name. Jack answered, "No, he didn't."

"It's just his word against Stan's," Roz noted.

The interview then focused on how after Jack left Marvel in

1970, he went on to create dozens of other new characters. "Yeah," he said, nodding. "Stan never created anything new after that. If he says he created things all that easily, what did he create after I left? That's the point. Have they done anything new? He'll probably tell you, 'I didn't have to.'"

Then came perhaps the most controversial subject of all: "I created Spider-Man," Jack claimed calmly. "We decided to give it to Steve Ditko." Joe Simon's 1990 nonfiction book, *The Comic Book Makers*, had recently revealed that a proposal for Spiderman (no hyphen) had existed and that Jack once called and "confessed to an old indiscretion" that made Simon "responsible for bringing Spider-Man into the world." Simon claimed that he asked why and Jack told him, "I had no work – I had a family to support – rent to pay – what else could I do?"

Jack's claim of creating Spider-Man – always the one character Stan could point to and say he created – was enough to make Steve Ditko break his decades-old media silence and say Jack's claim was false. As Ditko told it in an essay, he didn't really know what happened between Stan and Jack before Stan told him – after *Amazing Adult Fantasy* No. 14 was completed – that they'd be introducing a new hero next issue. They'd call him Spider-Man, Jack Kirby would draw it, and Ditko would ink, the artist recalled. Though Stan denied it, Ditko maintained that Stan described Spider-Man as a teenager whose magic ring turned him into an adult hero and that Ditko told him it sounded like Joe Simon's character the Fly. Either way, Ditko added, "Kirby had penciled five pages of his Spider-Man. How much was pure Kirby, how much Lee, is for them to resolve."

In his essay, Ditko also explained that Jack's five pages – which showed an orphaned teenager at home with his stern guardians before entering a "whiskered" scientist's house – didn't have much to do with the Spider-Man he and Stan made famous. But he wound up noting that Jack's pages did include the hero's name, an orphaned teenaged alter ego (a rarity in those days, except for when Jack and Joe Simon used it in the Fly), and a doting aunt and uncle.

The *Comics Journal* interview, which would ultimately divide the industry again, then found Jack claiming that he came up with the books on his own without anyone telling him if they needed another one – a claim that completely went against Stan and Marvel's established history of those halcyon days. And about his margin notes: "That would be my dialogue."

In calmer tones, Jack explained why he'd created so many characters during the 1960s: He had to make a living; he was married; he had a home; he had children. To support them, he had to return to Marvel. He also admitted that he was happy when college kids started reading their comics. But everything soured when management realized he was earning more money. "I say 'management,' but I mean an individual," he clarified. "I was making more money than he was, okay?" And this person wanted to make more money, too. "And there was a man who never wrote a line in his life – he could hardly spell – you know, taking credit for the writing." Since he was in a bad spot, Jack said, he went to DC.

Jack kept quiet during the 1940s, he revealed, for the sake of his mother, and two decades later, for the sake of his wife and children. But it was hard to do. Sometimes he wanted to punch someone in the mouth. The quieter he stayed, he said, the more he saw Stan become a personality in the books and official spokesman for Marvel – due to his relationship with the owner, he added. It wouldn't have been so unfair if they had put "Produced by Stan Lee and Jack Kirby," Roz said. "But he didn't have to say 'Written by.' He didn't have to take the entire credit. He'd put down 'Drawn by Jack "King" Kirby and all that stuff.'"

"Yes," Jack added, "and he'd be very flippant."

"Jack took it with a grain of salt, but I was the one who was very hurt by it all."

Groth asked if they ever spoke to Stan about credit. "You can't talk to Stan about anything," Jack replied bitterly.

"Every so often he'd put down 'Produced by,'" said Roz.

Groth asked if he saw it coming during the 1960s.

"Well, you don't have to see a thing like that coming," Jack answered. "It was happening, and I didn't know what to do about it." As editor, Stan had influence at Marvel. Whom could he complain to?

After Groth noted how Stan always complimented him during interviews, Jack said he should: If he hadn't saved Marvel and come up with those features, he quipped, Stan wouldn't have had anything to work on. What hurt the most, he continued, was that Roz saw him create the characters but Stan kept saying he hadn't. Even his grandson Jeremy would ask, Why is Stan Lee's name all over? "Why shouldn't my family be hurt? I know my wife is sore at me –"

"No, I'm not sore –"

"Because I say these things, but I'm deeply hurt because it hurt my family. There's nothing I can do about it. I'm not going to be believed at Marvel. I'm not going to be believed anywhere else unless . . ." He stopped talking for a second, then finally admitted what had been gnawing at him for decades. "Actually, my own fears probably prodded me into an act of cowardice," he said. "It's an act of cowardice. I should have told Stan to go to hell and found some other way to make a living, but I couldn't do it. I had my family. I had an apartment. I just couldn't give all that up."

The interview ended on a high note, however, with Groth asking what was the most creatively rewarding period of his career. The New Gods, Jack replied. "I was given full rein on *Mister Miracle*. *Mister Miracle* was a fine strip."

After the interview, Roz called Mark Evanier to say she'd be receiving a transcript before the interview was published and that she'd like him to help remove a few of Jack's more inflammatory remarks. Evanier, however, has claimed that the *Comics Journal* printed the interview before Roz had a chance to see it. While Jack regretted saying half of this stuff, many people in the industry felt his comments about Stan were in poor form. "Jack was always nonconfrontational," said John Romita. "But I gather that when he was with his wife and some of his hangers-on, there would be all sorts of grumbling. The truth of the matter is a lot of the artists, including me, used to say Stan left a lot of the plotting to us."

Romita himself had told interviewers he struggled to create stories from a slim plot and wound up injecting his own ideas. "But I never went so far as to say that Stan never wrote anything original. Some of Jack's compatriots would say things like that, that Stan never did an original writing job on any of Jack's work, that he just used Jack's notes."

Even Evanier, one of Jack's closest friends and biggest supporters, couldn't believe what the artist had told the *Journal*. Some of the statements were inaccurate, others uncalled for. Following their biggest argument yet, they stopped speaking for a while.

Stan was just as displeased. People told him Jack regretted saying this stuff and that the magazine allegedly didn't show him the transcript before it was printed, but it didn't matter. Whether he saw a transcript or not, Jack had still said these things. "In all honesty, there were people who were goading Jack, who were telling Jack" – adopting the tone of a gruff, sleazy huckster – "'You know, Stan gets all the credit and Stan is making all the money and you're not,'" Stan explained. "There was a time Jack thought I was getting huge royalties, which I didn't. And Steve Ditko did, too. I remember once I said, 'Why don't you come back and draw Spider-Man, and Steve said something to the effect of, 'I will when I get all the royalties I'm supposed to get.' So yeah, everybody thought I was getting these tremendous royalties. Anyway, Jack at that time was not thinking too clearly or rationally, and I really think that the fellow who published that magazine is not my biggest fan. I don't know why. I don't even know if I ever met him. But he'll happily write anything bad about me. And I think they were almost putting words in Jack's mouth. I think there were a number of people steaming Jack up."

He read Jack's quotes in the *Journal* – "I've never seen Stan Lee write anything" and "If Stan Lee ever got a thing dialogued, he would get it from somebody working in the office" – and called Marvel's lawyer. "Should we sue him?" Stan asked.

The lawyer said they could. It would cost a lot of money, but Marvel could afford it, and it'd cost Jack a bundle to defend it. "Well, forget it. I don't want Jack to go broke," Stan answered.

"I'm not a guy who sues anybody, and I would never have sued Jack," he insisted.

Within months, Jack's lawyer called to say, "Jack would really like to make up, what do you say?"

"It's fine with me," Stan answered. "All Jack has to do is write a letter to the *Comics Journal* that says that the things he said weren't true and I'll be happy to make up." Even if Jack did retract his comments, Stan wondered if they could ever be friendly again. But he never heard from Jack again – and didn't expect to, either.

It was an exhilarating time for Marvel Comics: new owners, more titles, a remodeled office, and young new artist Rob Liefeld's *X-Force* No. 1 drawing 3.9 million customers and replacing McFarlane's *Spider-Man* No. 1 as the best-selling comic of all time. Then, just as quickly, July 1991's *X-Men* No. 1 (drawn by new artist Jim Lee) shipped with five different ("variant") covers and sold a historic 7.5 million copies. One evening in December 1991, however, McFarlane, Liefeld, Lee, and the other record-breaking artists informed the company president that they were leaving en masse. "When they first left Marvel, it was very amicable, it was, 'Well, we're going off to start our own thing; maybe we'll fall flat on our face or maybe it'll be a big success, but we're going to take the chance and do it,' and everyone wished them good luck," said Matt Morra. Within a short time, however, the defectors publicly attacked company policies regarding characters and creative ownership. "So Jack became their standard and the flag they'd wave. 'We're doing this for Jack, we're doing this for the memory of Jack, so that creators can finally get their own rights.'"

Marvel had already gone public (owner Ronald Perelman and Stan stood next to someone in a Spider-Man costume on the floor of the New York Stock Exchange). With the company's biggest moneymaking artists now gone, Marvel tried to reassure shareholders by using similar gimmicks – shipping comics in plastic bags with the same multiple covers, trading cards, McFarlane-like art, and tinfoil "platinum" covers that had helped earlier works break all-time sales records. For a while, collectors were satisfied with the dressed-up inferior comics: When they made their weekly trip to tiny comic shops nationwide on Wednesday, they stocked up on their beloved Marvel titles. Not even losing their top talents could stop Marvel at this point.

In California, Stan missed writing comics. Film and television were great – he made friends and had seen some Marvel characters make it onto television or the silver screen – but now he was tiring of attending meetings that led to options, only to wait years to see if a project would ever enter development and preproduction. With comics, he saw his ideas reach an audience within four months. Now, with Marvel expanding and sales rising (even on titles drawn by replacement artists for the defectors), Stan pitched Marvel an idea for a line of books: existing characters Dr. Doom, the Punisher, the X-Men, and Spider-Man fighting crime one hundred years in the future.

Before he pitched the idea, Stan's most recent comic writing included 1980's *She-Hulk* – he created the spin-off character, but a Saturday morning cartoon never materialized – and 1988's *Judgment Day*, a sixty-three-panel Silver Surfer story with John Buscema that again pit the Satan-like scoundrel Mephisto against the gleaming, virtuous hero. Despite the fact that fans largely ignored the exorbitantly priced ($10.95) *Judgment Day*, Stan followed it up that same year with another Surfer story, a two-issue miniseries with French artist Jean "Moebius" Giraud that rehashed how Galactus first came to planet Earth. But where Stan and Jack had presented the towering traveler as a being simply looking for food to survive, Stan's elaborate new take on the story involved Galactus claiming he was a god, a religious fanatic urging his converts to commit suicide, and an uncharacteristically slim Surfer riding his flying surfboard with arms and legs in a Christ-like pose. This also went relatively unnoticed by fans.

Now, Stan wanted Marvel to publish a line that placed well-known heroes in the future, much as Frank Miller's *The Dark*

Knight Returns did with Batman. Like Miller, Stan intended to show people in the future living in a world without heroes. "Every one of them has disappeared and now suddenly heroes are popping up again, starting with *Spider-Man 2099*, *Ravage*, of course, and a *Doom 2099*, *Punisher 2099*, then later, *Ghost Rider 2099*, and *X-Men 2099*," said Morra, who worked with Stan on the line.

Marvel asked Jim Salicrup – editor of the record-breaking McFarlane *Spider-Man* comic – to work with him, but Salicrup declined. "Stan was able to edit the original Marvel Universe all by himself," he explained. "He certainly didn't need me. Then with Tom DeFalco [on board], it seemed as though two editors too many were involved." Much like Jack with his Fourth World, Stan hoped to edit the books from California. Once it became clear that he'd also write one of the books, *Ravage*, Jim Salicrup and Tom DeFalco wondered if Steve Ditko would draw it.

Ditko had returned to Marvel in the late 1970s. By then, a legend had sprung up around him: Rumors claimed he was a devoted fan of Ayn Rand's objectivist novels *Atlas Shrugged* and *The Fountainhead* and that he believed people were either all good or all bad, no in between. Ditko refused to compromise or work on comics that included ideas he felt were questionable.

During the 1980s, he'd drawn issues of *The Legion of Super-Heroes* and *Adventure Comics* for DC. After DC bought the rights to most of the Charlton Comics heroes of the 1960s, editor Dick Giordano – who, like Ditko, had also worked for the low-paying Connecticut-based publisher – asked him to return to *Captain Atom* (the space age hero whose powers derived from radiation – years before Stan and Jack used this gimmick in *The Fantastic Four*). At a meeting, Ditko said he didn't like the proposed story because "superheroes should not take the place of the United States military." Giordano then asked him to work on *Firestorm*, a comic about a middle-aged male scientist and a teenage boy whose bodies fuse to form a red-eyed costumed hero with nuclear powers and a flame on his head. When Ditko rejected this assignment as well, Giordano said, "I guess we really don't have anything to discuss."

"I guess we don't," Ditko answered coolly, then rose and left Giordano's office.

By the late 1980s, Ditko was back at Marvel, stunning freelancers and employees with his willingness to discuss Spider-Man. He just wouldn't draw the hero again. According to Marv Wolfman, "He always felt that Spidey should never be older than sixteen because that was the last year a kid could totally screw up." Other people claimed he wouldn't ever return to his most famous character, because doing so might encourage the idea that he'd peaked decades ago.

Ditko wowed comic readers with his run on *Rom the Spaceknight* (based on Parker Brothers' popular robot doll, a gleaming silver warrior who hunted shape-shifting aliens on earth and, with the use of his space blaster, banished them to a "limbo" that evoked his avant-garde landscapes in *Dr. Strange*). During his tenure on the title, some of the industry's biggest inkers lined up to work with him. "Here's Craig Russell inking Steve Ditko, here's Brett Breeding, here's Bob Layton," editor Roger Stern explained. "It was cool!"

Ditko also worked on other licensed titles: *The Further Adventures of Indiana Jones*, and Mego Toys' *The Micronauts*; he had drawn the occasional cover or fill-in issue for *Daredevil*; he had created backup stories included in *Spider-Man* annuals – but without drawing the hero – and an annual for *The Avengers*. But he wouldn't include Spider-Man or work on projects that presented immoral characters as heroic, liberal values, or the glorification of behavior he deemed questionable.

And he continued to avoid the media spotlight. If reporters called his studio, he might chat for a few minutes, yet he'd decline to be interviewed. When a journalist and author tried to write a book about his life and art, contacting his brother for an interview, he was furious. Since he didn't grant interviews, rumors continued to describe him as eccentric. "He's just a very private guy," Stern felt. "He believes the work is the important thing."

* * *

With Stan about to develop *Ravage*, Jim Salicrup decided to call Ditko at his studio in midtown Manhattan. "Hey, there's a new project that we're interested in having you work on," he began.

Ditko, he said, was his usual blasé self. "Yeah, yeah."

"We want to have a meeting with, uh, you and the writer."

"Yeah, okay."

"Stan will be coming in for it."

Ditko was silent for a moment.

More silence.

Breathing . . .

"Okay," Ditko said. "When do you want to meet?"

At the appointed time, Stan and Salicrup sat in Marvel president Terry Stewart's office. Ditko entered the room, a tall, well-dressed older man, wearing glasses. After greeting him warmly (DeFalco claimed with a brotherly hug), Stan outlined his idea of a Judge Dredd type in a grim world. Ditko wanted nothing to do with it. "He wanted a more positive, heroic view of the future rather than saying the world would be destroyed and the hero would be a garbageman," Salicrup explained. "After Steve dismissed the *Ravage* project, Stan said, 'What about we do a *Spider-Man* graphic novel? Think of the money we'll make, it'll be great,' and blah blah blah." Ditko tried to explain why he couldn't return to the character, Salicrup continued: "With the Marvel work, *Dr. Strange* and *Spider-Man*, Steve had reached that point where he was involved with the plotting and penciling and inking, and felt he was putting so much into it, and cared so much about it." The tiniest revision affected him personally. "It's hard to explain," Salicrup said, "but in other words, when you care that much about something, if it's not gonna go your way, you'd just as soon walk away from it. And I think that's what happened with Steve. And I think he was trying to explain to Stan that there was no way he could ever get back into that mind-set of caring about something so much again. I think he's rightfully proud of what he did before, and why bother trying to come up with something?" The meeting ended amicably, and Ditko left. A lot of money was dangled in front of him, Salicrup added, "and he just stuck to his guns and said, 'I don't want to, I don't want to do it.'"

Salicrup left the company "because Marvel at that point did not want to acknowledge that we were anything more than employees, and I was even told at one point that *Spider-Man*'s success was just a fluke, which is not the type of thing to endear me into wanting to continue working that hard on another project." Stan then saw his title for the line change to *2099*. After hashing out plans for the initial launch of the new books during a conference with Tom DeFalco and Salicrup's replacement, Joey Cavalieri, Stan started working on *Ravage*. The hero, a garbageman named Paul-Phillip Ravage, learned that the corporation that employed him was polluting the environment. Upon gaining superpowers and fleeing from the corporation's killers, Ravage met a boy whose father was also murdered by his former employer, Alchemax, in an attempt to conceal controversial waste disposal methods. "Stan had the concept of pollution building up because it was all dumped on this one place called Hellrock and all the pollution was creating this weird radiation and technochemical petroleum crap," said Morra. After this unquestionably *OMAC*-like origin, Stan filled *Ravage* with evil multinationals, villains like Dethstryk, and fiendish "mutroids" that lived in Hellrock. The hero himself had long hair, trash heap armor, and an arsenal of guns, knives, and chains. "I used to think violence was the last resort of a savage," Stan had him say. "I still do. But when the world's a jungle, the savages take over."

The new hero struck some employees as Stan's attempt to blend in with harder-edged heroes like the revamped Ghost Rider, the gun-blasting Punisher, and a Wolverine who routinely murdered his opponents with the indestructible claws John Romita placed in his knuckles. "I don't know that it ever came through, though," said Morra. "I don't think that's the kind of character Stan could ever write. And it certainly wasn't what artist Paul Ryan was drawing."

The December 1992 first issue arrived with a "gold foil" cover and a press release that said, "Stan Lee, writer/creator of *Spider-Man* and *The Fantastic Four*, high deacon of all Marveldom, creates with Paul Ryan, regular artist for *The Fantastic Four*, the New York of *Ravage*: a rampaging raider with the ultimate price on his head: death!" The release then noted, "Ballistic fans of the Punisher, Wolverine, and Judge Dredd will eat this up. Number one issue in New Marvel 2099 Line. Foil Cover!" Despite the promotional push, the foil cover, and the comparisons to other ultrapopular, ultraviolent heroes, comic fans were indifferent. So were a few editors. "I actually never even read the book," said Lia Pelosi, who also worked on the series. "I certainly never read any of the earlier stuff. When I was editing toward the end, I *had* to read them. But I don't know. I guess it never just worked out. As a character, it just never hit." Stan himself, she noted, wasn't real pleased with the character, either. "Nobody was. *Ravage* was sort of the child nobody wanted to talk about. You sort of *had* to do it. The character was really nothing we were into. Nobody really wanted to work on the book."

When he met his new editor, Matt Morra, at the San Diego Comic Convention, Stan grabbed a pen and paper and gave him an autograph. "To Marvelous Matt," he wrote. Morra was overwhelmed. "Meeting Stan in person was amazing," he said happily. "As a kid I used to read the old books. I used to read 'Stan's Soapbox!' And he became this almost mythical figure." For Morra, "the reason we loved Marvel Comics was that man. We had our favorite artists, but it was his stories, his characters, that became a part of our childhood." But even Morra felt that *Ravage* was nowhere near as memorable or successful. Stan himself had no way of knowing that the character would one day be invoked by his critics to settle arguments about him being a hack.

While fans enjoyed Stan's writing, Morra claimed, they detested new artist Paul Ryan's old-fashioned art. "I think Stan would have preferred it if the art was a little more in-your-face, a little more Kirby, maybe, you know?"

At a writing conference in early 1992, Stan met Pat Mills and Tony Skinner, who were doing *Punisher 2099*, John Francis Moore (writer of *X-Men 2099*), and Peter David, then handling *Spider-Man*

2099. After pulling Mills and Skinner aside, Morra recalled, Stan asked if they'd be interested in taking over his series.

"Essentially Stan wanted to launch it but never planned to do it for more than a year," Morra continued. "He had a limited time frame to begin with, and as you know, he cut it short – he certainly didn't even finish out the year."

Many readers were saddened over his departure. *Ravage* lost direction. His replacements didn't know what to do with the character. "I just don't think Stan was as passionate about *Ravage* as he was about some of his classic characters," Morra reasoned. Neither were most comic readers. Stan retreated from writing again but wasn't done just yet.

Chapter 20

Jack and Roz celebrated their fiftieth anniversary in 1992. For half a century she'd cared for him, made many of the major decisions, and was careful to see that he didn't work himself to death. When he pulled all-nighters at the board, she'd wake up, enter the office, and say, "Put the pencil down and come to bed already." In restaurants, after he placed an unhealthy order – he loved chocolate cake – she'd cut in and tell the waiter what he'd really have. When he stopped smoking his Roi-Tan cigars in 1980, after decades, she offered encouragement and support. For fifty years she'd been the best partner he'd ever had, and they were still inseparable.

While describing their marriage for friends and family, they were like an old-time comedy team. She'd tell the story of how he was driving one sunny afternoon, became distracted by story ideas, and slammed right into the back of a police car. He'd recount how he was drawing at his desk in his home office one day and she was driving home from the store: Her foot slipped on the brake, he looked up from his drawing and saw her car smashing through the back of the garage and coming right through the wall.

Now, at their anniversary party, in black tuxedo, his hair almost white, face somewhat drawn, shadows under both eyes, he stood near their first wedding picture (with Roz on the other side of it) and smiled for the camera. "It was kind of sad, because my father at the time was in remission from his cancer, and he didn't look well," said his daughter Lisa. "But they got up there and renewed their vows, and they danced." Throughout his illness, they didn't want people to know he felt bad. Roz, whose own health was failing, behaved the same. Both projected courtesy and optimism.

At home, Jack would sit in his favorite chair and watch TV. He'd head to the video store, rent four movies, then return the next day for more and hear the clerk say, "I don't know if I have any new ones for you, Jack." Occasionally, Mike Thibodeaux would come over with videotapes of movies based on his characters. Jack watched *The Fantastic Four* in silence: The actors looked like the characters but wore the dark blue uniforms artist John Byrne designed during the early 1980s. The Thing resembled a big piece of foam rubber. They got Dr. Doom right, but the costume looked cheap. "I think he was just kind enough to sit through it," Thibodeaux recalled. "The special effects weren't very good." Jack also watched the *Captain America* movie. He attended the premiere with Mike by his side and thought the beginning – Cap fighting during the war – wasn't that bad. Once the film moved to the present, however, showing the Red Skull on an island, he was appalled. "He fought to get his name on that thing," Thibodeaux said. "But when he came out of the theater, Jack was saying he wanted his name off the movie."

Thibodeaux tried to show him new Marvel books, but Jack wasn't interested. They represented the past. "He was happy just to have his grandson come over and swim," said Steve Sherman. "And tell war stories. Toward the end, that's all he wanted to do, tell World War Two stories, everything from the time he was drafted and inducted into basic training till they sent him home on a ship."

While undergoing chemotherapy, he couldn't draw as much as he used to, but during Thibodeaux's weekly visit, he looked at his friend's newest drawings and offered advice. One afternoon, Thibodeaux held up a drawing of a heroine on skates. "Jack, look at this."

He told Thibodeaux to call her Helen Wheels and make her the queen of all skaters. Then he explained how she could fit into

Thibodeaux's group the Malibu Maniacs, which he and his business partner, Richard French, hoped to self-publish through their company, Genesis West. When Jack heard Thibodeaux wanted to revive a comic he'd once done, *Last of the Viking Heroes*, he offered even more advice: Establish these new characters – competitive skater Thrasher, stuntman Andre, and Helen Wheels – then cast the spotlight on the Vikings. And publish three to four books a month.

Thibodeaux replied, "Jack, I'm not fast enough!"

Jack ignored him. "Mike, you have an epic brewing here. Start with the *Malibu Maniacs*, then bring in Darkfyre and Mystiko from *Phantom Force.*" Add another character to the cast, revive the *Viking Heroes*, juggle plots for two years, and wrap everything up with an emotionally charged finale.

Before Jack knew it, other companies wanted to publish more of his work. "He had become a great surviving superstar of the industry, and people were coming to him to do posters, lithographs, and limited-edition prints," said Mark Evanier. Jim Salicrup, who edited *Spider-Man* No. 1, now worked for Topps, a trading card company looking to sell as many comics as Marvel or Image Comics, the imprint started by the artists who left Marvel en masse. "I believe some guys representing one of Kirby's projects contacted Topps," Salicrup recalled. "Before they contacted me, I was thinking, Superheroes, Marvel, Image, DC, what can we do?"

The Kirby Company – two young entrepreneurs who had sold a few limited-edition statues based on Jack's designs and worked with Jack to develop a scenario and story lines – told Salicrup that Jack was involved and would receive about half of the profits; but Salicrup wanted to work directly with him. He convinced Topps to sign a deal to publish the Kirby Company's project, set it aside, and started discussing a separate deal with Roz Kirby that would bring her and Jack 100 percent of the money. "And Jack had a bunch of characters lying around, some of which were left over from that stash of drawings from the late sixties, even," Evanier said. Though Jack didn't feel well enough to write or draw any books, Roz negotiated what Salicrup called "a licensing deal, as if Kirby's characters had appeared in a movie or were toys." He wouldn't work on these comics, but he would receive royalties.

Salicrup, the chairman of Topps, the vice president, and the creative director then flew to California to meet the Kirbys at their home. Jack showed Salicrup old sketches and outlines for new heroes, and Salicrup grew a little nervous: Some might have been created for animation studios or other comic publishers. Jack handed him his old Secret City synopsis, sketches of a team called the Teen Agents, his earliest design for a huge cosmic bus used in *Jimmy Olsen*, and sketches of a group called Satan's Six, created when he was doing *The Demon*. He also offered characters that resembled experimental designs for the *Super Powers* toy line and comic. "I don't want to talk too much about that because I don't want to get anyone in trouble," Salicrup explained. "But at this point, he was older, he'd been ill. I don't want to sound as though he were trying to trick us in any way, but I was aware that he had given some of these characters to another company. And fortunately, I think that other company held Jack in such high regard that they were willing to look the other way."

Chapter 21

One afternoon in 1993, Steve Sherman came over to the Kirbys' house. He excitedly told Jack about work he was doing with new computers. "Jack, you should be trying computers, because you can do your collages and all this stuff."

Jack answered, "Nah, I'm not interested. I don't care."

Sherman was surprised. In the past, Jack would have been first to leap up and yell, "Oh! Let's see, let's do it!"

But now, licensing characters to Topps was enough. The deal brought in money for him and Roz, and it let him see unfinished creations in print. His name would also appear on every book. After Jack signed the deal – giving Topps the right to republish *Captain Victory*, *Silver Star*, and, technically, since Marvel owned the character but he held the copyright to it, the *Silver Surfer* graphic novel – Topps's chairman sent them fresh bagels from New York, and Salicrup reached out to Ditko and Heck to create this new "Kirbyverse."

In many ways, it was similar to what he had tried to accomplish at DC twenty-two years ago: Sell a publisher ideas, then have other writers and artists actually create the books. "And everyone made a lot of money off it," said Jim Salicrup. "I was happy that Don Heck, for example, got his largest royalty check ever from Topps. But another part of me felt, 'That's not right. These guys should have gotten a lot more from Marvel.'"

Soon, Jack greeted comic fans and professionals at a convention in Los Angeles. He glimpsed Don Heck – whom he had always wanted to work on the Fourth World series and had just done a great job on Topps's *Night Glider* – and in front of a convention crowd, the two old friends rushed to each other, hugged, and cried. Then each told onlookers that the other was the bigger talent. During dinner that night, Jack kept thanking Salicrup. "I had to finally say, 'Stop! Jack, this is crazy! If there's anyone who should be thanked, it's you! I wouldn't be here if it wasn't for your work! And everything I'm trying to do is in my own way trying to thank you!' And I meant that," Salicrup explained.

Jack then appeared at the 1993 San Diego Comic Convention and was stunned to see how far the industry had come. In the enormous convention center, forty thousand fans and professionals met, publishers unveiled new products, and comic dealers stood behind tables, selling rare comics and art by fan favorites. Everywhere he looked, he saw trading cards, T-shirts, collectible toys, superhero statues, videotapes, cinematic Japanese comic books (*manga*) and cartoon movies (anime), and pages of original art stolen ages ago from Marvel or DC. Since the Kirbyverse books were still being assembled, he didn't have to sit in one spot and sign autographs or field questions. Instead, he strolled through the cavernous space, observing modern fandom: There were comics he hadn't seen in fifty years; fans waiting on line for artists to autograph their books; promotional videos on huge monitors hyping strange new titles. "Jack was sort of wandering around, sometimes feeling kind of lost and not a part of it," Salicrup noted.

At Topps, Salicrup called Stan Lee's office in Los Angeles. He knew it probably wouldn't happen, but he wanted to ask Stan to script a Secret City story. Stan said he'd love to but couldn't owing to his exclusive contract with Marvel. "There were a lot of things people wanted me to do," Stan explained, then recalled how Goodman forbade him from teaming with one entrepreneur for a chain of "Stan Lee's superhero shops" that would have paid him royalties.

When Roy Thomas agreed to work on the books, Salicrup said, "It was a dream come true for me." Though he didn't like everything in the materials Topps provided, Thomas closely followed Jack's ideas. So did Tony Isabella, who would call Jack at home to run his latest Satan's Six ideas by him. Jack told Isabella to make the book his own, but Isabella kept calling. When Isabella named a bodyguard Bjorn Again, Jack thought it might offend people; he said make it Bjorn Happy. After Isabella said he named the devil's lawyer Odious Kabodious and told a few lawyer jokes, Jack asked, "Geez, you don't think lawyers are gonna get upset?"

Before Jack knew it, Image Comics also wanted to work with him. Since CNN and *Barron's* first announced the birth of Image in February 1992, the artists who left Marvel en masse in December 1991 had given Marvel and DC a run for their money. Though Marvel's resources could easily push a small publisher out of the direct market, Image's superhero comics – Rob Liefeld's *Youngblood* (a media-savvy fusion of DC's *Teen Titans* and Marvel's *The Avengers*), Todd McFarlane's 2-million-copy-selling *Spawn*, Erik Larsen's early Marvel-like *Savage Dragon* (a cop who resembled one of Jack's Inhumans), Jim Lee's hit team book *WildC.A.T.s*, Jim Valentino's less popular (but 750,000-copy selling) *Shadowhawk*, and other titles – continued to do well. After speaking to Thibodeaux and his business partner, Richard French, at their company Genesis West, Image offered to print *Phantom Force* and pay Jack some money. "He was just pulling whatever he had in the file or whatever Mike would help him with," said Sherman.

During this period, Sherman stopped by for a visit, and Jack took his former assistant aside and said, "That's it. I'm done."

Sherman was bewildered. "You're not gonna draw anymore?"

"Nope."

"Really? You're just going to give it up like that?"

"That's it," Jack repeated. "I'm done."

He made a few bucks doing cover reproductions – tracing old covers – but his eyesight was bad, his hand shook, and he just didn't have it anymore. "You have to figure, the guy was seventy-one years old, so it was about time," Sherman said.

In April 1993, Topps unleashed the first wave of Kirbyverse books: one-shot issues of *Captain Glory*, *Night Glider*, and *Bombast*. They were followed by the four-issue miniseries *Jack Kirby's Secret City Saga*. Topps shipped the comics in plastic bags, with "Kirbychrome" trading cards based on his designs but drawn by other artists. Topps then rolled out two more four-issue miniseries, the comedic *Satan's Six*, and *Jack Kirby's Teen Agents*. "Since Jack wasn't really involved, I don't think they captured his vision all that well," Thibodeaux said. "With the exception of a few covers and ten interior pages, Jack didn't do much at all." Jack, however, felt they were great. Many of his loyal fans agreed. "That first issue of *Satan's Six* sold two hundred fifty thousand copies," said Isabella. "My royalty check was the biggest I'd ever gotten in comics."

At that summer's San Diego Comic Convention, Topps heavily promoted Jack and his new books. With his daughter at his side, Jack ran into Gene Colan. The previous year, Colan had asked, "Jack, do you have your badge?" Jack had replied by imitating the bandito in John Huston's *Treasure of the Sierra Madre*, joking, "Badge? Badge? I don't have no stinkin' badge!" Now Colan noticed he didn't have his badge on again. "I asked him if he had it, and he said, 'What badge?' And he started to feel around and he wasn't sure of himself. I could see a different man there. He had been ill. And he was being helped in there with his daughter. It was different. I was trying to spoof with him a little, but I could see he took everything too seriously."

At a table in the Topps booth, surrounded by comics and trading cards, Jack met fans, answered questions, cracked jokes, let people videotape him, and posed for photos next to huge promotional displays. "He just came alive," Salicrup recalled. "He had a big smile on his face; he was having the greatest time."

After the Inkpot Awards ceremony, he and Roz joined one thousand other professionals and fans at an after-party. He noticed the crowd part and Stan Lee – tall, with graying hair and rose-colored glasses – quickly enter the room. Jack felt a little nervous. In the three years since the *Comics Journal* interview, they hadn't spoken. Even so, he called Stan over. "I was always friendly with him, no matter how he felt," Stan recalled.

Stan approached. Jack looked up at the taller, younger guy. Stan flashed his trademark grin. They hugged each other. "And Jack said something strange to me," Stan recalled. "He called me over and he said . . . and again, I felt Jack wasn't fully with it, you know . . . he said to me" – sternly – "'You have nothing to reproach yourself about, Stan.' And it was such . . . kind of a strange thing for him to say. I was glad to hear it, but I didn't expect it. And that was about it. And then some people came over and interrupted us and he went away and I went away. That was the last time I ever spoke to him." Stan Lee couldn't believe what he'd heard. Maybe deep down, he thought, Jack had always felt something positive about him. "And I think we worked so well together that if he had stayed with me, there's no end to what we might have accomplished, you know?"

To a new generation of comic book creators, Jack Kirby was a legend. And they wanted to pay tribute to him by including him as a character in the comics they were doing. He appreciated the sentiment but didn't want his face in anything copyrighted by DC or Marvel. Creators stuck him in their stories anyway and presented him with the finished comics. "Thank you, thank you," he'd say. "I'm honored." He didn't want to offend anyone.

At home, he continued to stick to his usual schedule. He'd sleep late, wake up, get the paper, eat breakfast, go through his mail, talk with Roz, and chat with a few people on the phone. Fans and friends called often, and someone was always visiting the house. "But his health was really starting to get to him," Sherman remembered. "His hair had turned snow white."

When he first met Jack, Sherman said, you couldn't tell his age. He was fifty-three at the time, but one might think he was twenty or twenty-one. "Not that he looked that way, but the way he acted throughout the entire twenty or thirty years I knew him. He was one of the few guys who was the same age as your father but didn't act like your father. He was into comics and fantasy and science fiction and could talk to you about that stuff and also talk about science and everything else. So he was like your friend, not just someone who was older and interested in this stuff. But in the last year of his life, his health had just sort of gotten to him. You could see he was a seventy-one-year-old guy. He didn't wanna really talk about comics anymore. He didn't want to talk about the characters. If someone asked, *then* he'd talk about the old days, but as far as talking about the creation of Marvel Comics and all that, he felt he'd said it all. He would say, 'You want to know about it? You can read it. It's in the books. Go read it.'"

For years, author Janet Berliner had worked with Jack, trying to turn his ambitious, horrifying, and somewhat fragmentary novel, *The Horde* – which he'd begun shortly after moving to California decades earlier and abandoned once he saw that scenarios he dreamed up were actually being reported on the nightly news – into something workable. Though a few other people got involved and Janet finally left the project, she dropped by to see him and Roz one rainy afternoon in December 1993. He was feeling ill but wanted to tell her a little more about the war. Roz urged him to relax and save his strength, but soon she got them all some coffee and homemade cookies. In the kitchen, Jack tried to tell them about what he'd seen, while the rain pounded on the roof and the windows, and Janet Berliner laughed and cried and laughed some more and looked as happy as she had when she'd first fallen in love with both of them.

Around this time, Joe's son, Jim Simon, claimed that Jack called his first partner to apologize for showing the Silver Spider proposal to Marvel Comics. "Maybe Jack felt guilty, I don't know," Jim said, "but Jack sent him the original Spider-Man that he still had in his possession when my father had created his version of Spiderman in 1953." He added, "They were talking on the phone, and I think Jack said he had it and he sent it back to my father. And I have it here someplace. It's a very large logo. It says 'Spiderman.' The only difference is there is no hyphen between 'Spider' and 'man.'"

"You know what?" Mike Thibodeaux said. "I was just recently up at the Kirby archives and there was a logo in there, a Spider-Man logo, which they've had forever, so I don't understand what this is about. Are they saying they got something back from him?" He added: "I think that's false. I think I would have heard about this because I was the guy usually mailing stuff back to people. I had to mail out all the artwork to whomever. This never happened."

After early issues of *Secret City* sold about two hundred thousand copies during the spring of 1993, Topps released two more mini-series – revivals of *Captain Victory* (now called *Victory*) and *Silver Star*. But when Topps canceled both after one issue, in early 1994, Salicrup called Roz, who then relayed the bad news to Jack. "Eventually, the market forces were overwhelming us," Salicrup explained.

Roz handed Mark Evanier a file that held sketches and half a dozen concepts for new comics – some developed, some barely there – and asked him to find another company to license them. Knowing that Jack could use the money during his retirement, Evanier dutifully promised to try his best. Though Topps's books were being axed, Jack sensed that *Phantom Force*, published by Image, would sell phenomenally well and yield a huge royalty check. "He had nothing but respect for those guys," Thibodeaux recalled, and the Image guys reciprocated. "They took out a double-page ad one time that really moved him. It was just about Jack. It had a picture of him and big letters that said 'Trailblazer.'" And Jack enjoyed their work. In their big guns and heroic figures he saw the brashness and boldness he had brought to his own work during the 1960s.

But his health continued to deteriorate. "I remember him one time saying he wanted to draw," said Thibodeaux. "He wanted to create. I think this was so ingrained in his soul. These are the things I remember him talking about, just wanting to draw again. Those last few months he wasn't doing anything at all."

Thibodeaux tried to show him some new Marvel comics, but Jack refused to accept them. Instead, he thumbed through hard-bound volumes of his stories from previous decades. "And he did drawings inside these books." Throughout his life, Jack never read any of his old comics – he might thumb through a copy if he needed to see a picture of how he'd drawn someone's costume. For some reason, holding one volume open, Jack started reading a copy of his 1940s work *In Love*. "That was the only time I remember him looking back at something. I was sure he was actually reading it because he was slowly turning the pages."

On Friday, February 4, 1994, Thibodeaux arrived at the house to take Jack and Roz out to lunch. That day, they laughed, joked, and ate. "And there was nothing out of the ordinary. He seemed pretty healthy," Thibodeaux recalled. On Sunday, Jack woke up, left his bed, and, as he always did, went outside to get the paper. He'd read it, eat breakfast, talk with Roz, and maybe accept a few phone calls. Opening the door, he stepped out of the house. Then he turned and went back into the house and into the kitchen and –

Roz found him. She immediately called Mike Thibodeaux. "She was crying. She couldn't talk at first. Then she said that Jack just passed away." He'd been trying to maintain his everyday routine and collapsed and had a heart attack in the kitchen. "She told me to make the phone calls. I made a few and raced over there. The rest of it is just a blur. I really didn't like that time."

"I felt terrible," Stan recalled. "I wasn't surprised because Jack had been ill. I could tell that last time I met him and a time before when I saw him at a convention he wasn't the old Jack Kirby. He wasn't with it somehow."

Someone was telling people Stan was banned from the funeral – though he had just attended Jack's birthday party – so Stan contacted author Harlan Ellison, who knew Jack's friends, and asked him to call Evanier and see if he could attend. Evanier asked Roz and she said yes, she definitely wanted him there. In his dark suit and glasses, tall, slim, dashing, and uncharacteristically downbeat, Stanley Martin Lieber entered the funeral to one or two looks of surprise. Ignoring them, he greeted Roz quietly. "Thank you for coming," she said sincerely.

"She appreciated it because even though they fought and had all these disagreements, they were all from the same era," Sherman noted.

After the funeral, a small group stayed behind to watch Jack Kirby's coffin descend into his grave. "It was pretty awful, a very somber and quiet moment," said Thibodeaux. "It just seemed so final; he was gone. This is it: This guy's gone." By his side was rock musician and Kirby fan Glenn Danzig, who said, "Long live the king."

Thibodeaux nodded, appreciating the remark. A young newcomer who had recently inked Jack's work then handed Mike a bottle of wine and said, "We need a toast."

Thibodeaux cleared his throat. He said, "May Jack's stature as an artist rise to the level of those legendary masters Michelangelo, da Vinci, and Van Gogh." After taking a sip, he passed the bottle around, then grabbed it and poured some out for Jack. "The one thing that struck me as sort of ironic is that he left Max Fleischer when he was like eighteen, because it was like a sweatshop that his father worked in, doing piecework," Steve Sherman recalled. "And he said he never wanted to do piecework in his life; he didn't want to end up like his dad. Yet, if you think about it, he ended up doing piecework. Even though he didn't work in the sweatshop, he still ended up working, just turning out page after page after page, you know, for a salary. . . . But if he didn't turn the pages out, he didn't get the salary. I don't know if he ever really achieved the level that he was hoping he would, where the work would generate an income without his having to sit at a table and draw."

Roz returned to the house in Thousand Oaks. Jack's art was still on the walls. His table was there. So were his science magazines, hardbound volumes, and old comics. She was lonely but had friends and family to make sure she was well and that she wasn't burdened by people who could be nuisances. And soon, Stan Lee called to ask her to lunch.

At the table, he apologized for a few things he'd said about Jack in public. In the past, he had told one reporter that Jack's writing for DC was amateur; that Evanier had to have ghostwritten anything good in there; that this proved that he, not Jack, had written the Lee-Kirby stories. Another time, he told a reporter he thought Jack was experiencing mental illness. In other interviews, Stan claimed he'd created everything alone, Jack had drawn what he told him to; that he'd even stood over Jack's shoulder and told him how the costumes should look. "It was a very pleasant, nice meeting, and I'm so glad that happened," Stan said.

Chapter 22

In 1995, a year after Jack's death, Hollywood continued to express major interest in characters Jack and Stan co-created. Four years after he was said to be directing the film, James Cameron finished his far-reaching treatment for a movie about Spider-Man, delivered it to Carolco, and things seemed to be moving forward. Twentieth Century–Fox, meanwhile, was attracted to movies about the X-Men, the Fantastic Four (with Chris Columbus as producer), Daredevil, and Iron Man. At Universal, producer Gale Ann Hurd wanted to develop a Hulk movie. Columbia Pictures wanted Dr. Strange; New Line wanted Blade: Vampire Hunter; producer Bernd Eichinger (who had handled the first *Fantastic Four* film) wanted a movie about the Silver Surfer; and Pressman Productions optioned Luke Cage. If all went well, Marvel heroes would appear in superior movies, and Stan – who was still busy pitching all these heroes to film and television executives – would consult and receive co–executive producer credit.

In addition to tirelessly promoting Marvel, Stan worked with a small staff – supposedly including Roy Thomas and Kurt Busiek, both of whom worked on the Kirbyverse books – on another self-contained comic line, Excelsior Comics: four new titles he hoped Marvel would publish sometime during 1996.

Stan had wanted to get the new books out for a while now, but Marvel was trying to license the characters to a company that made video games. Until that deal was signed, nothing would happen.

The delay was getting to him – he'd been developing Excelsior Comics for a year now – but Marvel executives said he simply had to wait until the right time.

The Excelsior titles were unlike the violent and brooding X-Men, Image, or Malibu comics dominating the sales charts. They were almost old-fashioned, closer to what fans called "retro." Though he publicly praised the new style of comics, Stan actually preferred the retro ones (including *Marvels*, Busiek's faithful retelling of Stan and Jack's earliest stories from the viewpoint of a newspaper photographer of the 1960s). Accordingly, they would have nothing to do with the traditional Marvel Universe. "In other words, it's unlikely that Spider-Man or the Hulk or Ghost Rider will be guest-starring in any of our books, or vice versa," Stan said at the time. "Of course, that may change, but that's the plan right now."

Potential for growth, however, was enormous. Each book was named after one title character but featured dozens of supporting players and villains. And instead of New York, Stan would set the stories in modern-day Los Angeles.

As with the *2099* line, Stan would limit his writing to one title – at least one first issue. Other writers and four different artists would handle the rest.

Stan wanted to discuss specifics, he told a reporter, but preferred to wait until the books were ready and Marvel made its big announcement. "I will say that I created the concepts for all four books. I more or less created all the characters and incidental characters, that is, the original ideas of what I wanted and how I wanted them done." But from this point on, other writers would handle three of them while he'd serve as an editor in chief.

Unfortunately, Stan was preparing – and banking on – a bold new line just when Marvel was experiencing financial woes, and the industry itself was finally, inexorably, on the verge of collapse. After many of their artists left to form Image Comics, and Image ate into the company's market share, Marvel had tried to lure "hot artists" with higher rates. "They went public shortly before we left," said the talented Erik Larsen. "Their stock took a big hit when we all pulled out of there. And they did a lot of things to try to keep the impression they were growing and becoming bigger and selling more comics every year." This included plenty of new spin-off Marvel titles. In addition to *The Fantastic Four*, readers could buy *Fantastic Five* and *Fantastic Force*. Marvel published double-size "unlimited" titles; they offered regular books, expensive annuals, and the *2099* line. Few, if any, however, matched the sales of record-breaking debut issues of *Spider-Man*, *X-Force*, and *X-Men*. Many of these later comics, Larsen felt, were actually "worthless in terms of entertainment value or anybody wanting them."

Marvel also kept including enhancements, trading cards, foil covers, and plastic bags (now viewed by legitimate fans who actually read the comics as worthless junk geared for collectors) with their titles. "But like any other trick, it gets old fast," said former employee Matt Morra. "Let's face it, they were slapping a 'prismatic foil-embossed dye-cut cover' on *Silver Sable* number twenty-five, as if anyone really was a big *Silver Sable* fan to begin with." Collectors and speculators – who could once be counted on to greedily buy multiple copies of certain bagged comics – had long since stopped collecting, owing to Marvel's multiple printings, which reduced demand for their so-called investments. And Marvel's penchant for presenting long-drawn-out stories that crossed over into dozens of titles became far too expensive for the average comic reader to afford to follow. "At that point, this sort of feeling that the Marvel Universe was something you could share in kind of snapped," said former journalist and comic writer Mark Waid. "I think that was a very important turning point for Marvel, when they started publishing more things than you could collect." After a precipitous dip in sales, a demoralizing mass layoff ensued. "The first round was very cheerful and gentlemanly, actually," Morra recalled. "You were given a couple of days to clean out your office and a pretty good severance, too. I received two weeks for each year of service, quite a few months of severance."

Next, a wave of comic shops shut their doors. The way it worked,

Marvel created and printed the books, then sent them to its distributor. Marvel and its distributor sold the books to comic shops for a discount off the cover price (about 40 percent). But comic shops bought the books on a nonreturnable basis. They'd get the bargain but take a loss if it didn't sell. With collectors out of the market, Marvel and other publishers learned that at least 30 percent of the comics ordered by shops were still sitting in stores. Because they spent money on books that didn't move, thousands of shop owners couldn't afford to pay their bills and closed down.

This explained why the last two years had seen industry sales plummet from $850 million to $650 million. Of course, $650 million was higher than 1991's $350 million, but Marvel could no longer ignore that the industry was in decline. The company couldn't even count on former readers to shore up sales. Since opening its doors in 1992, Image had taken 15 percent of Marvel's market share. With Image now foundering, these readers didn't return to Marvel products. By December 1994, Marvel reacted to the downturn in sales by canceling twenty-four comic series and firing half the editorial staff in a single day. Fired employees were encouraged to leave immediately; six editorial offices stood vacant by the close of business.

After shrinking from 110 to 50 titles, Marvel decided to buy its distributor Heroes World, Tom DeFalco explained, "because they felt that they could cut out the middleman and make more money – which was insane." Marvel bought the East Coast distributor and, in March 1995, told comic shop owners they could buy Marvel products only from Heroes World and that Heroes World would no longer carry books by competing publishers. Instead of paying Heroes World for a shipment of comics from various publishers, comic shop owners now had to pay five or six distributors to obtain the variety they once got from one company. Many shops dropped Marvel but found that without customers buying Marvel's popular titles, they couldn't pay their bills. For other shop owners, many of the Marvel titles they had sold in high numbers had been unceremoniously canceled. Fans of these defunct books slowly stopped coming by, until these owners also couldn't afford to stay open. Over the last three years, an estimated 5,500 American comic shops had closed down. Only 4,500 – less than half – remained. With the industry edging closer to its grave and the once high-flying publisher facing money problems, Marvel canceled plans for Stan's Excelsior line, said Matt Morra (then working for another Marvel-related company). "Stan was working on this mysterious line, and one editor left New York to go work for him. And no one ever saw what it was."

"I actually had some strips drawn," Stan explained. "The problem was, I didn't want to hire any of the people Marvel was using." He tried using new artists, but in the end, he couldn't work with them as he had with the old bullpen guys, he added. "And when some of the strips were done and I looked at them, they were okay, they were good enough, but I wanted something better than 'okay' or 'good enough.' So I just figured I'd forget about the project, and I never did them."

In January 1996, Marvel laid off the editors of the *2099* line, and another 30 percent of their staff. (After a few final issues, the entire *2099* line was canceled.) Editors who still had jobs would go from editing four books to seven. There'd be no more expense account lunches with freelancers or exorbitant use of Federal Express. No more long-distance story conferences on the telephone, either. Editors now had to punch in three-digit codes before placing long-distance calls. "I would assume that if the bill was too high, they could say, 'Oh, here's the guy who did it, let's find out why,'" Morra quipped. There would also be no more free drinks in the soda machine. Half of the production staff – many of whom earned $18,000 annually – had abused the privilege, Morra added. "You said the word *free* to them, they were practically walking off with cases."

As the money problems continued to worsen, the new owners didn't know how to turn things around. "You didn't have to be a genius to figure out, 'Well, gee, this *X-Men*'s selling pretty well, we'll come out with another one,'" said former *X-Men* editor Jim

Salicrup. "That's great when things are going well. Unfortunately, when Marvel finally did start to decline, these people didn't know what to do. They just kept doing the same thing. 'Well, what do we do? Sell or bid?' 'I know! We'll come out with another *X-Men* book!'"

Where the stock had once done great, Marvel began to rack up a crushing amount of bank debt by buying companies that wound up going bust, said Tom DeFalco. And when stock analysts came in to assess the company, he recalled, they routinely told owners the stock was falling for specific reasons, one of them being "because Marvel lost the Image artists." This, however, was incorrect, said DeFalco. "In fact, when the Image artists left, they created such a controversy and spotlight on the industry that all of our sales went up." *X-Men* and *Spider-Man* sold better without Jim Lee and Todd McFarlane. "But the stockbrokers assumed, 'Oh, they lost some major talent. That must be why the company is hurting.' So every time they did a review of the stock, they would always say it's bad because Marvel lost the Image artists . . . So they went and did a deal and brought them back, because they thought stock analysts would stop pointing at the Image artists. That was all just a publicity thing to try to help the stock sales."

In a deal that evoked the company's earliest days with First Funnies Inc. and Joe Simon and other packagers, the Image artists – Rob Liefeld and Jim Lee – were called in to Marvel and given carte blanche. After deciding which two books each artist would handle, and coming up with the title *Heroes Reborn*, they quickly redesigned everything about the Fantastic Four, Iron Man, Captain America, and the Avengers and explained the differences by ending another long-drawn-out crossover ("Onslaught") with the original versions of the characters banished to another dimension for a year.

Liefeld's first *Captain America* arrived with four different covers, and Lee's *Fantastic Four* impressed film producer and director Chris Columbus (who asked Lee's opinion about what a film version should look like), but *Heroes Reborn* didn't catch on. If anything, in-house editors felt slighted by the company's decision to use outsiders to improve sales of four of their most famous titles. A few creators, who had worked on the books for years and developed loyal followings, shared this opinion. "None of what they came up with was especially exciting, interesting, or different," Morra said. "I don't want to bad-mouth anybody, but it wasn't broken to begin with. They're good characters. Yeah, they need some new blood every now and then, but the idea of 'Let's nuke it and start from scratch,' the way Rob Liefeld did, just doesn't make sense."

Despite *Heroes Reborn*, Marvel continued to teeter on the brink. Now, writers and artists weren't even sure if they'd be paid for their work. "The mood in the office was complete and total defeat," revealed Mark Waid, then consulting editor. "You could measure the morale with an eyedropper."

Marvel tried to cut even more operating costs: eliminating the coffeemaker; getting rid of Federal Express and other forms of shipping; restricting use of the Xerox copier machine. "They actually limited the number of long-distance phone calls that editors could make, which was patently absurd, because almost every freelancer who works for Marvel works outside of New York," said Waid.

Fans conducted what they called the "Marvel Death Watch." *Forbes* commented on the low stock price and implied that the new owner was demolishing the entire industry. During autumn of 1996, Marvel went into utter free fall, losing $437 million that quarter alone. On December 27, 1996, with comic sales dropping by over 70 percent, Marvel Comics, after fifty-seven years, finally declared bankruptcy.

Marvel also fired many of its freelancers and employees. After Herb Trimpe, who'd been with the company since late 1966, was fired via Fed Ex, he tried to contact Stan, said Trimpe's wife, Linda Fite. "Stan was out on the West Coast. He was no longer in control of the print side of things. They were using his name, and I'm sure they were paying him for that, but he could not throw his weight around. And if he tried, and then they slapped him down, do you understand how shameful that would have been? 'Cause then you'd really know you were more toothless than you'd even feared, you know? They cut him out of the loop."

Soon, Stan himself received a letter that said his lifetime contract with Marvel, which brought a high six-figure annual salary, was canceled. Within days, Stan was invited to meet with Ike Perlmutter, one of the company's new owners. After a warm greeting, Stan claimed, Perlmutter stressed how important he was to Marvel and that he'd be making more money than ever. "I was told that it happened to all the employees because during the bankruptcy they had to do it, but not to worry, they would give me another contract. So I took their word for it," he said. The new contract was for two years and much less money. "It was a big drama for me because the contract that they offered wasn't as good as the one I had had," Stan explained.

He called his attorney.

After Jack died, Roz Kirby's health worsened. "She was lost without him," recalled Steve Sherman. That Jack's artwork was all around her in the studio made it even more difficult to live in the house. Fortunately, her children – Susan, Barbara, Lisa, and Neal – and extended family looked out for her. "Especially Mike Thibodeaux, who was there to take her to the doctor and to make sure that she wasn't alone," Sherman added.

Roz – curly-haired brunette, warm smile, sparkling eyes, elegant dresses, plainspoken and fearless – also attended annual Fourth of July picnics thrown by her son, Neal, and had people call her on the telephone or visit during weekends. The market crash took the good books, the bad books, and most of Jack's Topps books with it, but fans kept contacting her. Jack never realized how important or big he was, she told Thibodeaux. Now she was a fan icon herself, and this, Thibodeaux believed, kept her healthy. "It kept her going. It made her feel as if Jack were still there."

She looked forward to attending conventions. "The only problem was, it was later in her life, and we used to have to take a wheelchair 'cause she wouldn't walk too much. After about ten minutes, I'd have to put her in a wheelchair and wheel her around." But even then, fans still came up to speak with her and ask questions or request an autograph.

One weekend, Tony Christopher of Landmark Entertainment got her a few tickets to the Las Vegas show O. Thibodeaux drove Roz and her sister, Anita, to Vegas. That night, the sisters played blackjack until two in the morning. While entering the elevator, being wheeled past the open doors and into the car, Roz told Thibodeaux that she wished Jack were there. "I think it was one time when she really felt him gone. They were inseparable."

Wanting to provide for her children and grandchildren, however, kept her going. "She was going to find a way to make money for them. She felt she needed to be there for them." When her grandson, Jeremy moved in, and he wanted to enter the comic business by making bumper stickers, she said, "Oh, go for it; get this done." Later, she supported his dream of writing and self-publishing an all-new *Captain Victory* comic to keep Jack's characters and memory alive.

One day, Mark Evanier came by to tell Roz that producers would include a few New Gods in DC's new *Superman* cartoon. She was thrilled. Jack's heroes would live on – and she'd receive payment for the use of the characters. But best of all, the "Father's Day" episode aired with Jack's name in the credit line. She then learned that Warner Brothers was developing an animated *New Gods* feature; Evanier, hired as a Kirby consultant, informed her that the studio had redesigned the characters and begun to question the story. As he told it, half of the executives said *New Gods* was too much like *Star Wars* and they couldn't produce it. The other half said it wasn't enough like *Star Wars* so they couldn't do it. After a few Warner Brothers' animated projects tanked at the box office, the studio abandoned the project.

Roz's life continued with a certain amount of emptiness, Evanier recalled, though fans continued to invite her to tributes, to call, to come over and pay their respects. "And in a strange way, I always felt that it was kind of nice that she had that moment in the spotlight." When he took her to the San Diego Comic Convention and introduced her, the audience cheered and gave the same standing ovation they once gave Jack. "And it was nice that she got a little solo moment . . . because she was very important to his work and career. I always said Jack was a two-person operation. Only one of them sat at the board, but two of them did the work. She took care of him, she dressed him, she drove him around; they were absolutely inseparable. It was an amazing marriage and partnership."

On Sunday, September 28, 1997, Roz's daughter Lisa decided to throw her a seventy-fifth birthday party. The guest list included Evanier, Marv Wolfman, Mike Royer, Steve Rude, Len Wein, Mike Thibodeaux, *Lost in Space* actor Billy Mumy, singer Glenn Danzig, and Steve Sherman, among others. "A lot of people came up to the house, and that was probably the last big party we had before she became ill," Lisa said later. "She was really shining during that time; she was so appreciative of everybody being there."

Three months later, Roz caught a cold. Once it traveled to her chest, she was taken to a hospital. Mike Thibodeaux showed up the night of Sunday, December 21, 1997, and thought she seemed fine. She was coherent. After chatting for a while, he told her, "I'm gonna say a prayer for you, for a quick recovery."

"Don't worry about me," she answered. "I'm not going anywhere. Too many people are counting on me."

"Stay healthy, Roz."

At four in the morning, Thibodeaux's telephone rang. Roz's granddaughter, Tracy, said Roz had passed away in her sleep. That night, Mike stayed up and considered how Jack and Roz had changed his life. "See, I grew up with a very violent father," Mike explained. "He was pretty wild; he liked to fight a lot, not a good father. I didn't know there were men as kind as Jack, and that influenced me somehow – that a person could be as kind and caring and solidly good a soul. And Roz: I've never seen a cooler couple in my life." He wouldn't be able to visit Jack anymore or bring him videos or chat with Roz on the phone. He'd miss them both. He would also be forever grateful to them.

After her death, Mark Evanier called Stan Lee and invited him to the service. On Friday, December 26, friends and family gathered at the Chapel of the Oaks at the Valley Oaks Memorial Park in Westlake Village. A few people from the comic industry also showed up: Mike Royer, Mike Thibodeaux, Steve Sherman, Alfredo Alcala, Buzz Dixon, Sergio Aragonés, Paul Smith, Len Wein, and others. Evanier concluded his eulogy by saying, "Today, we're all sad to lose her. But we're glad he's got her back."

Epilogue

For fifty years, Jack Kirby drew more pages than any other comic book artist. He also never ran out of ideas. Every decade of his career found him taking the medium in bold new directions. The 1940s saw him work on *Captain America*, DC's *Sandman*, and the lucrative Simon & Kirby creation of the romance comic. The 1950s brought *Boy's Ranch* (a "kid gang meet *Shane*"), *Fighting American*, a more exciting *Green Arrow*, *Challengers of the Unknown*, the *Sky Masters* strip, and (with Simon again) the less successful but highly influential *The Double Life of Private Strong* and *The Fly*. The 1960s ushered in the Lee-Kirby era, bringing to life The Fantastic Four, The Incredible Hulk, the mighty Thor, the astonishing Ant-Man, the invincible Iron Man, Sgt. Fury and His Howling Commandos, The Avengers, The Uncanny X-Men, Galactus, The Silver Surfer, The Inhumans, and the Marvel Universe. In a span of just a few short years, Kirby and Lee forever changed the American comic book by introducing angst-ridden heroes, sympathetic villains, and a dynamic style that inspired everything that followed. "They were doing the best mainstream comics since EC," said *Comics Journal* publisher Gary Groth.

If he'd retired back then, Jack would have already done more than enough to merit *Wizard* telling its readership, "Without any doubt, Jack Kirby is the single most important creator in the history of American comic books."

But in subsequent decades, Jack continued to try to move comics closer to the mainstream, creating the entire Fourth World, the modern crossover, *The Demon*, *OMAC*, and *Kamandi* for DC; *The Eternals*, *Machine Man*, *Devil Dinosaur*, and Herbie the Robot for Marvel; villains for *Thundarr*; new comic heroes Captain Victory and Silver Star during the 1980s; and another ambitious trilogy, as well as his own "Kirbyverse," during his final days in the 1990s.

It's a testament to his genius that, forty years later, the Marvel Comics heroes he created or designed continue to draw readers. Though modern artists use less creative styles and tell darker stories, *The Hulk* is still about mild-mannered Bruce Banner turning into a rampaging green monster; *Thor* is still about a god using his fabled hammer, Mjolnir, to protect planet Earth and Asgard; the characters in *The X-Men* remain outcasts with strange powers (and include many of Stan and Jack's founding members); *Captain America* is still about a patriot lobbing his shield at enemies' faces; and *The Fantastic Four* heroes continue to square off against cosmic villains.

As for some of Jack's other heroes, Machine Man, the Eternals, and the Black Panther still appear in Marvel books, the sentient robot, under his original name X-51, anchoring the critically acclaimed *Earth X* miniseries; the Eternals are currently the subject of a mature-themed comic; and the Panther remains one of Marvel's most popular draws. Other concepts such as the Watcher, Galactus, Dr. Doom, and the Red Skull are all vital components of the Marvel Universe. Though Marvel has in recent years moved away from the Jack-like "Marvel style," opting instead to emulate the animation seen in Japanese cartoons, his art style continues to inspire artists like Steve Rude, Jose Ladronn, Walter Simonson, John Byrne, Erik Larsen, and Mike Mignola.

Marvel also continues to reprint Stan and Jack's early work in enormous telephone-size reprint volumes called *Marvel Essentials* and to use many of these stories as the foundation for works like the enjoyable tribute *The World's Greatest Comic Magazine*, the revisionist *The Ultimates*, the nostalgic *Hulk: Gray*, and the novelistic *Marvels* (whose artist, Alex Ross, called Jack "more or less the

Picasso of comics"). Marvel editor in chief Joe Quesada has said that Jack's legacy "is seen in every cover and every page of superhero sequential art today."

At DC, meanwhile, Jack's Fourth World heroes are part of the publisher's mainstream universe. Mister Miracle has been in *The Justice League*; Orion received his own series; the rest of the New Gods starred in *Jack Kirby's Fourth World*; the Demon wandered through literary works like *Sandman* and *Swamp Thing* and received a new series; Darkseid is still one of the most powerful villains; and DC, ironically, seems to employ more freelance artists whose work evokes what artist John Totleben called Jack's "expressionistic shorthand."

Jack's influence in comics is inescapable, even in highbrow series like Neil Gaiman's *The Sandman*. Though Gaiman's work is typically reviewed as a groundbreaking departure from superhero comics – which many critics frown upon – Jack helped create *The Sandman*'s core idea and many of the guest stars in Gaiman's all-important early issues. Gaiman himself has said that the cover of Simon & Kirby's *Sandman* No. 1 during the 1970s intrigued him and that he'd been inspired by Simon & Kirby's "idea they somehow pursued people into dreams."

Another DC-related literary favorite, Alan Moore's *The League of Extraordinary Gentlemen*, closely follows *The Fantastic Four* formula (an invisible member, a meek man who can become a monster, and a bickering male-and-female couple battle villains with late-nineteenth-century high-tech weapons). And Moore – also a Kirby admirer – has drawn on the Lee-Kirby style for his short-lived *1963* line of comics, which revived the style of Stan's brash advertising copy, "Bullpen Bulletins" column, and archetypes like Thor.

The self-deprecating, dramatic, and poignant superhero stories routinely featured on television cartoons *The Powerpuff Girls*, *Dexter's Laboratory*, *The Fairly OddParents*, and Disney's *Teamo Supremo* also speak of Jack's enduring legacy, as do other series about the Silver Surfer, the X-Men, the Avengers, the Hulk, and

Iron Man. Even the New Gods have found their way onto DC's *Superman* cartoon (through the work of Kirby fan and producer Bruce Timm).

Jack himself continues to be the subject of well-received magazines the *Jack Kirby Quarterly*, the *Complete Jack Kirby*, and the award-winning *Jack Kirby Collector*, and his personal history inspired some of the most riveting moments in Michael Chabon's Pulitzer Prize-winning novel, *The Amazing Adventures of Kavalier & Clay* (artists having their fictional comic hero, the Escapist, slug Hitler, face death threats from Nazis, and be cheated by an old-time publisher). Chabon himself dedicated this masterpiece along with everything he's ever written to Jack, which led to more media mentions and one memorable *New York Times* profile of Chabon identifying Jack as creator of the Incredible Hulk.

In Hollywood, the phenomenal success of Fox's live-action *The X-Men* (which earned $100 million in a quick eleven days) and its sequel ($85.6 million in two days) was followed by other blockbusters: *Spider-Man* (a record $114.8 million its debut weekend), *Daredevil* (over $40 million), and *The Hulk* (a historic $62.6 million in forty-eight hours). Though based largely on the revisionist 1990s version of the hero, the latter film (by Oscar-winning director Ang Lee) included an extended sequence that pit the computer-generated Hulk against military helicopters in the desert. Even though *The Hulk* is the most faithful adaptation of Jack's vision ever to reach the silver screen, Mark Evanier recently noted that Jack would most likely "have resented the hell out of all these movies if they meant a lot of people making tons of money off Kirby work . . . with little or none of it going to anyone named Kirby." Even so, Hollywood studios continue to develop Marvel properties, including *The Fantastic Four*, expected to arrive in theaters by late 2004.

If Disney's computer-generated *Dinosaur* isn't reminding Jack's fans of *Devil Dinosaur* (right down to its tale of a dinosaur and a lemur uniting for a heroic expedition), if Neo, the hero of *The Matrix Reloaded*, isn't knocking dozens of clones in black suits off his back or pounding his right fist on the pavement before flying (scenes seemingly torn from Jack's old *Hulk* and *Thor* pages), the machine-lined walls, metal surfaces, explosions, acrobatic fight scenes, computer screens, and technological wonders in most big-budget action movies bring Jack's old drawings to mind. While most of his peers have been quietly relegated to comics history, Jack has had his work exhibited in France's National Center for International Comics museum and been the subject of heated bidding during auctions at Sotheby's; and no less than the Smithsonian Institution requested to have the old battered desk at which he sat and worked.

Stan Lee remains an energetic, exuberant, and bombastic spokesperson for the entire industry (which is again facing low sales), but among many comic book fans, his image as sole creator of the Marvel heroes remains subject to debate. For a time, the magazine *The Jack Kirby Collector* printed a series of articles entitled "A Failure to Communicate," in which author Mike Gartland analyzed Jack's original artwork pages, examined handwritten notes by Jack that seemed to suggest dialogue or captions, and noticed also that text in published versions credited as having been "Written by Stan Lee" in numerous cases corresponded to Jack's notes. Many fans took this to mean Jack did more writing than Marvel let on and began to denounce Stan. It didn't help that artist Gil Kane said, "Jack made up all those stories, and I'm positive he'd made up practically all the characters, with very few exceptions."

Then there was Will Jacobs and Gerard Jones's nonfiction book, *The Comic Book Heroes*, which conceded that Stan's basic plots, dialogue, and captions contributed immensely to the success of the Marvel heroes but added, "As for who created the characters themselves; who plotted all their adventures; who gave them their basic essences, and their tragic dilemmas, and their mythic force . . . that had to be Kirby."

After noting how the first issue of *The Fantastic Four* mirrored *Challengers of the Unknown*, right down to its structure of a full-length tale divided into four chapters, Jacobs and Jones wrote that without Jack, there would have been no Fantastic Four, Dr. Doom, Watcher, Black Panther, Galactus, Surfer, Skrulls, "Him," the Kree,

Hulk, Thor, Loki, Hercules, Asgard, Avengers, Captain America, Ant-Man, Giant-Man, Wasp, Nick Fury, S.H.I.E.L.D., Hydra, Red Skull, X-Men, or Magneto. "What would there be?" Jacobs and Jones continued. "Dr. Strange; Iron Man; maybe Spider-Man. There would only have been villains like the Eel, the Porcupine, the Melter, and the Matador. There might have been a Daredevil . . . if the company had managed to drag itself along until 1964. But: it's doubtful."

When Jack's fans witnessed Stan alternate between describing himself and Jack as "partners on almost everything" and taking full credit, their criticism was merciless. It was so scathing, so below-the-belt, that even Jon B. Cooke of the *Collector* felt the anti-Stan sentiment among fandom was getting out of hand. "I don't think Marvel Comics would have happened without Stan," Cooke explained. "I don't think it would have happened without Jack, either, or Steve Ditko. But my feeling is, enough already, in a lot of ways. I think that Stan, maybe rightfully so, took a beating in the 1980s. I don't know if it was particularly necessary to continue to do it now, just out of pure respect. The guy's – what – seventy-eight, seventy-nine years old?"

While the entire industry honors the incredible contribution of Jack Kirby, it should be remembered that Stan Lee served as editor, writer, art director, *and* company representative during the Silver Age of Marvel Comics. Stan brought Marvel the corporate industry identity that distinguished it from DC and other companies. The humorous nicknames for artists, dramatic cover captions, engaging "Bullpen Bulletins" column, shared universe in which heroes met one another, "Stan's Soapbox!," various Marvel fan clubs and phonograph records, the welcoming tone of the letters page, the concept of heroes with tragic flaws – these were all created by Stan Lee. Stan created hundreds of characters for titles like *Iron Man*, *Human Torch*, *Ant-Man*, *Spider-Man*, and *The Avengers*. Stan gave every hero a unique identity. Stan was also the best talent scout the industry has ever seen – John Romita, John Buscema, Gil Kane, and others are today considered some of the greatest ever to work in the medium.

Stan also discovered new talents like Jim Steranko and Barry Smith, whose work eventually changed the look of comics. These artists credit the collaborative process for inspiring greater creativity and many classic stories and characters.

Officially, however, Marvel's position seemingly remains that Stan Lee is the sole creator of the Marvel Universe. After his lifetime contract was canceled during the bankruptcy of 1996, Stan and his attorney, Arthur Lieberman, negotiated a new employee agreement (on November 18, 1998) that might explain why the image of Jack as only a penciler continues to be promoted despite evidence that suggests otherwise. In addition to paying him $1 million annually for ten to fifteen hours of work on Marvel's behalf each week, the agreement lets him serve as spokesman for Marvel, receive production credit on Marvel-based movies, retain the title of publisher, let him decide if he wants to be named chairman emeritus of the movie or television company, and gives him the right, for publicity, advertising, public relation, historical, and any related purposes, to claim he is the founder or creator of whatever characters he created or founded on behalf of Marvel, but only if these claims are "substantially identical to prior Marvel uses."

Despite his contract and reported seven-figure salary, Stan himself also goes without official creator credit in Marvel's comics. "Some people have said to me, 'Yeah, but you don't own any of the stuff that you did,'" he said. "That's true, but nobody robbed me, nobody cheated me. I knew going in I was working for a company and whatever I did would belong to the company. And I was free to walk away at any time if I didn't like it. But I enjoyed doing what I was doing. I feel I've always been well paid."

During the years since Jack's death – and the deaths of original bullpen members Gil Kane, Don Heck, and John Buscema – Stan has become quicker to name Jack and Steve Ditko as co-creators of the classic heroes. "He has since become this really mellow guy," Denny O'Neil revealed. "I see him every couple of years and it's always a very cordial meeting: We have lunch or just hang out and talk for a few minutes." Recently, when Stan agreed to create the foreword for O'Neil's book, *The DC Comics Guide to Writing Comics*, O'Neil said, "The one change he asked me to make was to give Steve Ditko more credit for the Spider-Man stories they did, which I thought was extremely gracious of him."

Marvel and the media might have handed him all the credit – and he might have not corrected media reports that named him sole creator – but Stan Lee has made efforts to emphasize Jack's many contributions. During interviews, he has called Jack the most talented, imaginative, and creative person he ever met in comics and an endless source of stories, concepts, and ideas. He's called his art "one of the most powerful, dramatic styles you could ever find" and explained repeatedly that Jack's pages typically included "things that Jack would have added that we never discussed, which were all wonderful." He's said that writing dialogue and captions was easy "because the characters looked as though they were saying things that mattered." He's added, "It's hard to explain, but it was just such a pleasure to write stories based on the artwork that Jack had done." Too bad Jack wasn't here to see it.

ACKNOWLEDGMENTS

I'd like to thank the following people for their support, encouragement, generosity, and candor. First and foremost, I'd like to thank Caroline Carney, agent extraordinaire, for her support and belief in my work. I'd also like to thank Karen Rinaldi and Colin Dickerman of Bloomsbury for believing in this story, and editor Panio Gianopoulos for helping to improve it. I'd like to thank my daughter, Rachel Lauren Flores, for her unconditional love and company when Daddy had to sit at the desk and wade through piles of transcripts.

In addition, I'd like to thank Stan Lee for sharing his memories of Jack and Marvel and for the many classic stories he wrote. Next comes Mark Evanier, all-around Kirby expert, brilliant writer, and author of a forthcoming Kirby biography every reader should purchase. John Morrow of Twomorrows Publishing kept Jack's memory alive with his definitive journal, *The Jack Kirby Collector*, and responded to my e-mails and requests for help in locating interview subjects.

Steve Sherman, Greg Theakston, Mike Thibodeaux, John Romita Sr., Joe Sinnott, Gene Colan, Jim Steranko, Tom DeFalco, Dick Ayers, Frank Miller, Paul Gulacy, Matt Morra, Lia Pelosi, Jon B. Cooke, Steve Gerber, Marv Wolfman, and Roy Thomas all agreed to share their memories of Stan, Jack, and Marvel Comics. So did Mike Royer, Will Eisner, Mark Waid, Herb Trimpe, Linda Fite, Flo Steinberg, Tony Isabella, Steven Grant, Steve Rude, Steve Gerber, Scott Edelman, Jim Salicrup, Roger Stern, Neal Adams, Carmine Infantino, Julius Schwartz, Erik Larsen, Larry Lieber, Joe Ruby, Ralph Bakshi, Jim Simon, Gary Groth, Denny O'Neil, D. G.

Chichester, Rich Buckler, Bob McLeod, and Janet Berliner. The members of Yahoo's! Kirby-L mailing list – including Dr. Michael J. Vassallo, and Stan Taylor – and many of the site's protracted Lee vs. Kirby disputes also inspired me to keep writing.

Tales to Astonish is based primarily on all-new, original interviews. But in some cases, when an interview subject (for instance, Buscema, Heck, Chic Stone, or Gil Kane) was deceased, ill (Joe Simon), or otherwise unavailable for comment (Jim Shooter), a few research materials came in handy. To the authors of each of the following publications I extend my gratitude, not only for a quote or two – if applicable – but for the hours of sheer enjoyment their work provided.

The following works are all highly recommended to anyone seeking more information about the American comic book industry: Joe and Jim Simon's *The Comic Book Makers*, the monthly magazines *The Jack Kirby Collector*, *Comic Book Artist*, and *Alter Ego*, William Savage's *Comic Books and America 1945–1954*, Les Daniels' *Marvel: Five Fabulous Decades of the World's Greatest Comics*, Bradford W. Wright's *Comic Book Nation*, the *Comics Journal Library, Volume One: Jack Kirby,* Michael Mallory's *Marvel*, Dan Raviv's *Comic Wars*, Amy Kiste Nyberg's *Seal of Approval: The History of the Comics Code*, Roy Thomas's *The All Star Companion*, the Marvel *Essentials* volumes (telephone-book-size reprints of the earliest *Fantastic Four*, *Thor*, *Ant-Man*, *Uncanny X-Men*, *Iron Man*, and *Hulk* stories), and DC's reprint volumes of *The New Gods*, *Mister Miracle*, *The Forever People*, *Jimmy Olsen*, and *Green Arrow* (special thanks to Marvel alumni Bill Rosemann, and Peggy Burns of DC). I'd also like to thank the new regime at Marvel – Avi Arad, Joe Quesada, Tom Breevort, and others – for keeping the heroes alive and the movie adaptations faithful to the source material. Finally, I'd like to thank Jack "King" Kirby for inspiring me to adopt a superheroic pseudonym and pursue my dream of becoming a writer.

A NOTE ON THE AUTHOR

Ronin Ro is the author of *Gangsta: Merchandising the Rhymes of Violence*, the award-winning international bestseller *Have Gun Will Travel: The Spectacular Rise and Violent Fall of Death Row Records*, and the novel *Street Sweeper*. He has written for *Vanity Fair*, *USA Today*, the *Los Angeles Times*, the *Boston Herald*, *Playboy*, *Rolling Stone*, *SPIN*, and MTV. He lives in New York City.